THE SEVEN SINS
OF WALL STREET

THE SEVEN SINS
OF WALL STREET

Big Banks, Their Washington Lackeys,
and the Next Financial Crisis

BOB IVRY

PublicAffairs
New York

PublicAffairs books are available at special discounts for bulk purchases
in the U.S. by corporations, institutions, and other organizations. For more
information, please contact the Special Markets Department at the Perseus
Books Group, 2300 Chestnut Street, Suite 200, Philadelphia, PA 19103, call
(800) 810-4145, ext. 5000, or e-mail special.markets@perseusbooks.com.

Book design by Linda Mark

Library of Congress Cataloging-in-Publication Data
    Ivry, Bob.
    The seven sins of Wall Street : big banks, their Washington lackeys, and the
next financial crisis / Bob Ivry.
        pages cm
    Includes bibliographical references and index.
    ISBN 978-1-61039-365-2 (hardcover : alk. paper)—
    ISBN 978-1-61039-366-9 (e-book)
    1. Finance—United States. 2. Banks and banking—United States.
    3. Financial crises—United States. 4. United States—Economic policy.
    I. Title.
HG181.I97 2014
332.0973—dc23
2013048863

First Edition

10 9 8 7 6 5 4 3 2 1

For Janelle

CONTENTS

SCORECARD

Ladies and gentlemen, the six largest American banks, listed in alphabetical order:

Bank of America
Home: Charlotte, North Carolina
Scouting report: Hits below its weight. Kryptonite: mortgage servicing
TARP borrowing: $45 billion
Peak Federal Reserve borrowing: $91.4 billion on February 26, 2009
Total assets, 2006: $1.36 trillion
Total assets, 2013: $2.17 trillion
Percentage change: +60

Citigroup
Home: New York
Scouting report: Can't get out of its own way
TARP borrowing: $45 billion
Peak Federal Reserve borrowing: $99.5 billion on January 20, 2009
Total assets, 2006: $1.59 trillion
Total assets, 2013: $1.88 trillion
Percentage change: +18

Goldman Sachs

Home: New York

Scouting report: Biological imperative: money

TARP borrowing: $10 billion

Peak Federal Reserve borrowing: $69 billion on December 31, 2008

Total assets, 2006: $759 billion

Total assets, 2013: $959 billion

Percentage change: +26

JPMorgan Chase

Home: New York

Scouting report: Performance-enhancing drugs suspected

TARP borrowing: $25 billion

Peak Federal Reserve borrowing: $68.6 billion on October 1, 2008

Total assets, 2006: $1.34 trillion

Total assets, 2013: $2.39 trillion

Percentage change: +78

Morgan Stanley

Home: New York

Scouting report: Smallest of the six and getting smaller

TARP borrowing: $10 billion

Peak Federal Reserve borrowing: $107 billion on September 29, 2008

Total assets, 2006: $960 billion

Total assets, 2013: $801 billion

Percentage change: −16

Wells Fargo

Home: San Francisco

Scouting report: Quietly eating its competitors' lunch

TARP borrowing: $25 billion

Peak Federal Reserve borrowing: $45 billion on February 26, 2009

Total assets, 2006: $492 billion

Total assets, 2013: $1.44 trillion

Percentage change: +193

THE COST OF DOING BUSINESS

My daughter called me from school one day and said, "Dad, what's a financial crisis?" And without trying to be funny, I said, "It's something that happens every five to seven years."
—Jamie Dimon, chief executive officer of JPMorgan Chase, January 13, 2010

WHEN REBECCA BLACK BOUGHT THE THREE-BEDROOM house at 698 Hazelwood Road in southwest Memphis in May 2005 and moved in with her two teenage sons, it was a quiet community. Children played in the street, and neighbors tended their yards. She could afford the $57,000 mortgage if she skipped oil changes for the car and served the boys store-brand groceries.

Then trouble came.

Her next-door neighbor died, and his family lost the house. Across the street, there were two foreclosures. One morning, the abandoned house three doors down had gang graffiti spray-painted on the side. A girl in the neighborhood pulled a gun on her son.

In 2010, it was Black's turn to go. She'd gotten one of those 2–28 mortgages that slowly strangled so many borrowers—two years of a low, fixed interest rate followed by twenty-eight years of rising payments—and she'd reached her limit. "I was crazy about that house, and so proud of it," said Black, a US Army veteran. "I just didn't have enough money." She got a letter from her mortgage company saying it was starting the foreclosure process, and rather than hear a knock on the door one morning from a sheriff's deputy ordering her to get out, Black packed whatever she could fit into her Chevy Astro and left the home she loved so well. By 2011, the property two doors down had sold for $3,000, and Black was in bankruptcy.

If homes are living things, sustaining their inhabitants and contributing to the vitality of their communities, then Hazelwood Road is dying. On nine of the fifteen parcels on Black's side of the street, houses sit empty or have been bulldozed flat, or the lots have reverted to a tangle of sumac and poison ivy.

I visited Hazelwood Road in the hottest part of 2012, four years after bad mortgages triggered a meltdown in the world's most resilient economy. The biggest banks were reporting record profits, and government agencies were trumpeting statistics showing that a robust recovery from the worst hard times since Dorothea Lange's "Migrant Mother" was just around the corner. And though Hazelwood Road was never a paradise—a place where Black could buy a three-bedroom house for $57,000 couldn't be described as anybody's ideal of "location, location, location"—conditions there indicated that something essential about America had shifted in the aftermath of the 2008 financial crisis. An economic and political apartheid had emerged. Perhaps fairness had been an illusion and upward mobility just a dream before things went to hell. Still, hope for advancement was that much tougher for most people to sustain after 2008. And just as the crisis was no accident but rather a tragic convergence of stupidity, poor oversight, and, more than anything, a neighbor-versus-neighbor waging of financial warfare, so too were its consequences a result of calculation. Washington, in the form of the federal government and the Federal Reserve, the country's bank for banks, had sacrificed the common good for the profit of the few. By coddling the biggest banks—by rewarding their mischief rather than at least laying down roadblocks of disincentives for them to quit their misconduct—Washington made certain that the country continued down a path of self-aggrandizement that led to a perversion of American capitalism and the slow demolition of democracy.

THE LARGEST FINANCIAL INSTITUTIONS ARE LIKE WATER— they find the lowest point. Just about all the low behavior by the biggest banks and their Washington fellow travelers described in these pages occurred after the 2008 financial crisis. It's my aim not to relitigate the bailouts but to illustrate their legacy. I've divided the book into seven chapters, each corresponding to one of Catholicism's seven deadly sins. Wall Street's seven sins—size, secrecy, regulatory capture (when government supervisors identify more with the industry they police than with the people they're supposed to protect), excessive pride, complexity, impunity, and a predatory greed weaponized for the war fought by the rich against the poor and middle class—have us pointed toward the second avoidable economic cataclysm of the baby boom era. I've written this in the hope that recognizing the danger we're in will be an essential step toward correcting our course. It won't be easy. We've dug ourselves a deep hole. The digging out might be the most urgent challenge facing this generation of Americans.

After Rebecca Black left Hazelwood Road, one of her old neighbors complained about a snake that got into her kitchen. Memphis city workers mowed Black's grass. Vandals roamed the neighborhood ripping out copper plumbing, appliances, anything left behind, so the city workers nailed plywood over Black's old windows and doors. For the plywood and the yard work at 698 Hazelwood, Rebecca Black got a bill for $520. She hadn't lived there for more than a year, but she got the tax bill too. Her lender, a division of JP-Morgan Chase called EMC Mortgage, never took ownership. The house was technically still hers.

Out of this misery and confusion, we expect the US economy to sprout wings and fly. We know the healthy flow of credit stoking a go-go real estate market is the surest way to a sustained recovery. So we examine graphs of home prices, home sales, and construction starts, trying to ignore the unskiable downward slopes of 2006 to 2009. We point instead to the wormy tail ends of 2012 and 2013 so that we can declare the nightmare over. We suspect, but seldom say, that the evidence is telling us that the line on the graph is really a fuse. It leads to a suicide bomb of our own design. We're stuck between a desire for all these houses to sell and a fear that too many mortgages given to too many borrowers like Rebecca Black will push us back to the brink. Yet so few people are better off financially than they were before the 2008 crisis, and we've learned so few of the lessons that the near-death experience could have taught us, that it feels as if it'll take another terrifying plummet to get the people in charge to do something meaningful to repair this broken system.

One foreclosed borrower, Harry Subers, once told me that the mortgage industry had done more damage to America than Osama bin Laden. We cleaned up Ground Zero and built on the ashes. When it comes to struggling home owners, we've cut the grass. But the grass keeps growing, and the snakes have come back. Rebecca Black and the 7 million other mortgage borrowers who've lost their homes to foreclosure since 2008 have become a forgotten footnote, a buzzkill best ignored on the way to greater profits for the lucky few, their futures written off as the cost of doing business.

This was the actual, if unstated, policy of the US government and the Federal Reserve since the first subprime mortgage borrower quit paying. The Treasury Department did seem to understand that without a housing recovery the US economy would never shake its funk. How do you bail out the lenders and then let the borrowers twist? This is how. In 2009, Treasury earmarked $50 billion to help failing home owners. By October 2012, the department had spent $5.5 billion, with another $5 billion committed. That might seem like a staggering bounty, until you compare it to assistance for the banks, which in 2008—the depths of the financial crisis—collectively got $1.2 trillion of loans from the Federal Reserve on a single day. Overnight borrowing by JPMorgan Chase, Rebecca Black's lender, peaked on October 1, 2008, at $68.6 billion. Jamie Dimon, the lender's chief executive officer, got $23 million in compensation for 2011.

All Rebecca Black got was the landscaping bill.

America needs strong banks. But banks need a strong America too. In the wake of the last crisis, only one side of that ledger was fortified. We need to bring the teeter-totter closer to equilibrium. As a first step toward recovery, in the psychic as well as the economic sense, let's own up to what really happened in 2008: a bloodless coup. We call it a financial crisis, but it was really a leveraged buyout of the United States. Washington occupied Wall Street, and Wall Street captured Washington. Sure, there was some rhetorical sniping in both capitals about fat cats and overregulation and a bit of ludicrous whining when one Wall Street billionaire compared changing the tax code to Nazi Germany's 1939 invasion of Poland, as if taxing income as income (35 percent) instead of investment gains (15 percent) was the first step on the road to Stalingrad. (The whiner was Stephen Schwarzman of Blackstone Group, and he later apologized. But the tax law wasn't changed; it remains in Schwarzman's favor.) Park Avenue and Pennsylvania Avenue realized that they wore the same clothes, golfed the same courses, let the same $38 burgers congeal half-eaten on their plates, sent their children to the same schools, and shared the same lawyers. In some cases, they *were* the same lawyers. You were unlikely, if not unable, to break laws if you wrote them. Five years after the financial crisis—five years!—central bankers still hadn't quit printing money to bolster the banking system. No super political-action committee could compete with the $85 billion a month the Federal Reserve was sending the big banks by buying their Treasury bonds and mortgage securities. Like the European aristocrats fighting on opposite sides in World War I, depicted by filmmaker Jean Renoir in *The Grand Illusion*, they skirmished when appearances warranted but always, when the chance arose, clinked glasses to mutually advantageous goals—in this case, clearing all obstacles on the road to the kind of wealth that would have made Croesus demur. At the same time, most Americans worked harder but watched their incomes stagnate or fall. The people, in the Abraham Lincoln sense of the word, had been cut out of postcrisis prosperity. Those riding high atop the reinvigorated political-financial complex in the 2010s forgot the lesson taught by Henry Ford a century before: the way to get rich and stay rich is to make sure your fellow citizens have the means to buy your product.

In the years leading up to the Great Bubble Burst of 2008, unprecedented wealth had preceded the unprecedented loss of wealth. In the next crisis, no such luck. Ordinary folks had sunk most of their money into their homes, and the real estate bust took a giant chomp out of those small fortunes. If home owners regained some of what they had lost as home prices inched back upward, they weren't very well going to fall for the same trick again. And if they were, what crazy lender would float them a loan? For the banks, there was plenty of money to be made elsewhere. Thanks to the Federal Reserve, side betting on price fluctuations, also known as derivatives trading, was a lot less risky and tons more lucrative than handing over $57,000 mortgages to millions of small-time credit risks such as Rebecca Black.

In the months and years after the financial crisis, the top people in Wall Street and Washington had engineered a closed loop that ensured their feet never touched the dirty ground. Wall Street would originate the mortgages, and Washington would buy them. (The government was involved in nine of every ten home loans in 2013.) The Treasury would sell debt, and Wall Street would buy it, then sell it back to the Federal Reserve. (This was called "quantitative easing.") The Federal Reserve would print money, and Wall Street would use it to push up prices on stocks and all sorts of commodities (leading to record highs in corn, cotton, silver, gold, and the S&P 500). Bankers traded derivatives, those poorly understood bets that blew up local governments and sewer projects from Newport Beach to Birmingham, without anyone in the outside world catching a glimpse of the details. (The secretive market expanded to its biggest size after the crisis.) Ordinary people only got in the way— they were unreliable bill payers, they clogged up the customer help lines, they demanded payback from pension plans they'd contributed to, they yelped antiquated socialistic notions about everyone being in the same boat, and they interrupted shareholder meetings and congressional hearings with their caterwauling—so they were simply disappeared from the equation.

Bankers were an easy target for the rest of the country's disapproval, but they saw the kind of treatment they received in Washington and responded. It was impossible for them not to feel entitled. Their partners in the political capital rolled out the red carpet for them at every opportunity. The Federal Reserve swelled its balance sheet to $4 trillion, just to transfer cash to them. The Treasury and the Fed reworked their "stress tests," just to make sure their firms passed. Lawmakers invited them to hearings to chastise them and ended up asking them for investment advice. While many Americans undoubtedly had a hand in pushing the US economy to the brink of ruin in 2008, banking was one of the few professions for which the government guaranteed a profit in the aftermath. Nothing in the rule book prohibited Washington from funneling cash to strapped home owners rather than flush banks. But in the feedback loop of the New York–Washington–New York *Acela Express* train route, strapped home owners existed only if one deigned to squint out the railcar's tinted windows. The little people's failures were best written off as the cost of doing business. Bring in the accountants to wave their magic wands, and let's move a little faster down the track.

Wall Street paid for some of this largesse, through campaign contributions, sponsorships, and grants from its foundations, paid speaking gigs, and jobs and consultancies aplenty once the nobility of public service smacked hard against the reality of putting the kids through college. But what bedazzled regulators at hello—what was a more direct cause of regulatory capture—was simply the prestige that men making millions of dollars could bring when they visited Capitol Hill. In Washington, the American conviction that money equaled honey had gone too far. Sacrificed at Mammon's altar was any notion of the common good, or restraint, or that people who work shouldn't be poor, or that children need to eat, or that college students and the jobless can use temporary help from their country that will repay multiples in the future. There were individual exceptions, to be sure, but most of the time, if you wanted to stick it to Wall Street, you had no one from either the Democratic or the Republican Party to vote for. Practically the only bipartisanship shown on Capitol Hill in the 2010s entailed members of both parties bellying up to the same pay window, brought to you by the financial services industry. Lincoln's ideal of popular government had perished from the earth.

Bankers and those in their employ loved to tout the 2008 bailouts as a moneymaker for the US Treasury. Banks had paid back the Troubled Asset Relief Program, also known as TARP, and returned $20 billion in interest, they said—as if the country should go through it all again as a way of turning a profit. But the legacy of the financial crisis wasn't stronger banks. It was a weaker country. We paid a price beyond dollars for rescuing the behemoth financial institutions. Keep the $20 billion, I say, and give us back our government. Make banking boring again. Obey the spirit of the law. Buy a moral compass with your millions. Quit ripping us off. And lawmakers, policymakers, and their staff, quit making it easier for bankers to do whatever they feel like doing.

WHEN MATTHEW WINKLER HIRED ME AS A REPORTER FOR Bloomberg News's newly constituted real estate coverage team in October 2006, I'd been a film critic, a book reviewer, and a newspaper feature writer—the kind who writes about a snowstorm on Monday, New Jersey Devils hockey on Wednesday, and the death of a seven-year-old girl from the flu on Sunday. I knew only one thing about real estate: a housing bubble that had given home owners like me a wild ride was about to end. I'd bought a home in northern New Jersey in June 2005 with the intention of moving to a bigger place as soon as I could. Almost immediately I saw articles and TV news reports that made me cross my fingers in hope that the mad price rise would last two more years, two more years, please give me two more years. Going on a decade later, top bankers, respected regulators, and relied-upon credit raters claim they had no knowledge of a bubble. That no one did. That "market forces" caused lenders to lose money in the bust. That they were shocked—shocked!—to find that garbage mortgages had been peddled. That they were victims of the credit crunch and not partly to blame for it. I became a financial reporter not long before this load of crap started to get unloaded from the bullshit train. No wonder I was suspicious of what bankers told me. If I'd been aware of the real estate bubble as a civilian in 2005, surely the generals of finance knew about it too. The list of those pleading cluelessness could fill the economics faculty at an Ivy League university. It included two

Federal Reserve chairmen and the chief executives of the majority of the biggest Wall Street firms.

As my editor on the real estate team, Rob Urban, used to say, "All they had to do to know about the boom and bust was read their Bloombergs."

I had patient teachers at Bloomberg News. Rob had covered Enron and the Russian debt crisis of the late 1990s and knew a scam when he smelled one. He confirmed for me, over and over, that my being new to finance didn't mean I didn't see what I saw. I pestered Christine Harper, the chief financial correspondent, and she invited me along on her meetings with bankers. From her I learned that an undercurrent, deep below the surface, affects the ebb and flow of money. And it usually has to do with personalities. And somehow I fell in with Mark Pittman. I'd met him on my first day at Bloomberg News. He sat next to an old colleague of mine, Shannon Harrington, and when I found my way through the rows of desks to say hi to Shannon, there was this hulking linebacker of a guy in his late forties with a heavy-metal haircut—shaved close on the sides and long enough on top to be gathered into a ponytail in back. Pittman, a corporate bond reporter at the time, showed me that the truth, or a reasonable facsimile, lurks not in what people say but in what they do. For that, you needed documents, regulatory filings, spreadsheets, and prospectuses. The exciting work he did was built on hours of wrecking his eyesight poring over hieroglyphs.

"Where it impacts regular folks, you gotta do something about it," Pittman said. "Make sure the rules are fair."

How's this for fair? From June 2009, the end of the recession, middle-class income declined while the biggest banks made more money than ever before. Still, bankers agitated for loosening rules that might prevent another implosion on the grounds that regulation would crimp their profits. The irony is, without the help of regulators, taxpayers, and lawmakers, they would have lived more like the rest of the country—struggling to stretch their paychecks to the end of every month and saddled with credit scores that made it unlikely they'd ever be able to borrow anything but hedge clippers from the neighbors.

Without Washington as its midwife, a new Gilded Age, with its strong whiff of the robber barons of the 1890s, would never have been born. Bankers' rights expanded immeasurably after the crisis. Today, some of them don't pay taxes at the same rate that the rest of Americans do; they can use cash from customer deposits to roll the dice in the derivatives casino; they can mix trading oil with the business of drilling for, shipping, refining, and selling it; they can continue to defraud the same US government that bailed them out; and they face scant consequences for the fibs they tell investors or federal investigators. In 1997, the humor site The Onion made a joke about VIP citizenship available to those who qualified as privileged. It was funny, but it was also prophetic.

The heart of the predicament was the unprecedented growth of the biggest banks. Before the crisis, at the end of 2006, JPMorgan Chase, Bank of America, Citigroup, and Wells Fargo had $5.2 trillion in assets on their books. In 2012, they had $7.8 trillion. That's a 50 percent increase. In 2012, Wells Fargo, by itself, wrote one of every three residential mortgages in America. Usually, growth is a good thing. But this was unnatural and out of control. The big boys had gotten so freakishly huge that if they coughed in New York, financiers felt a breeze in Singapore.

Even the highly touted 2010 law called the Dodd-Frank Wall Street Reform and Consumer Protection Act, which was supposed to provide a way for regulators to put a large bank to sleep without bailouts, only added multiple layers of bureaucracy to the oversight of financial firms. It didn't end the phenomenon of banks being perceived as too big to be allowed to fail. In fact, it enshrined that very idea, bestowing that official designation on selected firms with the euphemism "systemically important financial institution," or SIFI. Bond buyers, the people who put their money on the line, gave the biggest banks borrowing discounts simply because they believed the government would step in if they faltered.

Though it would have made more sense for Congress to mandate that the biggest banks shrink or split into manageable, acceptably profitable entities whose problems would affect only their employees, shareholders, and creditors and not taxpayers—a plan endorsed in concept by a half dozen current and former Federal Reserve branch presidents, a couple of Bank of England bigwigs, senators from both political parties, and both men who created the "financial supermarket" Citigroup—the Obama administration opposed and defeated attempts to get such rules enacted.

REBECCA BLACK MOVED INTO A ONE-BEDROOM APARTMENT in a Memphis senior citizen's complex, a living space less than one-third as big as her home on Hazelwood Road. Because of her bankruptcy, she couldn't get a better deal than 12 percent on her car loan. "Money you don't even have, they want it," she said. Her embarrassment over losing the house curdled into a shrugging defeatism. "I don't want anybody taking care of me," she told me with an incongruous smile. "I'd rather be gone," she said, meaning dead. Such sentiment, attained at a high cost, was rare in Gimme-Now Nation.

Her brand of rugged individualism, if not her surrender, could be detected in the public pronouncements of the bank chieftains and their supporters, many of whom championed free market Darwinism for everyone but themselves. Their actions betrayed a willful denial of the fact that they owed their ongoing existence to people like Rebecca Black, whose mortgage payments made them rich, whose tax payments kept them afloat and furnished them with cheap loans, whose tolerance made it possible for them to enjoy wealth the world had never seen—and whose support for another round of taxpayer bailouts, should the big banks screw up again, was less than zero. That ought to scare the hell out of the rest of us as we careen toward the next financial crisis, which, according to Jamie Dimon of JPMorgan Chase, is due any day.

We must survive the next upheaval in order to wrestle back control of our financial and political institutions, to ensure that they serve society rather than society serving them. To make sure Wall Street will not write off the failure of America as its cost of doing business.

ONE

GLUTTONY

Size: Sherry Hunt and the Champions
of Responsible Finance

T HE TECHIES AT CITIMORTGAGE'S O'FALLON, MISSOURI, headquarters were told to drop what they were doing and gather outside. They filed out of the fluorescent light of the building and into the sun, where they lined up on the sidewalk at the edge of the vast parking area of the suburban office campus—three attached buildings with *Truman Show* landscaping between a golf course and clusters of townhouses, two megamalls west of St. Louis. Together they watched as a cortege of three black Cadillac Escalades made its way from the Interstate 40 access road to Technology Drive, then turned toward them and drove through the parted sea of parked cars. The Escalades stopped. Doors opened. The techies began to applaud. One of them gave a high-pitched whoop. Out of the back seat of the middle Escalade stepped a man, lean and slender necked, with wire-frame glasses and a shock of white in his dark hair. He acknowledged the warm greeting by ducking his delicate chin, flashing a smile, and giving a quick, self-conscious wave. With the other hand he buttoned the top button of his suit jacket. He was Vikram Pandit, Citigroup's chief executive officer, boss of all bosses, come from New York to review the troops.

When he'd disappeared inside the building, the techies quit clapping and filed back to their cubicles.

Perhaps it was too much to expect Pandit, buckled inside the SUV or circling above the O'Fallon offices in Citi's jet, his polished feet touching the sidewalk only long enough to be showered with ginned-up adulation, to know what was really going on at CitiMortgage. A thousand miles separated the cherrywood conference rooms of the bank's Midtown Manhattan command center from the concrete and reflective glass of CitiMortgage headquarters in Missouri. Connecting the mother ship with the far-flung outpost was a corporate ladder whose every rung was populated with go-getters who lived to please those above them and step on those below. The only glimpses New York had into what O'Fallon was up to were periodic reports on the quality of the home loans CitiMortgage was processing. The reports told Pandit how well this spark was moving the piston of Citi's moneymaking machine. From soon after Pandit was chosen to lead the bank in December 2007 until the winter of 2012, the reports conveyed the message to the top that the mortgage factory was well greased and purring. Performance was improving every day.

Mortgages keep America's banks in the black. For decades, they promised steady profits for relatively low risk. Even when they're short of cash for other things, the great majority of home owners pay their mortgages on time every month. Nobody likes to see an eviction notice stapled to the front door. It's no coincidence that the biggest banks in the country are also the biggest residential lenders. And as far as loan factories go, Citigroup's was among the biggest of the big. In 2012, the 3,200 CitiMortgage workers in O'Fallon were joined by 2,800 more in Irving, Texas, and another 1,000 in Ann Arbor, Michigan, with 2,200 more spread among four other facilities. They processed millions of mortgages every year. Big banks like Citi not only pay hundreds of employees to sell mortgages directly to customers out of storefront branches but also buy premade mortgages from outside brokers, other loan companies, and other banks. Among its many tasks, the O'Fallon office makes sure these mortgages are kosher, that every precaution is taken to ensure that borrowers won't quit paying. If the mortgage papers are in order, chances are the mortgages are too. And if the mortgages are in order, they'll probably be repaid. The stakes are high. Before the financial crisis of 2008, CitiMortgage was buying as much as $90 billion a year of home loans from outside sources. In the years since the crisis, with about half the brokers and mortgage companies having gone belly up, that number has shrunk, and for a time there was mounting pressure from top executives to feed the hungry beast. Mortgages pay the banks' bills.

After the financial crisis of 2008, residential lending pretty much stopped. No financial firm wanted to risk advancing money to American home buyers, who had turned into deadbeats in record numbers. With little fanfare, taxpayers stepped in and became the nation's mortgage bankers. Since then, the taxpayers' role has only grown. In 2013, Fannie Mae, Freddie Mac, or the Federal Housing Administration (FHA), the three government-controlled mortgage companies, either bought or guaranteed about nine of every ten mortgages in the country. In a scenario that repeated itself many times during the crisis and after, private debt was transformed into public obligation: when a Citigroup borrower in Springfield USA quit paying, Washington picked up the tab. Only when the government could prove the loans were fraudulent or had missing paperwork to begin with—a costly and resource-sapping undertaking that can take years—could it force banks like Citigroup to cover the government's insurance losses.

That makes cutting corners on mortgages potentially damaging to the whole country. And as long as there have been mortgages, corners have been cut. It's a lot easier to identify the home loans with messed-up paperwork before they quit paying. In the industry, messed-up paperwork is called a "defect," and defects come in different flavors—a signature left off an important document, a ridiculous appraisal, a mismatch between a borrower's income on the mortgage application and on the tax records. Other more serious problems may also indicate fraud: bank statements on which the bank's name is misspelled, tax forms where Wite-Out has been smeared over a number, borrowers who list employers that don't exist, borrowers whose identities can't be confirmed.

Here's the crazy thing: whereas Fannie and Freddie double-check samplings of the mortgages they guarantee against defects, the Federal Housing Administration does not. Or, at least it didn't in any meaningful way from 2009 to 2012. The FHA, part of the cabinet-level Housing and Urban Development Department, expanded the number of loans it guaranteed from $700 billion in 2007 to $1.1 trillion in 2012. And it delegated all quality control to the lenders. From at least 2009 till 2012, government mortgage guarantors simply didn't double-check the mortgages coming in.

In other words, the FHA left it up to the foxes in O'Fallon, Missouri, to make sure taxpayer hens didn't get stuck insuring bad loans.

According to O'Fallon, Citigroup was doing a world-class job at making sure all the paperwork was in order and borrowers would most likely repay their loans. Ask executives at the bank's New York headquarters how their US mortgage business was doing, and they stood a little taller. "The quality of our mortgages is among the best, if not the best," they'd crow. I'd watched as a CitiMortgage guy tapped a finger on multicolored bar charts that compared Citi with the other biggest lenders—JPMorgan Chase, Wells Fargo, and Bank of America. "See that? We're number one," he said with pride.

The bar charts were based on data from O'Fallon. The numbers from O'Fallon were increasingly encouraging—miraculous even. Here was Citi, a financial gargantuan that lost $36 billion in just fifteen months back in 2007 and 2008, mostly because of bad mortgages. It received a bailout of $45 billion from the US Treasury Department, was promised another $301 billion from the government to prop up its bad investments, and received dozens of overnight loans from the Federal Reserve that peaked at $99.5 billion on a single night in 2009. Those big numbers made Citigroup the most bailed-out US-based bank. Financial world rock stars such as Sheila Bair, former chairman of the Federal Deposit Insurance Corporation, or FDIC, have intimated that the government and the Federal Reserve orchestrated the entire bank bailout extravaganza of 2007 to 2010 in order to save Citigroup, with the checks to the other banks mere window dressing to camouflage the singular insolvency of Citi. President Barack Obama told author Ron Suskind that he favored shutting Citi down in the spring of 2009 and auctioning off its parts to the highest bidders. Only through the intervention of Treasury Secretary Timothy Geithner did Citi survive in its present form, Suskind found. And here they were in 2012, just thirty-six months removed from their deathbed and a figurative Dr. Kevorkian with his hand on the plug, ready to pull, and Pandit and his lieutenant, Sanjiv Das, chief executive of the CitiMortgage division, could brag that everything was peachy. Not perfect, they'd say, but a source of delight and the benchmark by which their competitors ought to measure themselves. They were the comeback kids. They'd survived the nightmare of the third week of September 2008, when more than one high-placed man in American finance made a phone call to his wife, telling her to go to the ATM and withdraw as much cash as she could, because it looked like the ATMs might run dry. And now, in 2012, the quality-assurance reports from O'Fallon were telling the New York executives that they were heroes.

Citi celebrated its two hundredth birthday in 2012, and New York toasted CEO Pandit with gallons of champagne that summer in recognition of the bank's charitable giving. Lionel Richie and Chaka Khan sang for him at a benefit dinner for Harlem's Apollo Theater. Josh Groban performed at a party for a children's mentoring organization. The Museum of the City of New York hosted a black-tie dinner where it presented Pandit with a leadership award.

"We are proud to support the great institutions that make New York City, our home for two hundred years, a better place," Pandit said about the galas.

O'Fallon had made a mockery of his so-called leadership.

The quality-control reports looked rosy because they were cooked. The truth, in fact, was ugly. Citi was still screwing up. Managers in Missouri simply changed the numbers or had their underlings farther down the corporate ladder apply figurative dabs of Wite-Out to inconvenient findings. Their reasons went beyond good old-fashioned sucking up to the boss. It was a matter of livelihood. Compensation was based on the reports. Happy numbers meant more presents under the Christmas tree. Besides, what "defect" couldn't be fixed? Missing paperwork in the mortgage applications could be found. Questionable appraisals were carefully informed opinions on ever-changing local real estate conditions. The two signatures only looked different. The nonexistent employer listed by the borrower was clearly a simple mistake. A transposed digit, an incorrectly copied address, a dotted line unsigned: What was the harm?

The government didn't seem to care. There's an expression in the finance business attributed to billionaire J. Paul Getty: If you borrow $10,000 from the bank, that's your problem. But if you borrow $10 billion from the bank, that's the bank's problem. The US Treasury had sunk all those billions into Citigroup, along with the asset guarantees and those overnight loans from the Federal Reserve, not to mention the political capital spent on keeping Citi's air passages above water. It wanted Citi to succeed. It would guarantee any mortgage Citi shipped over to Fannie, Freddie, and the FHA, no questions asked. As long as Citigroup swore twice a year on its FHA certifications that it had the best interests of the American taxpayer in mind, that was good enough. The government trusted Citigroup. It had to. Their fates were intertwined. And besides, 2008 was a long time ago. This was the new Citi—the Citi of responsible finance. Vikram Pandit, in a series of advertisements aimed at winning over a citizenry—and potential customer base—that was mad as hell about having to bail out a bunch of spoiled and ungrateful bankers, said as much. "We're going to stand for the financial services company that practices responsible finance—making sure we're transparent, making sure we're honest, making sure we manage our shareholders' money prudently," Pandit said on a video posted on the Citigroup website. Transparency, honesty, prudence: those were the new watchwords. The crisis was over. The economy was recovering. Citigroup had paid back its government loans. People were buying houses and refinancing their mortgages. Defaults were down. All was well. Everybody was happy.

Until Sherry Hunt.

OF THE HUNDREDS OF VICE PRESIDENTS AT WALL STREET banks, Sherry Hunt might have been the unlikeliest. She was a country girl, born and raised in southwestern Michigan, where her father taught her to fish and her mother showed her where in the woods to find wild mushrooms. She listened to Marty Robbins and Buck Owens and came to believe that God had a plan, that everything happens for a reason.

She got married at sixteen and didn't go to college. When she found herself, a little more than a year later, with a baby, living in Alaska, she asked a friend to help her get a job. That's how she started processing mortgages, in Fairbanks, Alaska, in 1975.

Over the next thirty years, Hunt moved up the ladder to mortgage-banking jobs in Indiana, Minnesota, and Missouri. On her days off, when she wasn't fishing with her second husband, she rode her horse, Cody, in Wild West shows. Sometimes she dressed as Annie Oakley, sometimes as Calamity Jane, firing blanks from a vintage rifle to entertain an audience. She liked the mortgage business, liked that she was helping people buy houses. She was good at it. She believed in people, and she also believed they ought to get loans they were likely to pay back.

In November 2004, at the age of forty-seven, Hunt joined Citi-Mortgage. At first, she felt like a mouse in a maze. She wasn't used to the sea of cubicles stretching out in all directions at the O'Fallon headquarters. "You only see people's faces when someone brings in doughnuts and the smell gets them peeking over the tops of their cubicles," she joked.

It looked like a great career move. The housing boom was on, and Citi was the country's sixth-largest residential lender at the time and headed upward. She'd made the big time.

Her job was supervising sixty-five mortgage underwriters—the people who check for mortgage "defects" and make sure borrowers are able to repay their loans. She and her colleagues inspected home loans Citi wanted to buy from outside sources to make sure they met the bank's standards. Citi would vouch for the quality of the loans when it sold them to investors or approved them for government insurance.

In the soaring market of the mid-2000s, Citigroup couldn't process the mortgages fast enough. Investors loved buying bundles of home loans, called mortgage-backed securities, because they received a decent return and were considered low risk by the credit-rating companies. O'Fallon's job was to keep the assembly line going to meet the demand. Hunt and her team were expected to keep the process moving. They couldn't check every loan.

By 2006, Hunt's group was responsible for overseeing $50 billion of mortgages that Citigroup bought from brokers and independent loan companies. They were finding all sorts of defects in the mortgages: doctored tax forms, missing signatures, phony appraisals, and liar loans, where the borrower's income was obviously picked out of the air so he could qualify for the loan. Hunt tried reporting the defect rate to supervisors, but somehow her warnings never made it past that rung of the corporate ladder, and the flow of defective mortgages never seemed to slow.

CitiMortgage wasn't the only lender more concerned with quantity than quality. The mortgage bubble was inflating, and everybody was along for the ride. Citigroup was paying bonuses based on the number of mortgages that employees processed. O'Fallon workers bought their boats, their flat-screen TVs, and their Disney cruises, just like the borrowers who cashed in on their home equity by refinancing their loans.

By late 2007, Hunt's team was finding flaws or fraud in 60 percent of the loans they checked, an astounding number in an industry that tries to keep problem loans to 5 percent of the output or less. The defects put the bank in danger. When Citi packaged the loans into securities for sale without government guarantees, it promised to make good on any defective ones whose borrowers quit paying. The flaws in underwriting were exposing Citi to millions, maybe billions, in so-called buybacks. Hunt wasn't just a stickler for meaningless rules. She knew these violations could cost the bank some serious money.

Hunt couldn't convince anyone with any authority to toss a wooden shoe into the mortgage-processing machinery—until one day she sent a summary of her findings to Richard Bowen, a supervisor in Citi-Mortgage's Irving, Texas, office.

Bowen was a deeply religious man, a former Air Force Reserve Officer Training Corps cadet at Texas Tech University in Lubbock, and a certified public accountant. He comes across as something of a Boy Scout, so it's a mild shock when he mutters an obscenity, which he's apt to do when he talks about mortgage defects. Bowen took a look at what Sherry Hunt sent him and came to the same conclusion she had: these bad mortgages were putting Citigroup at risk.

Bowen tried his best to raise alarms. But he didn't get anywhere.

On the morning of November 3, 2007, with his wife telling him to hurry up or they would be late for a wedding they were attending, Bowen shot off an e-mail from his home computer to top Citi brass in New York. It went to the bank's chief financial officer, Gary Crittenden, and to Citi's senior risk officer, who was in charge of making sure perils such as flawed home loans didn't cost the bank, and to the bank's chief auditor. But Bowen's main target was Robert Rubin, who at one time had been the Michael Jordan of the economy—popular and successful with an untouchable resume. Rubin had headed Goldman Sachs, the New York investment bank, before becoming President Bill Clinton's Treasury secretary. *Time* magazine, in a 1999 cover photo, called Rubin, Federal Reserve Chairman Alan Greenspan, and Clinton economic adviser Larry Summers "The Committee to Save the World." Rubin was instrumental in convincing Clinton to support legislation allowing banks to commingle gambling activities with customer deposits, which had been a no-no since the Great Depression. After his stint in Washington, Rubin went to work for the biggest beneficiary of that legislation, Citigroup, as chairman of the executive committee. Bowen figured Rubin was savvy enough to heed his warning once he became aware of the problem, so he put the words "Urgent—Read Immediately—Financial Issues" in the e-mail subject line.

"The reason for this urgent e-mail concerns breakdowns of internal controls and resulting significant but possibly unrecognized financial losses existing within our organization," Bowen wrote. "We continue to be significantly out of compliance."

In other words: Danger ahead! Rotten mortgages!

Bowen said he was interviewed by lawyers from an outside firm doing work for Citi and then demoted. He said he went from supervising more than two hundred employees to supervising two. By early 2009, a little more than a year after his e-mail, he no longer worked for Citigroup.

Citigroup denied retaliating against Bowen. Brad S. Karp, chairman of the law firm Paul, Weiss, Rifkind, Wharton & Garrison in New York, representing Citi, said in a letter to the Financial Crisis Inquiry Commission, the panel Congress created to plumb the causes of the 2008 crash, that Citi acted on Bowen's concerns about defective mortgages. He said CitiMortgage fired a supervisor and changed its underwriting standards. He didn't provide specifics.

A week after Bowen sent his e-mail, Sherry Hunt and her husband were driving their Toyota Camry, going about fifty-five miles per hour on four-lane Providence Road in Columbia, Missouri, when a driver in a Honda Civic traveling in the opposite direction hit them head on. Sherry broke a foot and her sternum. Her husband broke an arm and his sternum. Doctors used four bones harvested from a cadaver and titanium screws to stabilize his neck.

"You come out of an experience like that with a commitment to making the most of the time you have and making the world a better place," Hunt said.

Soon after Hunt returned to work, lawyers from Paul, Weiss invited her into a conference room at the O'Fallon office and asked her about mortgage defects. At the time, she said, she had no idea it was related to Bowen's e-mail. But the lawyers' persistent questions and dogged digging for the smallest details gave her an idea. From that time forward, she decided to take notes every day. She kept the notes on a spreadsheet on her home computer. The notes would come in handy when, like Bowen, she decided that she had to speak up.

CITY BANK RECEIVED ITS CHARTER IN 1812, THE YEAR THAT two New Madrid earthquakes, epicentered in Missouri, rang church bells in New York. It was 101 years before the founding of the Federal Reserve. Dutch farmers still tilled the soil of the Bronx, and the buttonwood tree at 68 Wall Street, birthplace of the New York Stock Exchange, had yet to be swallowed by BMW of Manhattan. Trade was brisk at the time in Tennessee cotton, Caribbean rum, and African slaves.

The bank's first bailout came twenty-five years later, during the Panic of 1837. In the same way that billionaire investor Warren

Buffett came to the rescue of Goldman Sachs in 2008, tycoon John Jacob Astor and a group of wealthy merchants pumped money into City Bank to keep it afloat. There was no central bank at the time to dole out overnight loans the contemporary equivalent of $99.5 billion, though seventy-five years later, Frank A. Vanderlip, an executive of the bank then called National City Bank of New York, participated in the secret meetings on Jekyll Island, Georgia, that gave birth to the Federal Reserve.

City Bank was the first to amass $1 billion in assets, and in the 1920s, its chief executive, Charles Mitchell, was referred to as "Billion-Dollar Charlie." Mitchell is best known today for the grilling he received from a special prosecutor investigating the causes of the 1929 crash. Ferdinand Pecora, appointed by Congress to conduct hearings in 1933, prodded Billion-Dollar Charlie to reveal his role in pushing pump-and-dump stock speculation—touting shares of a company and then selling them—which helped inflate the investment bubble.

Pecora also discovered that Mitchell had paid no taxes on his $1 million 1929 compensation. Mitchell resigned.

Billion-Dollar Charlie's personal sacrifice was not in vain. In reaction to the crash of 1929 and the ensuing depression, Congress created the Federal Deposit Insurance Corporation, which guaranteed savings accounts, and the Securities and Exchange Commission, tasked with making sure investors got a fair shake. It also passed the Glass-Steagall Act, which forced banks to separate investment banking—underwriting stocks and bonds, cutting merger and take-over deals, and rolling the dice in high-stakes games of chance—from their taxpayer-guaranteed deposits. It would be nearly forty years before Citi begged for another bailout.

Bank analyst Mike Mayo lists the years the financial institution, known through the decades as City Bank, National City Bank, Citibank, Citicorp, and Citigroup, came close to failing: 1921, 1932, 1970, 1982, 1991, and 2008. "Citi has been involved in virtually every major financial screwup," Mayo said. Citi clamored to fund Enron and underwrote WorldCom. In the early 2000s, Citi's stock analysts, on whose independent assessments of the relative value of companies' shares investors relied, were convicted of hyping companies that Citi wanted to do business with. The bank lost its private-banking charter in Japan after improprieties there in the mid-2000s led Chief Executive Officer Chuck Prince to fly to Tokyo to offer his personal apologies. Mayo totaled all of Citi's fines, settlements, reserves, or write-downs in the twenty-first century and figured they represented about $1 for every $3 it made.

Historians credit Walter Wriston, a former Eagle Scout who led the bank from 1967 to 1984 (and through two bailouts), with bringing innovations to the industry such as the automated teller machine and the negotiable certificate of deposit. But the most significant moment in the recent history of banking would come more than a decade later, when Wriston's successor, the patrician John S. Reed, picked up the phone to take a call from Brooklyn-raised Sanford I. Weill.

DICK BOWEN'S DEPARTURE FROM CITIMORTGAGE IN EARLY 2009 left Sherry Hunt feeling lonely and isolated. Bowen was a good man, she believed. He'd called Sherry after her car accident, offering his help and prayers. To see a decent man like Bowen treated so shabbily made her angry.

It also scared her. She'd supplied Bowen with much of the data he'd used to blow the whistle on CitiMortgage's quality-control failures, and seeing how he had left the bank, she was terrified she'd lose her job. She couldn't afford that. She had medical bills and attorney's fees to pay. She decided to lay low.

That didn't last long. On April 1, 2008, Citi demoted her. She went from supervising sixty-five people to supervising none. She was now part of the "quality-assurance" team. There, she found plenty of dirt to fill up her spreadsheet. "Every time I turned over a rock I found a snake," she said.

One place particularly rife with slithering reptiles was Citi-Mortgage's Fraud Prevention and Investigation Group. That was where the quality-control team shipped loans they suspected of being more than just flawed. It was where loans with suspected fraud went.

The FHA rules about this sort of thing are clear. CitiMortgage was supposed to notify the agency if it found anything suspicious in a loan guaranteed by government insurance. And it was supposed to do it within a month.

In November 2009, a year after Citigroup's bailout, Hunt came across about 1,000 loans the quality-control team had flagged for possible fraud. Some of them had been in the queue with no action taken for more than two years. Not until July 2011, when the US attorney in Manhattan issued a subpoena to the O'Fallon office, did CitiMortgage finally tell the FHA about its secret stash of potentially fraudulent loans.

SANDY WEILL, WITH THE HELP OF A COCKSURE WINGMAN named Jamie Dimon, parlayed a Baltimore-based subprime lender into a financial empire that included the Salomon Smith Barney brokerage and the insurance giant Travelers Group. To grow, they needed cash. The easiest and cheapest source was customer deposits. John Reed's Citicorp could be the wellspring that ka-chinged Weill into the big time.

Weill's pitch to Reed was simple. Together they could create a financial services supermarket. Customers who came for a savings or checking account could get a mortgage and insurance for their home, a credit card to buy clothes and furniture, and a stockbroker to handle their retirement account. The supermarket would also have an investment banker to make deals and traders to keep the money rolling in. This Frankenstein monster could compete globally with the biggest banks of Europe and Asia and continue gobbling up smaller competitors.

Reed was game. The only trouble was, they needed to change the law. The sixty-five-year-old Glass-Steagall Act prohibited risking Grandma's Christmas Club account on the dice games of financial markets. Ironically—and Citi's history does not lack for irony—Glass-Steagall had been enacted in the wake of Ferdinand Pecora's harsh questioning of the man who'd had Reed's job in the 1920s, National City Bank's Charlie Mitchell.

But Glass-Steagall had been whittled down over the decades. Weill and Reed wanted it to sleep with the fishes. They signed their deal to merge Travelers and Citicorp in 1998, creating Citigroup, before the law was repealed. They felt confident that with influential friends like Treasury Secretary Bob Rubin to support them, the so-called modernization of the banking industry would prove a no-brainer for lawmakers and President Bill Clinton.

The Gramm-Leach-Bliley Act, as the repeal of Glass-Steagall was called, would enhance the stability of the American financial services industry, Clinton said in a statement accompanying his November 1999 signing of the legislation. It's the most important law for the industry since the Great Depression, Clinton said, and "America's consumers, our communities, and the economy will reap the benefits of this Act."

IN 2009, CITIMORTGAGE EXECUTIVES PUT TOGETHER A COM-mittee to refute Sherry Hunt's claims on mortgage defects. They called it the Quality Rebuttal team. In meetings they tried to convince Hunt that she'd judged some mortgage defects too harshly, that they really weren't as bad as she said they were. For instance, a signed document called a HUD-1 declaration is required for every FHA loan, and according to government guidelines, the loan ought to be rejected for FHA insurance if the document is missing. The

Quality Rebuttal committee insisted a missing HUD-1 declaration didn't make the loan a bad one. The members dug in their heels and wouldn't listen to Hunt, despite her twenty-five years' experience with government-guaranteed mortgages. They outvoted her. The loan was approved for FHA insurance. Hunt could only shake her head and make note of it on her spreadsheet.

CitiMortgage even went so far as to create new categories for loans. If a mortgage was defective, it was classified by the severity of its defect. That meant that the reports up the ladder would seem even better—Hey, look, our tier 1 defects are down 58 percent! (So what if tier 2 defects are up, say, 87 percent?)—except that the FHA, Fannie Mae, Freddie Mac, investors in mortgage-backed securities, and anyone else who would sue Citi if there were problems didn't give a rat's patootie whether Citi said a loan had a tier 1, tier 2, or tier 3 defect. They just wanted to know if it would continue paying and if Citigroup had done all it could to assure that it would. CitiMortgage's new classification system made sense only to CitiMortgage. Its executives could use it to show that they were the comeback kids, that Vikram Pandit and Sanjiv Das were heroes, that mid-level executives deserved their bonuses, and that the trucks could be bought, the flat screens installed, and the Disney cruise tickets booked.

Establishing the Quality Rebuttal team to make Sherry Hunt's life miserable was a turning point not only for Hunt but for Citigroup as well. Mortgages represent the best of our financial system, capitalism, America. Mortgages give shelter to families, enable people of modest means to improve their lives, and allow parents to pass along wealth to their children. A good mortgage means a solid home, and solid homes are the foundation of the healthy communities that together form a strong country and confident world.

Mortgages are generosity with conditions. They aren't gifts, which can be abused or taken for granted. They require discipline and foster responsibility. A good mortgage is a small miracle, an expression of faith, a testimony to the honesty and good will of all participants. They grow in value with each payment.

Mortgages can also be a straightforward way for people to do life-long harm to others. They—literally—hit people where they live. A number added here, a clause deleted there, and a fair mortgage becomes plunder, extortion, perpetual servitude, lost hope. They can do, and have done, lasting damage to people, to neighborhoods, to cities, and to the whole nation.

Before it decided to pour its resources into challenging its own quality-control standards, Citi might have been able to make the argument that it was trying. That it wanted its mortgages to help people buy homes and create strong communities. That it expected to make money but would do so only while doing what was right. After putting together the Quality Rebuttal group, Citi could no longer make that argument.

In January 2010, at a staff meeting, 1,000 CitiMortgage employees gathered to listen to pep talks and sales reports. Then it came time to announce the workers-of-the-month award. It went to the Quality Rebuttal crew. Members of the team received certificates and $25 gift cards.

Hunt, watching the Quality Rebuttal employees accept their rewards, felt her face grow hot.

GRAMM-LEACH-BLILEY ALLOWED THE BANKS TO GROW BIGGER and concentrated the world's money in the vaults of the top four US retail banks. In 2007, Citigroup, JPMorgan Chase, Bank of America, and Wells Fargo combined for $2.5 trillion in deposits, or 17.6 percent of the market. Five years later, they held $3.9 trillion, or 27 percent of the market.

Those four banks had grown to attain an exalted status: the US government would never let them collapse. They were, in the industry jargon, too big to fail.

Recall the saying about the bank that lends $10,000. It owns the borrower. But the bank that lends $10 billion? It's owned by the borrower.

Being a too-big-to-fail bank during the financial crisis meant the government made sure you survived. Being a too-big-to-fail bank in the years after the financial crisis meant the government made sure you prospered.

The biggest banks could do little wrong in the eyes of their benefactors. And when their behavior got too heinous to deny, they often got a slap on the wrist. Laundering money for sanctioned countries, mortgage fraud, violating rules against risky behavior, losing billions of customer money—"rogue" employees were to blame for such misdeeds. Insider stock trading for a $276 million profit got the wrongdoer a criminal trial; crashing the world's biggest economy and wiping trillions off global balance sheets didn't merit criminal charges at all.

The Dodd-Frank Wall Street Reform and Consumer Protection Act, the 2010 law that promised to end the phenomenon of too big to fail, in fact did the opposite.

As "systemically important financial institutions," big banks were required to write living wills. These documents were meant to provide a series of steps for government regulators to put a big bank to permanent rest in the event it ever got so sick it threatened the health of the global financial system. These steps, the thinking went, meant the government wouldn't have to bail out a bank ever again.

Yet the plan seemed hatched in a vacuum. First of all, what bank would declare itself so sick as to be beyond saving? Bankers are proud people who think of themselves as winners able to overcome any obstacle. Lehman Brothers insisted on Sunday, September 14, 2008, that it could survive, even thrive, before it filed the biggest bankruptcy in US history on Monday, September 15, 2008. Bear Stearns executives didn't believe their investment bank could plunge so quickly into insolvency; some were reportedly playing bridge and smoking weed while Bear burned. Morgan Stanley blamed short-sellers—investors who bet against them—for ruining the bank's stock price. It surely wasn't their fault that the bank was forced to take more than $100 billion in emergency overnight loans from the Federal Reserve, the biggest single sum of any bank.

If the bankers themselves couldn't be counted on to call it quits, maybe regulators, led by the Treasury secretary, could be the ones to make the hard decision. That was the intent of the Dodd-Frank legislation.

These were the same regulators who dished out a single-night peak of $1.2 trillion to banks needing overnight loans in 2009. Who were on the giving end of countless wrist slaps. Who either used to work on Wall Street or, in many cases, hoped to one day.

Even if all went smoothly on the assisted suicide, the Dodd-Frank wind-down plan would work only if a big bank ran into trouble on its own. That could happen. But the failure of one institution would more probably indicate the imminent breakdown of others. After all, they are trading partners. They are subject to the same market mayhem caused by terrorist attack, hurricane, or investor panic. They make similar bets in the same markets. In 2008, there was a chain reaction. First, Bear Stearns, the fifth-biggest investment bank, collapsed. Then Lehman Brothers, the fourth-biggest. Merrill Lynch, the next in line, was only able to stave off collapse by selling itself to Bank of America. Morgan Stanley and Goldman Sachs were next. Morgan Stanley got a shot in the arm from the Federal Reserve, and Goldman Sachs got a confidence boost from Warren Buffett. On the retail side, Wachovia, the fourth-biggest US bank by deposits, needed to sell itself to Wells Fargo or face the biggest liquidation the FDIC had ever undertaken. The bank didn't falter all by itself. Washington Mutual, the country's biggest savings and loan, averted meltdown by being sold in a panic to JPMorgan Chase. IndyMac, the second-biggest savings and loan, vaporized. Citigroup and Bank of America each needed overnight loans of almost $100 billion from the Fed to make it through.

But lenders love the SIFIs. They loaned the big banks money at a discount rate. They could see that Uncle Sam and the Federal Reserve would never let a SIFI go under, so they figured their loans would always be repaid. In 2011, the FDIC estimated that funding costs for US banks with more than $10 billion in assets—about two dozen fall into that category—were about one-third less than for the smallest banks, which had very little to do with the global financial meltdown.

In trying to do away with the phenomenon of too big to fail, Dodd-Frank made it worse.

Phil Gramm, the former Texas senator whose name goes first in the law that allowed the banks to get so big, said that the repeal of Glass-Steagall had nothing to do with the financial crisis of 2008. He didn't say, however, what role it might play in the next one. When Gramm said that, by the way, he was vice chairman of the investment bank unit of UBS, the biggest Swiss bank. Bankers call this kind of self-promoting statement "talking your book."

CitiMortgage's war on its own quality standards intensified. In November 2010, a senior executive e-mailed his subordinates, ordering them to make sure the percentage of flawed home loans declined from 7.25 to 5. He told them to "drive this rate down by brute force" if necessary.

The defect rates did go to 5 percent. The quality-control reports were getting better. The mortgages weren't.

Hunt was feeling beat up. Disrespected. Every day was a tussle. They weren't happy times. She started listening to a song that made her feel better: Rascal Flatts's "Stand." "Decide you've had enough," it goes. "You get mad, you get strong / Wipe your hands, shake it off / Then you stand."

She printed out the lyrics and pinned them to her cubicle. Reading them made her feel stronger. She studied the whistle-blower provision in the new Dodd-Frank law. She'd seen her friend Dick Bowen shoot before aiming. She'd do it differently. She'd do it right.

On March 22, 2011, a supervisor three levels above her on the corporate ladder asked Hunt and a colleague to linger behind in the conference room after a meeting. He was angry. His face was red, and he shook a finger at them. If they didn't get the mortgage defect rates down, he told them, "It's your asses on the line."

That tore it for her. Now Hunt felt she was being held personally responsible for fudged reports. It had to stop.

That night, she decided the time had come for her to take a stand. Hunt would follow the first step prescribed by Dodd-Frank: formally complaining to the company.

The decision kept her awake most of the night. She was risking everything—her livelihood, her career, her home. After leaving Citi, Bowen had landed a job as an accounting professor at the University of Texas, Dallas. But the injustice of his treatment still tore at him. He'd seen wrongdoing and summoned the courage to call it out— and *he* was punished. It didn't make any sense. As much as Hunt liked and respected Bowen, she didn't want to walk around with the weight of frustrated outrage on her shoulders.

A week after her irate supervisor had shaken a finger in her face, Sherry Hunt took a deep breath and marched into CitiMortgage's human resources department. She told them everything: how the bank had routinely bought and sold bad mortgages for years, how the fraud unit wasn't doing its job, and how the quality-control people were getting pressured to change their ratings.

She couldn't say a word about her whistle-blowing to her colleagues. She found a postcard of Leonardo Da Vinci's *Mona Lisa* and pinned it up in her cubicle next to the Rascal Flatts lyrics. Like La Gioconda, Sherry Hunt had a secret.

"I'm afraid of what I know," Hunt wrote the Securities and Exchange Commission in a May 24, 2011, letter. "I do not want to know what I know. I have nothing to gain from coming forward and have no hidden agenda." The letter was the second step in the Dodd-Frank law's instructions to whistle-blowers.

The next step was hiring a lawyer. She chose Finley Gibbs, who'd helped Hunt after her car accident. He was a partner in a seven-attorney firm in Columbia, Missouri, who'd never done securities litigation before. That didn't matter to Hunt. She trusted him. Gibbs notified the Justice Department of what Sherry Hunt knew and was willing to tell them. During the summer of 2011, she got out her spreadsheet and went over the details in four conference calls with government lawyers.

For two months Hunt and her lawyer sweated over whether to file a legal complaint. It would be what's called a *qui tam*, or false claims lawsuit, against Citi for defrauding the US government. False claims suits began during the Civil War, when merchants sold the Union Army tainted meat. An employee of a company ripping off the government can sue the company on behalf of taxpayers. Government attorneys can choose to join the legal action based on the evidence and their estimate of the chances for victory. Whistle-blowers have a hard time winning *qui tam* suits without government intervention, and only about one in five gets government backing.

In August 2011, Hunt decided she had to do it. Citigroup would never change its ways if she didn't. With no guarantee that the government would support her, she sued Citi in US District Court in Manhattan. The complaint was sealed.

Hunt still had to go to the office. Every morning she'd leave her house with its ten-acre lot, drive along a dirt road where cows and horses grazed in pastures, turn onto the two-lane county highway that passed over a river bridge barely wide enough for two vehicles, join the traffic on the interstate, and arrive at the sea of parked cars in O'Fallon. She navigated the rows of cubicles like a ghost. Nobody knew about the complaint. She felt vulnerable, as if she could lose her job over the smallest thing—a misplaced paper clip, a squeaky chair.

She knew the chances of beating the bank in court were slim. She was Calamity Jane. Citigroup handled overseas payments for the US government. She worked in a cubicle in O'Fallon, Missouri. The US government and its central bank had invested nearly half a trillion dollars making sure Citi survived.

Waiting for the government to decide whether to join the case was excruciating for Hunt. Then, on January 3, 2012, she got a phone call from Finley Gibbs, her lawyer. Her spreadsheet had impressed US Attorney Preet Bharara in Manhattan. The details were damning, the evidence overwhelming. The Justice Department had decided to join her in suing Citigroup.

The rest happened quickly. There was no testimony, no trial. On February 15, Citigroup agreed to pay $158.3 million—1.4 percent of its 2011 net income of $11.2 billion—to settle the charges. The bank also did something rare among the dozens of financial firms facing lawsuits for mortgage improprieties: it admitted wrongdoing.

Other banks had been slapped for screwing up their government-guaranteed mortgages. Also in February 2012, Bank of America paid $1 billion to settle a false claims suit—without admitting culpability. In May 2012, Deutsche Bank, Europe's biggest financial institution, settled a case charging it with misrepresenting loans to the Federal Housing Administration—like Citigroup had—and it too admitted wrongdoing.

The period in which the wrongdoing had occurred set Sherry Hunt's case apart. Bank of America and Deutsche Bank had been sued for bad behavior in the frenetic days of the precrisis credit bubble, when underwriting standards were ignored to keep the mortgage machine humming. Hunt showed that Citigroup had kept it up for four years *after* the financial crisis. The government's complaint made it clear that even up to the day of the settlement, CitiMortgage executives were pressuring quality-control employees to put a happy face on their reports. The government's lawsuit made it clear that the issues that led to the $158.3 million settlement hadn't been resolved.

As a whistle-blower, Hunt was entitled to part of the money. Because her spreadsheet made it easier for federal prosecutors to make their case, they cut her in for $31 million.

To the Citigroup communications department, Sherry Hunt didn't exist. They immediately started spinning the news. The press release they sent out in conjunction with the Justice Department's announcement stated in part,

> We are pleased to resolve this matter in conjunction with the National Mortgage Settlement reached last week among the five largest mortgage servicers and the Department of Justice and state Attorneys General. As with the larger mortgage agreement, we have fully provided for this settlement as of the fourth quarter of 2011.

One problem: the National Mortgage Settlement, a $25 billion agreement between five banks (including Citigroup), the Justice Department, and forty-nine states concerning the mishandling of foreclosures, had been signed the week previous. Hunt's complaint had nothing whatsoever to do with the National Mortgage Settlement.

For some reason, Citigroup insisted that its agreement with the Justice Department in the Hunt case was part of the legal resolution on foreclosures. Did Citi's public relations team think no one would pay attention to the Hunt case if they confused it with a much larger one? Citigroup's press liaisons never did give up the fiction that the two agreements were part of the same legal complaint.

The denial had begun.

"THE FHA WAS NOT DEFRAUDED."

Less than a minute into our conversation, Sanjiv Das's engine was powered up to full throttle. CitiMortgage's chief executive officer was off and running, defending the lender's representations to the Federal Housing Administration.

"Responsible finance is the single biggest tenet across Citibank, and it is something that we take extremely seriously," he said, referring to the advertising campaign his boss, Vikram Pandit, had initiated in 2010, promising transparency, honesty, and prudence. "And if you really think about the principles of responsible finance, it's about giving the right product to the right set of customers manufactured the right way."

Industry jargon tends to make my mind wander. I quit paying close attention to what Das was saying. Anyway, I had my voice recorder taping it, so I could always listen later.

I looked around the oval cherrywood conference table. We were somewhere in Citi's Manhattan headquarters, in a meeting room with a window overlooking Park Avenue. It was March 2012. Seated at the table on this chilly morning were Das, tall and slim, in a blue suit, two press aides, and an assistant. I took a chair to Das's right, and on my right was the Citi beat reporter for Bloomberg News, a scruffy young Irishman named Donal Griffin. I'd asked him along because he was capable and knowledgeable and possessed a finely tuned bullshit meter. Also, I figured I could use a wingman. I'm not always sure that my colleagues and I are on the same side—an ailment called capture makes a lot of journalists act funny around bank executives, as if they're part of the bank's information-dissemination team and not independent voices challenging the facts as the bank presents them. I had no doubts that Donal and I would be pushing in the same direction.

Most of Wall Street had colonized Midtown Manhattan. In 2008, Barclays Capital had inherited the Lehman Brothers building on Seventh Avenue and Fiftieth Street, near Times Square, replacing the Lehman green with Barclays blue. Morgan Stanley was a stone's throw west, over on Broadway and Forty-Eighth. Bank of America finished a new skyscraper on the corner of Forty-Second Street and Sixth Avenue and called it One Bryant Park, as if it had annexed the buttonwood-lined green rectangle diagonally across the street. Bear

Stearns had built a beautiful tower at Forty-Seventh and Madison with an octagonal shape so each floor could have eight corner offices instead of four. After JPMorgan bought Bear in March 2008, with the help of the Federal Reserve Bank of New York, where JPMorgan Chief Executive Officer Jamie Dimon was on the board of directors, JPMorgan's investment banking executives moved from the bank's own headquarters in an older building across the street, on Park Avenue, into the prettier, newer Bear Stearns octagon. The $1 billion estimated price tag for the building was about what JPMorgan had paid for the whole company, minus its rotten mortgages and other toxic assets, which the New York Fed had helpfully taken off its hands. Also on Park Avenue was UBS, the Swiss gargantuan accused of illegally manipulating worldwide interest rates. A few blocks north was Citigroup, where years after their retirements both Sandy Weill and John Reed still kept offices with bank-paid staff, a reward for their service to America.

"The mandate that we have is around making manufacturing quality of all kinds of loans, including FHA loans, absolutely pristine," Das was saying.

I was fully aware of the long-standing corporate practice of lulling listeners into lethargy with thick, impenetrable blocks of pure baloney. After twenty minutes, the well-trained corporate practitioner would typically stand up suddenly and announce that time was up, he was already late for an important appointment, and he hoped I'd gotten what I wanted. If I had any more questions, he'd say, I could address them to the press aides, who would or wouldn't return phone calls. I saw this scenario unfolding.

Hold up, I told Das. You said that there was no fraud. Yet Citigroup admitted wrongdoing in a lawsuit charging that your division had for years misrepresented the quality of its mortgages to the federal government. How is that not fraud?

"The business is a complex one, but the mandate is very clear," Das said. "The mandate is to manufacture loans the right way, and that was in the settlement. If you read the settlement, it was an explicit mandate to manufacture loans that are pristine."

"At Citibank," he continued, using the name of the systemically important financial institution's deposit-taking division, "the processes that were put in place, the people that were put in place—there's a whole new management team put in place"—he was referring to people he'd hired and promoted since taking over the division in 2008—"and the spirit with which this was done was to manufacture loans with manufacturing quality better than 5 percent, and that is something that has been said to you and to the industry explicitly as a mandate that we took on. We shared that with the FHA and with Fannie and Freddie, and we have a very proud trajectory of having accomplished that. Which is why this is not defrauding the FHA."

As I tried to find the switch on my own bullshit meter, which I had on vibrate and which was now rattling my molars, Griffin mentioned that Citi's agreement with the Department of Justice said nothing about CitiMortgage accomplishing anything. In fact, the opposite. The complaint explicitly said that even as the settlement was being written, even in 2012, CitiMortgage was a "battleground" where employees continued to fight over reporting mortgage defects.

"It's a complex process," Das said, looking Griffin and then me squarely in the eyes. "This is a complex process."

When I asked him how he would assess the job performance of his employees, who'd cost the bank $158 million and brought the shame of a confession of culpability, he used the words "fantastic" and "incredibly strong team."

I decided to give him an out. I knew the FHA didn't check the loans for quality. Maybe this was a case of the government turning a blind eye to defects because it wanted to increase the volume of FHA loans, then reversing course and blaming Citigroup for the lousy quality of those loans. Did he or any of his employees ever feel pressure to do FHA loans, to increase the volume to satisfy some government mandate, regardless of the quality of those loans?

No, he said.

Why did Sherry Hunt not get satisfaction after taking her concerns to human resources at CitiMortgage? Why did this issue have to go to the Justice Department? Why couldn't you have resolved her complaints in-house?

Das seemed affronted. He brought himself up and knit his eyebrows. "Did you ask her if she spoke to me?" he said.

The answer convinced me that CitiMortgage's loan-processing machine wasn't going to clean itself up quickly, if at all. Sherry Hunt had followed all the proper procedures. She wasn't obligated to skip five rungs of the corporate ladder and speak directly to Das. Nor would she be expected to. Sitting there in a conference room on Park Avenue, I thought of all the crappy jobs I'd had when I was younger, the ones where the bosses had no idea what the underlings were up to. Restaurateurs clueless that the waitresses were serving beer to their underage friends. Warehouse workers who punched the clock for absent coworkers. Cabdrivers who exaggerated their proximity to customers' addresses to snag fares over the dispatch radio. The manager who was seducing as many workers as he could. The assistant manager who hired his friends, then left all the work to others. Yet, without fail, the bosses always spoke as if they had their fingers on the pulse, certain that their employees respected them and responded positively to their directives, that people paid too little and bossed around capriciously would put the good of the company ahead of their own interests.

Now imagine the funny business that could go on in a company with 250,000 employees in 160 countries, many of them playing with other people's money without consequence.

I switched off the bullshit meter. It was useless.

Das went on to say that Citigroup was either number one or number two in the industry as far as the quality of the mortgages it manufactured—he kept using the word "manufactured" when it came to mortgages, as if these thirty-year contracts were widgets welded together on an assembly line—and how difficult it was to make an FHA loan and how complex they were. He bragged about how proud he was that his and everyone else at CitiMortgage's compensation was based on the low defect rates of the loans, and he tied that dubious practice to responsible finance.

I knew time was wasting so I asked him the question I was most looking forward to hearing answered: Why had CitiMortgage set up a Quality Rebuttal group to fight the assessments of Hunt's quality-assurance team?

"An appraisal comes in at a certain value," he began. "Do you know that that number is 100 percent precise?" He looked at me as if he expected a response. "There are discussions that happen. Ask the folks in quality assurance whether they had veto power or not. The answer is absolutely yes."

Did he mean to say that Hunt's ass had not been on the line, as her supervisor's supervisor's supervisor told her that day in March 2011? That looking all pissed off and shaking a finger in a subordinate's face and telling her that her ass was on the line if the defect rates didn't decrease didn't mean, actually, that her ass was on the line? That somehow the supervisor had been—I don't know—kidding? That it was Hunt and not her boss's boss' boss who got final say on which mortgages would be bought and sold and which would be reported as defective?

"Go back and ask the guys at quality assurance whether they had veto power or not," Das said.

So I did. After Das stood up suddenly and announced he was already late for another appointment, I called Sherry Hunt and asked her whether she had had veto power.

I had to pull the phone away from my ear she laughed so hard.

THREE WEEKS AFTER THE HUNT CASE WAS SETTLED, CITI'S board of directors announced it would pay Vikram Pandit, the chief executive officer, $15 million for 2011, plus millions more as a "retention bonus." The directors cited his ethical conduct and his leadership in creating a corporate culture of responsible finance as reasons for the pay package, which put him in the middle of the pack for Wall Street chief executives.

The directors also applauded Pandit for cleaning up the US mortgage business.

It was true that Citigroup had repaid its loans from the government and the Federal Reserve, with interest, and Pandit had piloted a bank that reported profits during each of the nine quarters up to the time he landed the pay package. Pandit had also agreed to accept $1 in pay for 2009 and 2010—after he'd pocketed $165 million from the $800 million sale of his hedge fund to Citigroup in 2007.

Shareholders may have been thinking of the 90 percent decline in Citigroup stock during Pandit's tenure when they took the rare step of rejecting his compensation in a nonbinding vote at their annual meeting in April 2012.

They may have had in mind Sherry Hunt's victory too.

IN 2012, TWO OF THE MOST POWERFUL MEN IN CITIGROUP'S history took the opportunity to publicly change their minds and reject the 1999 law that allowed the bank to use Grandma's Christmas Club deposits to play at the traders' casino.

John Reed had already come out for breaking up the largest banks. In October 2009, he'd written what amounted to a mea culpa letter to the *New York Times*, saying that "some kind of separation between institutions that deal primarily in the capital markets and those involved in more traditional deposit-taking and working-capital finance makes sense." The separation, combined with requiring the banks to borrow less, he'd written, "would go a long way toward building a more robust financial sector."

In April 2012, two days after his sixteen-year tenure as Citigroup's chairman ended, Dick Parsons intimated that tearing down the wall between trading and customer deposits may have been a reason for the worst financial crisis since the Great Depression.

"To some extent what we saw in the 2007, 2008 crash was the result of the throwing off of Glass-Steagall," Parsons said at a Rockefeller Foundation event in Washington. "Have we gotten our arms around it yet? I don't think so because the financial-services sector moves so fast."

Later, Parsons told Bloomberg News that Citigroup might just be too big to manage.

"One of the things we faced when we tried to find new leadership for Citi, there wasn't anybody who had deep employment experience in both sides of what theretofore had been separate houses," Parsons said.

Why hadn't Parsons done anything while he'd had the chance? Perhaps because he'd been making gobs of money. And when his time in the fray had ended and he had a long retirement ahead of him with more of that money than one man could ever spend, that's when Dick Parsons changed his mind.

But the most astonishing about-face was Sandy Weill's. Weill, more than anyone, had become the banner carrier for Gramm-Leach-Bliley. He'd engineered the merger of Travelers and Citicorp, which blazed the trail for the rest of the industry. In a July 25, 2012, interview on CNBC, the financial news network, Weill said that taxpayers would be safer—and investors wealthier—if the biggest banks broke up. "What we should probably do is go and split up investment banking from banking, have banks be deposit takers, have banks make commercial loans and real estate loans, have banks do something that's not going to risk the taxpayer dollars, that's not too big to fail," Weill told CNBC. That way, he said, they'd be much more profitable.

It's often said that the Yiddish word *chutzpah* refers to the man who kills his parents and then throws himself on the mercy of the court because he's an orphan. It could also apply to a man who strong-arms a financial services supermarket into being, watches as the course he sets for it helps impoverish the most prosperous country in history while enriching those who had the most to do with the decline, then, when he's done sucking the last marrow from the bones, goes on TV to say, "You know what? I'd probably make more money now if we went back to the way it was before I changed it all. So let's change it back."

On October 16, 2012, Vikram Pandit stepped down as chief executive officer of Citigroup. Parsons, the man who'd hired him, had left the bank, and Pandit clearly didn't have the confidence of the new chairman, Michael O'Neill. After a 2012 rebound, the bank's stock price had still lost 89 percent since Pandit had replaced Chuck Prince in December 2007—about the same time that Dick Bowen's warnings reached the bank's top executives.

On his way out the door, Pandit gave himself a pat on the back for a job well done. "It's hard to come up with things we should have done differently," he told Bloomberg TV.

Though Citigroup withheld some of a $40 million "retention bonus" it had agreed to pay Pandit just months earlier and declined to provide him with an office and staff like it had for Weill and Reed, the bank rewarded his service with a parting gift of $6.7 million.

No techies lined up on Park Avenue to applaud his final exit.

TWO

WRATH

*Secrecy: Mark Pittman and the Patron Saint
of Goldman Sachs*

M ARK PITTMAN PLOPPED DOWN ON A BARSTOOL—ALL SIX
feet, four inches, and three hundred pounds of him—and
chirped, "We're suing the Fed!"

It was October 2008. A cool, misty rain fell on Manhattan. Pittman had walked without an umbrella one block north from the world
headquarters of Bloomberg LP, the business-data company where he
was the news division's best reporter. He'd arrived at his favorite wa-
tering hole, a dim dive on Sixtieth Street called the Subway Inn, and
ordered his usual: a bottle of Budweiser and a shot of Jack Daniel's.

I was the guy he drank with.

The Fed that Pittman was referring to was the Federal Reserve,
the central bank of the United States since 1913. Its board of governors decides how much money will circulate and what interest rates
should be. It's where banks put their money and where they get
loans. Think of it as a bank for banks. As the most powerful financial institution in the world, with almost zero accountability, it can
tell Congress, the president of the United States, and the American
people to take a flying leap.

To Mark Pittman, former cattle ranch hand and bar bouncer, the son of a Kansas Piggly Wiggly store manager and a school crossing guard, the Federal Reserve needed to be told, "No, *you* take a flying leap."

Congress, in the Federal Reserve Act, directed the central bank to oversee operations of the banks and to keep the value of the dollar stable. That meant curbing not only inflation but also deflation—when prices fall. Later on, Congress added the job of making sure Americans can find jobs.

In practice, if not as an explicit matter of law, the Fed has one other responsibility: protecting the country's biggest banks.

In the summer of 2007, that job got tough. Too many poorly underwritten home loans, like the ones Dick Bowen had warned Citigroup about, had stopped paying. Defaults were piling up. Nobody had ever seen numbers like it. So many independent mortgage companies were going belly up so quickly that one Southern Californian started a blog called Mortgage Lender Implode-o-Meter to keep track of all the roadkill. The biggest banks had financed those mortgage companies, and in some cases had bought them, to keep the mortgage machine rolling. They had gradually lowered lending standards to the point where mortgage brokers, some of whom were in their early twenties and had last been working at car washes, joked that anyone who could fog a mirror could get a loan. Lending to subprime borrowers, who had little or no history of repaying their debts, had soared to about 20 percent of all mortgages written in 2007. Many of these mortgages had been written in a hurry, with no regard for how much money the borrower made or how valuable the house was. One mortgage customer told me he had signed his loan documents on his car hood in a Home Depot parking lot. Now a lot of those borrowers were starting to have trouble keeping current on their payments. Delinquencies were rising, higher than they'd ever been. The whole mortgage enterprise had gotten so dubious that investors became suspicious. They rushed to sell anything connected with subprime.

The problem was, nobody could tell how much subprime debt a fund had bought or a bank had on its books or in its mortgage pipeline. With so much in doubt, lending stopped. Creditors couldn't be sure who would end up dead next, and with real estate values declining and borrowers falling behind, they didn't have ready access to cash they could lend. The movement of money through the financial system is as vital as blood flow is to the human body, and it had quit nourishing the extremities.

Not many people outside the financial world knew it yet, but a panic was on.

Even Federal Reserve Chairman Ben Bernanke was slow to understand. For the first seven-plus months of 2007, Bernanke had insisted that the subprime mortgage crisis would be "contained," that most people needn't worry about the contagious disease of faltering trust. The big banks and government-supported mortgage buyers Fannie Mae and Freddie Mac had sold the loans in bundles to hedge funds, pension funds, insurance companies, and other banks all hoping to get a little more money back in exchange for taking on the added risk of investing in subprime. The credit-rating companies—Standard & Poor's (S&P), Moody's, and Fitch—had given subprime mortgage securities top grades, meaning that they were considered as safe as Treasury notes. The US government had never reneged on a debt. Neither would subprime mortgage borrowers, according to S&P, Moody's, and Fitch.

Regardless of what the credit-rating companies said, by August 2007 even Bernanke could see that financial firms around the world didn't have faith in each other's ability to repay their debts. They were frightened, and most likely embarrassed, that all the subprime loans on their books, declining in value by the day, would render them insolvent. Bernanke had studied the Great Depression. He believed that the central bank had screwed up the economy back then by not making enough money available. So he decided to lend, lend, and lend some more. The whole philosophy could be summed up as "Go big or go home."

As the so-called lender of last resort, the Fed can make short-term loans to financial institutions nobody else will take a chance on. As long as a bank's not insolvent, it can qualify for a Fed loan. The Fed's oldest—and for ninety-four years the only—lending program is called the discount window. The loan recipients, by tradition, are secret. The Fed frets that if people could tell which bank was asking for emergency funding, they'd figure the bank was in trouble. Depositors and investors would pull their money, and counterparties would quit trading with the bank for fear that it would fail and they'd be stuck.

Because of that perceived stigma, the Fed created new programs to lend money to banks. From August 2007 to the end of 2008, in addition to the discount window, ten programs, each designed to dissolve a different clog in a crucial pipe of the world's financial plumbing, were busy making barrelfuls of money available to the financial system.

Banks took billions. No one outside the Fed and the walls of the borrower bank knew who they were or how much they'd taken. A problem emerged: How could investors in a specific firm, from the huge Citigroup to little Saigon National Bank in Westminster, California, know whether the bank executives' superior management skills were keeping the business above water or the firm's survival depended on access to seemingly limitless Fed loans? How could pension plans and mutual funds judge which banks were healthy enough to invest in and which were being dragged to dry land by a Federal Reserve lifeline?

How could taxpayers, who were ultimately on the hook, determine if this was the best use of the country's treasure?

Pittman had been bursting for details about the loans the Fed gave to the banks. When he asked the Fed for the data and the Fed refused him flatly, he only wanted it more. The back-and-forth between the behemoth reporter and the behemoth bank was familiar to me. I sat next to Pittman at the office. His loud phone voice frequently intruded on my daydreaming. We often worked as a team trying to clear the smoke screen of obfuscation and complication that the financial industry tended to cast in the path of anyone trying to dig deeper into their operations than their press releases allowed. We ate lunch together most days, ordering takeout from Little Thai Kitchen on Fifty-Third Street or picking up plastic containers of American-made sushi from the Japanese grocery on Fifty-Ninth. We often shared a drink or three in the evenings before boarding our commuter trains, Pittman heading to Yonkers, me to New Jersey. I'd gotten steady rants about his quest to get the Fed to cough up bailout data, and as his frustration with the central bank morphed into a mission, we'd collaborated on stories about the Fed's refusal.

What chafed Pittman back in October 2008 was his knowledge that Congress and President George W. Bush, at the urging of Treasury Secretary Henry Paulson and Ben Bernanke at the Fed, had made $700 billion available for the banks. Of course, $700 billion was a lot of dough. But it was only the visible tip of the iceberg. The Fed had been lending to the banks for more than a year. We knew that Bank of America, JPMorgan Chase, Wells Fargo, and Citigroup were getting $25 billion each from the Treasury Department and that Goldman Sachs and Morgan Stanley were getting $10 billion. But we had no idea how much individual banks were getting from the Fed. That was the problem. The central bank reported its loans only in aggregate. Each Thursday at 4 p.m. Washington time, when the Fed released its updated balance sheet, the numbers would grow, and they were big. But the updates revealed no details concerning where all those billions were headed.

Secrecy was a red flag flapping in the breeze for Mark Pittman. He'd already done groundbreaking stories on the screwups of the biggest banks. In 2007, months before it became obvious, he chided the credit-ratings companies, S&P, Moody's, and Fitch, for failing to sound the alarm for investors on subprime mortgage securities. Since the companies had deemed the mortgages a safe bet, insurance companies figured they must be sound enough to buy. But the rising number of subprime defaults meant investors were starting to lose billions of dollars. Pittman figured this out before S&P, Moody's, and Fitch—or at least he came out and said so before they did.

Pittman had also been the only one to chronicle the creation of the ABX, an exchange where traders could bet against, or "short-sell," American home owners. The series, on which I collaborated, was called "Wall Street's Faustian Bargain." Pittman explained how Goldman Sachs, in the best-known example, could sell a mortgage investment called Abacus to a German bank at the same time it was betting that Abacus would lose money. The ability to short-sell American home owners made billions for some hedge fund managers and spurred the big banks to churn out more and more bad mortgages, with tragic consequences.

Pittman loved piecing together the evidence. This was a guy who had his nose busted when he got coldcocked in a high school locker room after a big game. He vowed to never again be surprised, so he was always on the lookout. The stuff he uncovered made him a star. He pointed out that Hank Paulson, the Treasury secretary who was offering the billions in bank bailouts, was chief executive officer of Goldman Sachs at a time when the New York investment bank was creating the "complex" financial gadgets that were now going bad—a big reason that bailouts were perceived to be needed. And Pittman had reported that Paulson's successor at Goldman Sachs, Lloyd Blankfein, was in the room when Paulson, Bernanke, and Timothy Geithner, president of the Federal Reserve Bank of New York, decided to rescue AIG, the giant insurance company that was on the hook to Goldman Sachs for $16 billion.

Pittman took it personally.

"It's not the Fed's money," Pittman said. "It's our money. And we deserve to know where it's going."

THE FEDERAL RESERVE IS AN ODD ANIMAL, SHROUDED IN mystery—the okapi of financial institutions. It has a kind of particle/wave status as both an agency of the executive branch and its own independent thing. It's funded by its member banks, but the Federal Reserve Act of 1913 mandates that elected officials must have at least a scrap of oversight. With the consent of Congress, the president appoints the bank's chairman to a four-year term and each of its seven governors to fourteen-year terms. The chairman must appear in front of relevant committees of the House and Senate twice a year for a proper grilling. Aside from that, the Fed is basically free to print money, buy securities, lend dollars around the world, and set benchmark lending rates. It enjoys this autonomy because lawmakers couldn't trust themselves to keep from pressuring the central bank to flood the land with easy money every time an election rolled around. This keeps the Fed, in theory, mostly free of political interference. But it also means that living within the world's longest-running democracy is an nonaccountable servant of the big banks that can hit "CTRL+P" whenever it wants, pick winners and losers, lend money in secret, and keep elected officials—and everyone else—on the outside looking in.

The Fed deserves its reputation for secrecy. Its creation myth is a whopper. The country's top Wall Street backslappers and a very wealthy senator conceived its birth at a hush-hush 1910 confab on Jekyll Island, Georgia. Their aim was to smooth out financial panics by giving banks a pool of money they could tap when no one else dared extend them credit. Over the course of a couple years, they shaped their plan into the third central bank of the United States, the first two having been killed by populist uprisings in the nineteenth century.

The origin of the Federal Reserve in that secret Jekyll Island meeting has fed the imaginations of conspiracy lovers, who never tire of linking the cloak-and-dagger of the Fed's conception to a variety of dystopian world orders. It's possible to play a kind of multiple-choice Mad Libs with the nightmares espoused by the tinfoil-hat brigade. For instance,

An international cabal of _____

1. Jews
2. Trilateralists
3. Freemasons
4. Council on Foreign Relations members

created the Fed with the aim of _____

1. enslaving the world
2. making themselves as rich as Satan's bookie
3. subjecting us to the degrading rituals of their nefarious cults
4. ending time

by establishing _____

1. one world government
2. the income tax
3. fiat currency
4. evil robots

The folks who ascribe to any of the above may have booked seats on some fanciful one-way flights of make-believe, assigning villainy to milquetoast bureaucrats and dark motives to policies that in the real world have both positives and negatives, but their fruity Kool-Aid contains this shimmering droplet of truth: the Fed can do what it wants. And for decades, it never had to tell us what that was.

SECRECY WOULD LEAVE A LEGACY AS CORROSIVE AS THE bailouts themselves, but in 2008, the inside story was a hard sell to ordinary people. There was little patience among the general American public for breathless exposés on what had, for nearly a century, been a shadowy corner of the financial system. By 2013, handicapping the next Fed chairman was newsworthy, but even as late as the financial crisis, most Americans didn't know or care what the central bank did. Not many people were clamoring to read all about it. Pittman knew as well as anyone that simply speaking the words "Federal Reserve" at a backyard barbecue was all it took to clear a path to the food table. Pittman had plenty of friends in the financial industry—flacks, buy-side guys, stock analysts, and bond raters— who could, over drained glasses of scotch, yammer endlessly, and sometimes even provocatively, about such sexy subjects as yield spreads, mezzanine tranches, and credit hedging. They loved to kibitz about the central bank and its new and expanded role at the very center of American business and politics. They could enthrall Pittman with stories about the suckers at a Dusseldorf bank or the savvy women at a Pittsburgh money fund, and they could tell raunchy jokes that passed for metaphors of current market conditions that were so spot-on he might even remember them the next morning. But he had just as many friends—artists, upstate cop reporters, public relations guys, and Palisades Boat Club members—who knew only that something fishy was going on and had no patience for details beyond where in the stock market they should park their money, if that.

Part of the reason was the impenetrability of what observers resorted to calling "financial instruments." Financial firms paid the world's craftiest attorneys, accountants, and public relations representatives armfuls of cash to cast a haze over what they were doing. Prospectuses, the documents meant to provide details of investments for people thinking about putting in money, often ran to 1,000 pages and read like crimes against the English language. Press releases were no better. Neither were the banks' official reports, filed every three months with the Securities and Exchange Commission. University of San Diego law professor Frank Partnoy and journalist Jesse Eisinger tried in early 2013 to squeeze meaning from Wells Fargo's quarterly accounting and got more and more baffled the deeper they dug. When they called Wells Fargo for guidance, employees referred them back to the impenetrable report.

During the crisis and in its immediate aftermath, as Fed money was leaving through the back door, this lack of disclosure drove Pittman nuts. He especially hated when his colleagues in the financial media referred to "complex transactions" and left it at that. He wished more people had the desire to unscrew the inscrutable. He couldn't figure why so many reporters skipped the meatiest details. "This is the biggest story of our careers," he'd plead. "Not just *financial* story, but *story*." And while a big part of it lived in the inaccessible details, there was plenty of macro evidence abounding to fill a volume of grim fairy tales. In a blink, the Federal Reserve had reshaped the financial system. Hell, it had *become* the financial system. With a wave of his arm, Bernanke had transformed trillions of private debt into public obligations. The free market had ceased to exist. While few people were looking, bailouts became standard operating procedure. Profit went to the bankers; everybody shared losses. Central bankers believed that the biggest banks *were* the American economy. If they could rescue the financial institutions, the thinking went, the rest of the country would benefit too. At least, that was their story. And they stuck to it. The Fed backed up the money truck—beep, beep, beep—and basically told Congress, the president, and the American people, "We know what we're doing. Trust us." And just about everybody did trust them. Blindly.

That's what outraged Pittman. That's what drove him to parse the fine print of collateralized debt obligation prospectuses and pronounce them barnyard droppings. That's what made him examine mortgage performance records and label them fiction. The bankers had the audacity to tell him and everyone else not to worry, they had it covered—and these were the same clowns who'd gotten us into this mess. With an independent eye, Pittman could tell that the financial system had become a sham, a fake empire. Pittman bet that, at the very least, bankers were hiding bailout details simply out of shame. The New York branch of the Fed, headed by Timothy Geithner, was supposed to be monitoring the behavior of the Wall Street firms to make sure they didn't blow up. But blow up they did, first Bear Stearns, then Lehman Brothers, with wannabes like Fannie Mae and Freddie Mac caught in the undertow. The problem was far from contained. Wachovia, one of the country's biggest retail banks, and the two biggest savings and loans, Washington Mutual and IndyMac, fell like dominos. The Bloomberg News financial reporting team was working nearly around the clock. World bankers and their regulators were meeting what seemed like every weekend, trying to save another firm's bacon. How humiliating for the masters of the universe to have to beg taxpayers for help.

Pittman viewed the bailouts as a way for Bernanke to cover Geithner's ass. It was a risky and expensive way to save bureaucratic face. The same coziness between Wall Street and Geithner's New York Fed, which made it possible for the banks to do just about whatever they pleased during the mortgage boom, was extended in the bailouts into a blanket and inappropriate forgiveness for those harmful activities. The lie sprang up, spread by well-compensated operatives in the media, that "market conditions" had caused the big bank failures and near failures, that fearless and guilt-free plundering was just what boys-will-be-boys Wall Street did. If capitalism was all about winners and losers, we'd mutated in a matter of days into some bizarre hybrid that was altogether different, with unelected decision makers rewarding their buddies for making millions of dollars doing things that crashed the economy.

Without fluency in the particulars of the bailouts or the behavior that necessitated them, Americans were mere spectators, reduced to working out their frustration in a generalized and almost paranoid-seeming rage at the cronyism, the unfairness, and the nerve. The $700 billion earmarked for Treasury's Troubled Asset Relief Program, or TARP, came right out of Americans' pockets, and from the very start, they didn't like it—not at all. The infamous plunge of the stock market on the day TARP was, on the first try, defeated in Congress only served to show, once again, the growing disconnect between ordinary people and those with enough wealth to buy pieces of the market. And while whatever the Fed was lending wasn't, strictly speaking, taxpayer money, it was new money, fresh off the printing presses, and any college freshman who managed to stay awake during Econ 101 could tell you that increasing the money supply is bound to cause rising prices, creating a hidden tax on everyone, even if they are victims of the financial mess and not its beneficiaries. In essence, the country's financial leadership was telling the country, "Quit worrying about how big the tab is—just pay it."

If TARP had proven so unpopular, how would Americans react when they discovered the details of what was happening at the Fed? Setting aside the argument over whether it was necessary to attach the money pump to the banks and crank the dial to eleven, the not knowing how much and to whom was—well, it was kind of outrageous.

Pittman had grown up studying *Life* magazine's photos of Bull Connor's Birmingham firefighters pointing water hoses at children and watching on TV as Senator Sam Ervin's Watergate hearings revealed the liars and schemers who roamed the halls of the White House. He wanted to know the details of what the Fed was up to because he thought America ought to live up to its democratic ideal. That institutions, no matter how big, ought to be responsible for what they did. That it was only fair that the people know. Simple as that.

He knew what was at stake. Not just money. Not just economic policy. Not just the functioning of the world financial system. But the future of capitalism. The credibility of democracy.

Sure, it was corny. Corny as Kansas. Pittman was uniquely qualified to be the guy who carried the torch, who led the march into the murk. He felt just as much at home in front of a spreadsheet, squinting at the figures over his round eyeglasses, as he did on his boat on the Hudson River with his wife Laura and the girls, sipping a beer as the sun sank behind the Palisades. He'd been an engineering student. He was comfortable with numbers. He'd been a high school linebacker. He could take a little pain. He'd been a crime reporter. He could smell a rat. And he was at Bloomberg News, with its multiscreen Bloomberg terminal providing every financial statistic that meant anything at his fingertips. A son of the Midwest, he was born at a time when people still believed that in America, if you worked hard and kept out of trouble, you could make a decent life for yourself. There was no guarantee, but at least you could hold your head up. Pittman's Mennonite grandmother had helped raise him, and along with the sandwiches made of bacon grease and figs picked from the backyard tree, she'd fed him an unshakable sense of right and wrong. If you lied, cheated, or stole, you ought to be punished. To Pittman, a reporter wore a figurative badge and carried a metaphorical gun. He protected the good guys and nailed the bad guys. Then Pittman went to the Subway Inn after work and downed a beer and a shot—sins to a grandmother who disapproved of dancing and poker.

"Do me a favor," he once said to me. "If I ever get too confident about something, I need you to let me know."

Like I ever did.

In May 2008, in journalists' lingo, Pittman FOIA'd the Fed. In other words, he filed a Freedom of Information Act request with the central bank for the details of its emergency loans to banks. He asked the Fed to tell him the names of the banks that were getting the billions, how much they were getting, and what they gave the Fed as collateral in return.

Despite its independence, the Federal Reserve is subject to the same rules of disclosure as the rest of the executive branch of government. In theory, as long as the requested records don't violate any of the nine Freedom of Information Act exemptions, the 1966 FOIA says that Pittman or any other citizen can get its data.

The Fed resisted Pittman's request, arguing that naming borrower banks would brand them as outcasts. "Stigma" was the word it used. The Fed wanted to avoid any appearance of weakness on the part of the banks, afraid that it might spark a run. These were banks that in the middle of the 2000s had borrowed $20, $30, even $40 for every dollar they had on hand and were betting it all at the mortgage casino. A sell-off of shares, the calling in of loans, or other firms' refusal to do business with any of these obscenely indebted institutions could send them tumbling into insolvency in a matter of days. Bear Stearns had proved that.

The Fed said it couldn't give up specifics without risking a run, which would hurt the individual borrower banks and the whole banking system. In other words, the Fed told Pittman to take a flying leap.

Pittman appealed the Fed's decision, as was his right under the Freedom of Information Act. Again, the Fed said no.

If you're a reporter covering the financial industry, you get used to hearing that word. In many instances, a banker doesn't have any obligation to bare his soul, if he has one, to the intrusive jackals of the press. But this was a special case. This was a brewing catastrophe that Pittman predicted would result in "tumbleweeds blowing down Wall Street." It was important, imperative even, to start keeping track of the money before things really went haywire.

The next step outlined by the Freedom of Information Act was for Bloomberg to sue the Fed to force it to give up the data. This option appealed to Pittman. He'd gotten the idea from his boss, the

Bloomberg News projects and investigations editor Amanda Bennett. Bennett had run Portland's *Oregonian* and the *Philadelphia Inquirer*. At one time she had competed against men as a weightlifter. She was upbeat and driven, had won two Pulitzers, and came to Bloomberg with a mandate to win another. You think she didn't relish the notion of suing the Fed?

Bennett brought in Charles Glasser, the Bloomberg newsroom attorney. Glasser was a troublemaker with spiky salt-and-pepper hair and Hong Kong–tailored suits. He smoked fancy cigars, drank single-malt scotch, drove a supercharged Jaguar XKR, played Albert King–drenched solos on vintage electric guitars, and bragged that he was a descendant of the early-twentieth-century American Communist Emma Goldman, who was famous for saying, "If I can't dance, I don't want your revolution," though she actually didn't. As a news photographer in Nicaragua in 1980, Glasser had been photographed in the back of a pickup truck cradling an M-16. His mouth watered at the possibility of a lawsuit.

Bennett and Glasser met with Matthew Winkler, Bloomberg News's editor in chief. Founder Michael Bloomberg had hired Winkler in 1990 to start a news service to complement the data feed the Bloomberg terminal provided to traders. Winkler quit his job as a *Wall Street Journal* bond reporter to become Bloomberg News's employee number one. He'd shown up for his first day at 8 a.m.— considered numbingly early for anyone accustomed to the daily rhythms of a morning newspaper. The future mayor of New York asked Winkler in his typically wry manner if he'd enjoyed his beauty sleep. It's safe to say that for the next quarter century, Winkler was just about always working. On the day in 1990 that Mike had given him a chair and a phone, that was Bloomberg News in its entirety. By 2008 the organization had more than 1,000 employees working in 140 offices around the world. The long wrangle that began the day Pittman, Glasser, Bennett, and Winkler decided to sue the Fed would, more than anything, put Winkler's baby on the map.

For Bloomberg LP, the Fed FOIA was an attractive case because it dovetailed with its corporate ethos of transparency. Mike Bloomberg had started Bloomberg LP in 1981 to pull back the curtains on the otherwise secretive bond market. Before the company started publishing bond prices, just as stock prices had been public for decades, customers had to rely on bond salesmen for quotes. That simple but revolutionary change in how credit markets did business was the basis of the Bloomberg terminal, a pair of monitors with multicolored blinking words and numbers, rented by the month, set up on traders' desks. It gave them all the prices, yields, spreads, Fibonaccis, and fluctuations a trader needed to rip the face off the competition. The whole knowledge-is-power thing proved so popular that Bloomberg the man amassed one of the country's great fortunes. Bloomberg LP was bringing in more than $9 billion a year in 2008. Transparency had built the company and was one of its paramount values. Bloomberg LP's offices and conference rooms had clear glass walls. Employees joked that one day a work crew would show up and install glass walls in the rest rooms.

Bloomberg, who'd relinquished day-to-day command of the company when elected mayor of New York in 2001, was asked if he was okay with the lawsuit. "Do it," he said.

On that rainy October day in 2008, a couple weeks before his fifty-first birthday, at the Subway Inn on Sixtieth Street, Mark Pittman raised his glass of Jack Daniel's.

"We're suing the Fed," he said. Then he grinned. "And we're going to win."

For the past year our aim had been to nail the bastards who wrecked a financial system that was responsible for the highest standard of living the world had ever known. We lived in a mountain empire of high peaks and deep valleys, where the thrill of The Get ran smack into the limits of what we could do without real badges and guns. The life of the investigative reporter is one of subpoena envy. Our bravado kept us rolling from one story to the next, and at the Subway Inn, emboldened by the belly burn of Tennessee's finest spirits, thrilling things seemed possible. There we ranted about injustice, cursed idiocracy, mapped out reporting plans, bulldozed indignities, celebrated our involvement in important stories, and dreamed big.

I supported Pittman's quest; it was mine too. But I was more skeptical than he was. Suing the Fed was like setting out to seize the broomstick of the Wicked Witch of the West. No adversary in the ninety-four-year history of the US central bank had ever prevailed in court against this immovable object. Now that the financial crisis was in full downswing—Lehman Brothers had declared bankruptcy the month before, and every economic indicator was losing altitude—the system was on the brink, and the first casualty of war would be transparency. Pay no attention to that bearded man behind the columns of the Federal Reserve building. The world's most powerful financial institution had dismissed Pittman and his upstart demands for data with a regal flick. The courts would fall in line.

So when I raised my glass of Jack Daniel's and touched it to Pittman's, all I could muster was, "Good friggin' luck, dude."

His laughter boomed.

On November 7, 2008, Bloomberg LP filed suit against the Board of Governors of the Federal Reserve System for the release of the names of banks that borrowed from the Fed, how much they borrowed and when, and what collateral they put up in exchange. The quest for transparency would take twenty-nine months. The costs, of both the Fed's opacity and the fight against it, would be dearer than any of us imagined.

THIS IS HOW THE FREEDOM OF INFORMATION ACT IS supposed to work: Let's say you're a reporter doing research for a story about the first anniversary of the bankruptcy of Lehman Brothers, the New York investment bank whose September 15, 2008, failure stepped on the fingers of the economy as it tried to scale a Mount Rushmore–sized recession. You write a letter to the Federal Reserve detailing what you want—in this case, all documents generated by Fed staff doing analysis ahead of time on the possible failure of Lehman Brothers. Within twenty days, the Fed will let you know whether it will satisfy your request, and if all goes well, a few weeks later an employee of the central bank will ship you the documents, which you can then share with the world, ignore, or shred and use as kindling at your vacation campsite.

This is how the FOIA often works: Let's say you're a reporter working on that same story. The Fed will acknowledge receipt of your June 4, 2009, FOIA request, and then you will hear crickets. You will call the FOIA office to see about progress, and you will reach a human being who assures you that your request will be processed as soon as the office processes the dozen or so requests it's received before yours. One of the lesser known aspects of the FOIA is that if the Fed determines that documents generated by, say, JPMorgan Chase are pertinent to your request, an FOIA officer will contact JPMorgan Chase to ask the bank if it's okay for the Fed to release the documents to the public. That's because the Fed, or any other government agency, wants JPMorgan Chase to cooperate the next time it asks the bank for a confidential document. The Fed, or any executive branch agency, will then wait for JPMorgan Chase, or any company or individual, to respond. I have no official data on the frequency of a company's agreeing to release documents it sent to a government agency under the presumption of confidentiality, but I'll hazard a guess that the percentage approaches a number resembling a doughnut. So you wait and wait, then end up writing the story for publication the second week of September 2009 without the information you requested.

Time will go by, and because you've moved on to other projects, you will forget you ever made the FOIA request about Lehman Brothers in the first place. Then, on December 30, 2010, four hundred seventy-seven days after your story was published and five hundred eighty-one days after you sent the Fed your first letter asking for the information, you will receive a cardboard box in the mail from the Board of Governors of the Federal Reserve System. (You will resist the urge to shout, "What's in the box? What's in the box!?" like Brad Pitt in the movie *Se7en*.)

What's inside the box will be a pile of paper seven inches high. On top will be a letter from the secretary of the Fed board, Jennifer J. Johnson. It will tell you that the Fed staff did indeed monitor Lehman Brothers's condition and discuss contingency plans for the investment bank's failure. E-mails, letters, memos, and other records showing that discussion, Johnson will write, contain information exempt from the FOIA for a variety of reasons: they are related to internal personnel issues (which you can understand because nobody is particularly interested in what grades the Fed employees might have received on their annual reviews); they are unwarranted invasions of employee privacy (which is a good thing, too, because nobody wants to know what these people did over the weekend [unless it was attending a party thrown by AIG with taxpayer money]); they are privileged inter- or intra-agency memoranda (lawyers plotting, presumably); they contain bank supervision details (which would be nice to see but are explicitly excluded from public view by the FOIA); or they betray trade secrets.

Your heart will sink. But then you will look into the box and slide your hand down the inside of it, just to gauge how many pages there are, and you will estimate 1,000 or so, all double sided. You will feel excited by the prospect of discovering something no one outside the Fed knows. How happy you are! How happy your editors will be, and how grateful your readers! You will secure an empty conference room and tap an eager colleague to help you pore, and you will have difficulty lugging the box into the conference room because it's so heavy—and so full of possibility! But when you begin the laborious process of eyeballing the individual pages, you will be reminded of

Yossarian, the hero of Joseph Heller's World War II novel *Catch-22*. Yossarian, a crewmember on bombing flights over Italy who's been confined to a bed in a field hospital on a Mediterranean island because of a mysterious liver ailment, is assigned the task of censoring servicemen's letters home. To amuse himself, Yossarian one day declares war on modifiers, crossing out each one with a thick black pen. Another day, he leaves only the words "a," "an," and "the." Or he'll simply obliterate the whole body of the letter, leaving only "Dear Mary."

You paw through the first pages of your documents to find that a Yossarian in the Federal Reserve's FOIA office has placed a gray box over everything. It appears as if nearly the entire range of human commercial activity can be interpreted as a "trade secret." You and your embarrassed colleague go through one hundred pages, two hundred, three hundred, picking up speed as you realize the obvious—that there's very little but gray squares, gray rectangles, gray lines, gray, gray, gray, on every page. Your Fed FOIA Yossarian has declared war on everything. You marvel at a central bank that paid some hapless employee to go through 1,000 double-sided pages simply to annihilate their content, then dump them all into a cardboard box and ship it to you. It's something that might be done by a bored serviceman laid up in a hospital. A mental hospital.

THERE'S METHOD TO THE MADNESS. SENDING YOU THE BARREN fruits of your FOIA request allows the Fed to check a box. "Partial grant" is something government bureaucrats devoutly wish for. It pads their stats.

It's like the CitiMortgage employees who figured out that the quality of the home loans didn't matter as long as the reports looked good. In fiscal year 2010, the Federal Reserve processed 857 FOIA requests, granted 445, denied 42, and issued 82 "partial grants"— including your request for documents related to the Lehman Brothers bankruptcy. "Trade secrets" was the exemption most cited when the Fed denied a FOIA request.

But the numbers are meaningless, sunlight shined on a dark corner of nothing. The idea of a "partial grant" consisting of 1,000 double-sided pages of gray is a bureaucrat's idea of transparency, its Orwellian opposite.

I don't mean to pick on the Federal Reserve, at least in this instance. My experiences with the Securities and Exchange Commission and the Treasury Department have been similar. Perhaps the Fed's Lehman Brothers e-mails betrayed legitimate trade secrets, though it's hard to imagine them doing damage to a bankrupt bank. Anton Valukas, a Chicago attorney, led a team that wrote a 1,000-page explanation of how Lehman Brothers collapsed. Called the Valukas report, it contained damning information about the activities of Lehman Brothers executives and in some cases didn't clothe the bank's counterparties in glory either. Nobody went to jail, and nobody claimed the revelations held up the bankruptcy process. The Valukas report exposed the weakness of the Freedom of Information Act—it's only as good as the Yossarians in the agencies' FOIA offices allow it to be. FOIA has its own catch-22. If a reporter files FOIA requests, he must be after a secret. And if it's a secret, it can't be revealed. At the Fed, protecting the banks comes first. Transparency comes last.

On his first full day in office, President Barack Obama promised a new era of transparency in government. On January 21, 2009, Obama directed agencies to "adopt a presumption in favor of disclosure, in order to renew their commitment to the principles embodied in FOIA."

In 2012, Bloomberg News reporters Jim Snyder and Danielle Ivory undertook an exhaustive study of Obama's executive branch to see if the president had lived up to his promise. Snyder and Ivory sent FOIA requests to fifty-seven agencies for the fiscal year 2011 travel records of their top administrators. Since taxpayers foot the bill for these trips, and the wanderings of federal officials on the taxpayer dime are indisputably public record (with scant possibility of invoking the trade secret exemption), it would seem a no-brainer that the reporters would get the information in a timely way.

Only eight of the fifty-seven agencies responded to their requests before the twenty-day deadline, the reporters wrote. Six months later, they still hadn't received records from nineteen agencies. During the first year of the Obama presidency, Cabinet agencies used exemptions 466,402 times to deny access to information, a 50 percent jump from the final year of the George W. Bush administration.

ON AUGUST 24, 2009, LORETTA PRESKA, CHIEF JUDGE OF New York's Southern District, ruled that looking foolish is a cost of doing business, and banks appearing vulnerable to customers, counterparties, and investors—what the Federal Reserve called "stigma"—is less important than the public's right to know where its central bank is sending its money—especially with regard to so-called trade secrets, or Freedom of Information Act Exemption No. 4.

Bloomberg LP had won. The Fed had lost. The celebration was muted. Charles Glasser had vowed to smoke the foot-long cigar he'd been saving. It went unlit. Pittman didn't skip down the halls or wrap any interns in an Eisenstaedtian V-J Day embrace. I joked that this proved that a working-class kid from Kansas could beat the world's most powerful financial institution, as long as he had better attorneys. One of those attorneys, Thomas Golden, of the New York firm Willkie, Farr & Gallagher, who led the Bloomberg legal team, assured everyone at Bloomberg world headquarters that it wasn't over. He was certain the Fed would appeal.

Three weeks later, the Clearing House Association, a 156-year-old group of the biggest American banks—JPMorgan Chase, Wells Fargo, Citigroup, Bank of America, and Goldman Sachs among them—jumped to the central bank's defense. Together with the Fed they appealed the Preska decision. If anything, Bloomberg LP's lawsuit had laid bare the relationship between the Fed and the biggest banks. Their cooperation was now explicit. They were in cahoots.

BLOOMBERG LP'S SUCCESS IN COURT TOOK LAWMAKERS BY surprise. Pittman and I received calls from congressional staffers drafting what would become the Dodd-Frank Wall Street Reform and Consumer Protection Act. They were excited by the possibility that the Fed, America's most secretive nonspy institution, would be forced to throw open its books and allow Bloomberg News to see who'd borrowed what when.

Talking to them, I began to realize that interest in the financial system's transparency wasn't exclusive to either Republicans or Democrats. It cut crosswise ideologically. In fact, two of our most vocal supporters in Congress were Ron Paul, the Texas Republican, and Alan Grayson, a Florida Democrat. Paul, a free market acolyte of Ayn Rand and longtime critic of the central bank, was finishing his book *End the Fed*. He'd run for president on both the Republican and Libertarian tickets. Grayson was a first-term progressive who'd made a fortune suing corporate profiteers in the aftermath of the Gulf War. The two were polar opposites on the political spectrum, with Paul advocating a federal government small enough to drown in the bathtub and Grayson most famous for championing Obama's expanded health-care coverage. They agreed, however, that the Fed should be held accountable for the unprecedented bailouts.

Pittman and I spent an hour or so chatting with Paul and his press secretary, Rachel Mills, in Paul's Capitol Hill office. Paul had introduced legislation to audit the Federal Reserve in every session he'd been in Congress, dating back to the 1970s, and he'd rarely gotten anyone to listen to him. When we met with him in 2009, he was in the middle of collecting more than two hundred cosponsors.

Congress members were hearing it from their constituents. They wanted an end to the bailouts, the perceived cronyism, the secrecy. I remember best, from the afternoon in Paul's office, how he'd decorated his walls. Most congress members display photos of their families or themselves with famous people. Paul was different. Behind his desk, he'd hung framed black-and-white photographs of the so-called Austrian economists: Ludwig van Mises, Friedrich Hayek, and Murray Rothbard.

Grayson, intimidatingly smart and blunt, wasn't a fan of the Austrians, but neither was he a fan of the central bank's secrecy. When the Fed's inspector general, who was supposed to be keeping tabs on the bailout money but clearly wasn't, appeared at a hearing of the House Financial Services Committee, Grayson had roasted her. I almost felt sorry for the gazelle, yielding pathetically to the lion's jaws. A video of their confrontation, posted on YouTube, got more than 1 million hits.

On Capitol Hill, Pittman and I also met with staffers from the offices of Connecticut Democrat John Larson and New Jersey Republican Scott Garrett, whose brilliant young press aide, Erica Elliott, gave us her verdict on the first draft of the Wall Street reform legislation, which she'd received the day before we met with her and had studied all night. Dodd-Frank would not end the problem that the three of us agreed was the thorniest legacy of the Wall Street rescue: banks that have grown too big to be allowed to fail.

BLOOMBERG LP V. BOARD OF GOVERNORS OF THE FEDERAL RESERVE reminded me of what it's like raising children: the days are long but the years are short. In September 2009, the Fed and the Clearing House Association appealed Judge Preska's decision, and the following March the appeals court upheld Bloomberg LP's original victory. In May 2010, the Fed and the big banks asked the full court of appeals to reconsider, and in August the judges announced that Preska's ruling would stand. (For those keeping score at home: Bloomberg LP 3, Fed/big banks 0.)

In October 2010, the case went to the Supreme Court, but with a twist. The Fed decided not to appeal and left the case to the Clearing House Association. It was now Bloomberg LP against the country's biggest banks, with the Federal Reserve on the sidelines. The solicitor general, the administration's lawyer at the Supreme Court, even went so far as to argue that the justices should force the Fed to release the lending data.

In the meantime, Congress had passed the Dodd-Frank Act, which mandated the release of some details of the Fed's emergency lending. On December 1, 2010, the central bank disclosed recipients and loan amounts for most of the programs created to quell the financial crisis. For the first time, the Fed's veil was drawn aside. We discovered that a lot of European banks got a lot of money; firms such as Fidelity Investments and BlackRock helped put the programs together, then availed themselves of them; and the Fed was accepting mystery collateral, which it wasn't supposed to do. But Dodd-Frank hadn't forced the Fed to release discount window data, the most contentious part of the Bloomberg LP lawsuit. That's where the embarrassing secrets were. Also remaining hidden were details of a lending program few of us even knew about.

SENATORS TED KAUFMAN AND SHERROD BROWN DIDN'T WANT to wait for the voluminous Dodd-Frank. They decided in early 2010 to take a stab at doing away with too big to fail. They introduced legislation that was pretty simple. Banks with more than $500 billion in assets would have to sell them off gradually until they didn't have $500 billion in assets anymore. Called the SAFE Act, it would affect six American banks: Bank of America, Citigroup, Goldman Sachs, JPMorgan Chase, Morgan Stanley, and Wells Fargo.

Kaufman, a Delaware Democrat, was in the unique position of being able to speak his mind and do as he pleased. Kaufman never expected to be a US senator. He'd been a prosecutor, then an aide to Senator Joseph Biden. When Biden became Barack Obama's vice president, Kaufman was appointed as his successor. Kaufman announced at the outset he didn't plan to run in 2010. That meant he didn't have to spend half his waking hours dialing for dollars. He wasn't beholden.

When it came to breaking up the biggest banks, Kaufman knew he was swimming against the current. The freshly rescued banks had stepped up their lobbying. They wanted to stay as big as they were, remain competitive with the biggest overseas banks, and get even bigger. Their advocates knocked on doors and wrote checks. And they had help. Both Lawrence Summers, Obama's chief economic adviser, and Timothy Geithner, the Treasury secretary, stopped by Ted Kaufman's office to offer their opposition to SAFE. Summers argued, all evidence aside, that bigger banks were more stable than smaller banks and less likely to shake up the entire financial system if they encountered trouble. Geithner's gambit was more sophisticated. Leave it to the grownups, Ted, Geithner told him. We're negotiating international rules in Basel, Switzerland, as part of the new Basel III bank regulations. We'll put in size limits there.

Brown, an Ohio Democrat, said the main argument he heard from both lobbyists and fellow senators was that limiting bank size was "punishing success." Hadn't the biggest banks repaid the Treasury Department's TARP, along with the hefty interest rates the government charged, netting the American people a nice profit? They certainly had (though, as former FDIC chairman Sheila Bair pointed out, Citigroup alone among the big boys never paid back Treasury's $20 billion capital injection; instead, the government sold its stake to stock investors). Hadn't they also paid back the Fed, with interest? As far as we knew, yes. Brown told his detractors that it's a funny kind of success, when a business needs billions of dollars in rescue money from the US government just to stay afloat. But it was a losing argument. Brown and Kaufman only had TARP as an example. They didn't know how much the Fed was lending to the banks. No one did—not even, it turns out, the guys at the Treasury Department who had designed TARP.

IN MARCH 2011, THE US SUPREME COURT REJECTED THE Clearing House Association appeal, forcing the Federal Reserve to release details of its discount window lending during the financial crisis.

Ten days later, the avalanche came: 29,000 pages of data—all in PDF format. It would take weeks for Bloomberg LP's data scrapers to get the numbers into spreadsheets so that we could properly analyze them. Releasing the information in less-than-accessible form seemed like a petty thing for the world's most powerful financial institution to do. Meanwhile, for the first time, we could see why the Fed had been so possessive of the information. The American central bank had loaned money to the Bank of China, a bank partly owned by Muammar Ghadafi's Libyan government, and a Japanese fishing collective called Norinchukin Bank. It had funneled billions in loans to banks such as Goldman Sachs and JPMorgan Chase, whose executives had consistently insisted that their firms didn't need the money. But the most surprising revelation to emerge was the volume of money that went to the banks—much, much more than we thought. My Bloomberg News colleagues Bradley Keoun, Phil Kuntz, and John Voskuhl decided the fairest way to present the information was to calculate, for each bank, peak lending days, average daily borrowing, and the number of days the bank was on the dole. Other news organizations, watchdog groups, and academics had totaled the loans and come up with enormous, seemingly outlandish figures. For instance, if a bank borrowed $1 billion on a Monday, paid it back on Tuesday (not uncommon in the financial world), then took another loan for $1 billion on Tuesday night, and so on for a week, the other Fed watchers said the bank had taken $5 billion in loans. Since the bank never had more than $1 billion out at any given time, Keoun, Kuntz, and Voskuhl figured it was best to say that. Even so, they unearthed staggering numbers in the data. The peak lending day for all banks combined was December 5, 2008, when international financial institutions took a whopping $1.2 trillion in loans from the Fed.

That's on one day. And that's trillion. With a *t*.

THE PEEK INSIDE THE FEDERAL RESERVE'S DISCOUNT window also revealed the lengths to which the Big Six chief executives would distort reality when it suited them. Keoun, Kuntz, and I, with the help of editors Voskuhl and Robert Friedman, put together a graphic for *Bloomberg Markets* magazine showing what the CEOs were saying publicly about the health of their banks at about the same time their secret Fed borrowing was peaking. Let's just say there were contradictions.

"Morgan Stanley is in the strongest possible position," the firm's chief executive officer, John Mack, told investors on September 21, 2008. Hardly credible, because eight days later, on September 29, 2008, Mack's bank had $107 billion in emergency loans outstanding from the Federal Reserve, the most of any financial institution. Morgan Stanley, the country's second-biggest investment bank, has never disclosed these loans, though they amount to nearly eleven times the $10 billion it received from the TARP program. Without Bloomberg's lawsuit against the Fed and the biggest banks and the ensuing twenty-nine-month legal tussle, that loan would have remained a secret between Morgan Stanley and the Federal Reserve.

Vikram Pandit, Citigroup's chief, said on January 16, 2009, that his bank had "an irreplaceable franchise." If he'd meant the prodigiousness of its secret Fed transactions, he might have had a point. Four days after he said that, Citigroup emergency borrowing hit its peak of $99.5 billion.

On November 26, 2008, Bank of America's top man, Kenneth Lewis, wrote to shareholders that he headed "one of the strongest and most stable major banks in the world." He didn't say that his bank owed the central bank $86 billion on that day and would borrow a peak of $91.4 billion on February 26, 2009. Wells Fargo's chief, John Stumpf, assured investors on January 28, 2009, that "we couldn't feel better about the future." He never told them about the present: $45 billion in emergency overnight loans from the Fed on February 26.

Chief Executive Officer Jamie Dimon was bragging about JP-Morgan Chase's "fortress balance sheet" on February 23, 2009—three days before his bank hit its peak borrowing of $68.6 billion, nearly double what it received from TARP.

And CEO Lloyd Blankfein's comments about Goldman Sachs's "deep global client franchise, experienced and talented people and strong balance sheet" came on December 16, 2008, two weeks before his bank's Fed borrowing peaked at $69 billion. Goldman Sachs had taken $10 billion from TARP, at the same time complaining that it didn't need the cash from Treasury. Perhaps it didn't. Perhaps Goldman Sachs's borrowing from the Fed, in secret, was all it needed to stay solvent. We'll never know. Goldman has never said.

MONEY WASN'T THE ONLY THING AT STAKE IN SUCH GARGANtuan bailout loans. Americans grew more suspicious of their government institutions. Confidence ebbed in Wall Street firms that got away with disclosing exactly nothing about the loans they received in secret. Bankers acted with impunity, knowing their top regulator would stick up for them if they ever got into trouble. And legislation that would have broken up the Big Six—saving us from Dodd-Frank's convoluted prescriptions and myriad decisions by committee and the persistent peril of having financial institutions so complicated and huge that their troubles were everyone's troubles—failed.

"A funny kind of success," Senator Sherrod Brown had called it. Brown and Kaufman's SAFE Act was defeated 60–31, on May 6, 2010, without any of the lawmakers knowing the truth about the bailout—that it was bigger and longer and wider and more secretive than they imagined.

BRAD KEOUN, A BLOOMBERG NEWS REPORTER WHO'D ASSUMED an essential role in the Fed coverage, spotted it first. Buried in the 29,000 pages of the Fed's discount window release were bar graphs labeled with the names of the world's biggest banks—Goldman Sachs, Credit Suisse, JPMorgan Chase, Deutsche Bank, and the rest. The charts were fun to look at; the vertical bars were divided into sections of different, vivid colors. The bars measured billions of dollars over time, and each color represented a different Federal Reserve emergency lending program. The charts evidently showed how much each bank was borrowing from the Fed, broken down by lending facility. All of the programs were familiar to us—except one. It was represented by a hot-pink stripe labeled, mysteriously, ST OMO (RHS). For some of the banks, ST OMO (RHS) reached into the billions.

"What the hell is ST OMO?" Keoun asked me, pronouncing it "Saint Oh-mo." I didn't know. Nobody in the office knew. I phoned a source who used to work at the Fed. He said that ST OMO stood for "single-tranche open market operations." Well of course it did! He explained that in March 2008 the Fed wanted to buy mortgage securities because the market for them had frozen. Instead of designing a new lending facility, the Fed simply expanded a preexisting one. It had used a program called open market operations, which since the 1940s had been the mechanism for the Fed to buy Treasury debt and, later, the debt of mortgage buyers Fannie Mae and Freddie Mac, referred to as "the agencies." Open market operations allowed the central bank to regulate the flow of money into and out of the financial system—when the Fed bought bonds, it put cash into the system; when it sold them, it took cash out. For decades, the Fed's OMO had bought a maximum of $5 billion at a time, but in 2008, because of dire circumstances, my source explained, the Fed authorized loans of up to $100 billion at a time through OMO. The twenty-one primary dealers—the units of the biggest banks that trade directly with the New York branch of the Federal Reserve—were required to bid on the loans and put up mortgages as collateral.

"What about the 'RHS'?" I asked.

"That stands for 'right-hand side' of the chart," he said. "High school math?"

Okay, so I wasn't the smartest guy in the room. Imagine how I felt when I expanded the bar graphs on my computer screen to 700 percent and used a ruler to measure the amounts. That was the only way I had of estimating how much each bank had taken in loans from the expanded single-tranche open market operations. I asked the New York Fed for the details, but a public relations employee said the bank wouldn't give them to me. The spokesman seemed puzzled that I hadn't known about ST OMO.

"We put out a press release at the time we expanded the program," he told me. So I looked it up. Here's what the central bank had to say about it on March 7, 2008: "Beginning today, the Federal Reserve will initiate a series of term repurchase transactions that are expected to cumulate to $100 billion. These transactions will be conducted as 28-day term repurchase (RP) agreements in which primary dealers may elect to deliver as collateral any of the types of securities—Treasury, agency debt, or agency mortgage-backed securities—that are eligible as collateral in conventional open market operations."

It was incomprehensible to me, seemingly written in code, so I called Barney Frank, the man whose name is on the most sweeping financial reform legislation since the first administration of Franklin D. Roosevelt. "I wasn't aware of this program until now," the Massachusetts congressman told me. We had stumbled on an emergency lending program that not even the chairman of the House Financial Services Committee knew about.

We added it to our tally. When we published an article saying that the most successful securities firm in Wall Street history had exchanged mortgage-backed securities for a $15 billion loan, the biggest in the program, for as low as 0.01 percent interest—making the Fed bailouts as much about cheap money as about urgent emergency cash infusions—Tyler Durden, the major domo of Pittman's favorite website, Zero Hedge, quipped that ST OMO was "the patron saint of Goldman Sachs."

THE FINANCIAL CRISIS MADE THE FEDERAL RESERVE INFINITELY more transparent than it had been for nearly a century. The Fed chairman, Ben Bernanke, took the time to answer questions at a televised press conference. Policy makers have, for the first time, stated their goals as far as the unemployment and inflation rates. Central bank committees now explain their view of how the economy will behave in the future and how they plan to steer through difficulty. Ron Paul's legislation to audit the central bank is now law. Fed watchers—those who can't remember Jekyll Island but who lived through the almost metaphysical opacity of Bernanke's predecessor, Alan Greenspan—have reason to rejoice.

But the sunshine will continue seeping into the world's most powerful financial institution only through the future efforts of people such as Mark Pittman. We must always keep in mind that the Fed is an odd animal, a creature of the banks, and neither by law nor in practice obligated to make sure the rules are fair for the rest of us.

MARK PITTMAN DIDN'T LIVE TO SEE THE STORY END. HE'D suffered his first heart attack at the age of forty-three on Father's Day 2001, when his youngest daughter was just three months old. He never quit smoking his beloved Marlboro 100s. He drank daily and ate whatever he wanted. Such reckless behavior was his way of staying invincible in his own mind. "I lived every day in fear that it would be his last," said his wife Laura. "It sounds like a soap opera, but it's true." Laura made sure Pittman at least made regular visits to a cardiologist. During one checkup in the summer of 2009, the results of a stress test weren't so good. The doctor scheduled him for a procedure the next day to insert a stent to increase the blood flow in his chest. If he didn't lose weight, quit drinking, stop smoking, and get some exercise, he'd die, his doctor said. He followed the directions, except for the drinking part. He couldn't give up the glass of wine or the beers he'd have after work.

After the stent went in, Pittman wasn't himself. He'd always been a reliable reporting partner, but now he was making promises he didn't remember. He took the Delta shuttle to Washington to interview a former Bush administration Treasury official for a story we were doing together, and when he returned, he sent me incomprehensible notes. I asked him for the tape of the conversation and was surprised to hear that over lunch he hadn't asked one question whose answer we could use in the article. This was no ordinary journalist; this was the best I'd ever worked with.

The Friday before Thanksgiving 2009, I left town to visit family in Minnesota while Pittman partied at the annual dinner sponsored by the Financial Writers Association of New York, where he was a perennial pooh-bah. He was happy to see friends he hadn't seen all year.

A couple days later, he seemed to come down with the flu. The night before the holiday he stayed in to watch the girls while Laura went to dinner with friends. It happened so fast: Laura got a call at the restaurant. She arrived back home to find that Pittman had been vomiting blood and was close to passing out. "Help me," he told her. Then he was gone. When the paramedics arrived, they couldn't revive him. It was just after midnight on November 25, Thanksgiving Day.

I'd been hanging out with the family all the next day and had left my BlackBerry on the dresser in my in-laws' guest bedroom. When I fired it up, it was almost midnight Central Time, more than twenty-four hours after Pittman had died. I had gotten messages from a couple of colleagues, another from Amanda Bennett, our boss, and one from Mark.

I didn't know what to think. My first thought was that one of our stories had needed correcting—every Bloomberg News employee knows accuracy is the top priority, a directive drummed into us even more relentlessly than at other media companies, and having to issue a corrected version of an article is kind of like having committed a mortal sin. I called Amanda, who figured I'd already heard. I hadn't.

"Mark died," she told me.

It was not completely unexpected, with his bad heart, but still. My body felt like a totaled car. I'm not sure what I said to her or how I reacted. I felt like I was moving through darkness without headlights.

But what about the message I'd received during the day from Pittman? Was he communicating with me from the great beyond? It turned out to have been written on Pittman's BlackBerry by his buddy Billy Karesh, asking me to call Mark's wife as soon as I could.

ABOUT EIGHT HUNDRED PEOPLE TURNED OUT FOR THE memorial service at the majestic St. Paul's Episcopal Church in Yonkers. Laura's aunt, a minister, spoke. So did Laura. Billy Karesh delivered a eulogy, and so did I. Pittman's family had flown in from

Kansas—his father and mother and their spouses, his two brothers and their wives. Zero Hedge, Pittman's favorite website, had reported his death, and readers went back and forth on its possible cause. Many had given the multiple-choice Mad Lib a whirl and were convinced the Federal Reserve had murdered him. At first I dismissed this as knee-jerk tinfoil-hat lunacy, but when I stopped by the Pittman house to visit Laura a few days later, she asked me to talk to the medical examiner. The conspiracy chatter had made her anxious, and she thought it better to rule out foul play while we had the chance rather than to have it always shadowing her. There ought not be any secrets, she told me. I phoned the coroner and said that I was inquiring about the exact cause of death. I explained why I was asking, that Pittman had been a journalist trying to get the most powerful financial institution in the world to reveal secrets about some very connected people. "I'm from Russia," the coroner told me in slightly accented English. "I understand."

He called back a few hours later. "Heart failure," he told me. No signs of a CIA poison dart or toxic radiation. "His heart gave out." The doctor had googled Pittman and could see why I was concerned. "It seems like he was a great man," the coroner said.

Maggie, Pittman's twenty-six-year-old daughter from his first marriage, was moved to write to the conspiracy theorists on Zero Hedge. This is what she said:

This is Maggie Pittman, and Mark is my father. He would probably disapprove of me feeding the masses this information, but he taught me to always speak and seek the truth. He was not murdered. I do appreciate and understand your thinking and would probably think the same in other circumstances. However, he was not murdered.

He suffered from heart disease for many years and while this is extremely sudden and a loss for everyone, it is no conspiracy. I wish everyone could know his hearty and always available laugh, his wisdom and his sense of righteousness and his total commitment to me and my family.

I feel truly truly blessed to have this amazing man as my father and will do everything I can to make sure others follow suit and keep fighting on. I loved him more than anything in this entire world and I will miss him for the rest of my life. Thank you again and keep on.

He was fifty-two.

THREE

ENVY

*Capture: Jamie Dimon and Going Long Risk Some
Belly Tranches (Especially Where Default May Realize)*

IN MARCH 2009, AS THE US ECONOMY TOPPLED INTO THE
gutter after bingeing for years on cheap borrowed money, Mark
Pittman and I added up how much the Federal Reserve had committed to keeping the financial system alive. We came up with $7.77
trillion—half the value of everything produced in the country that
year.

It turned out that $7.77 trillion wasn't enough, and $1 was too
much.

The bailouts, in evolving permutations, persisted four, five, six
years after the crisis. Because they did, the banks never had to sober
up. As William McChesney Martin Jr., who was Fed chairman in
the 1950s and 1960s, once quipped, the job of the Federal Reserve
is to take the punch bowl away just as the good times get rolling.
Postcrisis, when the banks returned to the party, still woozy from
overindulgence and bruised from taking their drunken header, it
was as if they had never left. The punch bowl was still there, and
it was spiked with a couple of science-fiction-sounding elixirs: zero
interest rate policy (ZIRP) and quantitative easing (QE).

ZIRP and QE were the programs the Fed implemented that helped the banks get bigger and stronger after the 2008 crisis. They were the new bailouts—the bailouts that never ended.

Zero interest rate policy is exactly what it sounds like. Starting in December 2008, the Fed set the interest rate for bank-to-bank borrowing at a shade north of nothing. Not a bad deal, is it? That meant that all the tuition spent by Wall Street employees on Harvard MBAs and Princeton economics doctorates went to waste—a third-grader could see the potential for profit in stacks of money no one had to pay for. As for QE, it was the Fed's way to pump cash into the banks—by buying securities from them, such as Treasury debt and mortgage bonds. The Fed does this, on a much smaller scale, all the time. When the central bank wants more cash in the financial system, it buys securities. When it wants less, it sells them. QE was just business as usual, but on steroids. A lot of steroids. Between 2008 and the middle of 2011, the Fed bought mortgage securities and Treasury debt worth $2.3 trillion from the banks, and in September 2012 it began buying again, to the tune of $85 billion a month, with the promise of an infinite shopping spree into the future. Smart alecks dubbed the Fed's plan "QEternity." QE succeeded in pushing down mortgage rates, making home ownership cheaper for millions of borrowers, but it was less triumphant in spreading the wealth and getting people back to work.

All this freshly minted cash sloshing around was as plentiful as Monopoly money, but it was real enough. Home prices, spending on construction, and manufacturing data ticked upward, slid back, then ticked upward again. Any economic recovery the Federal Reserve hoped to spark depended on the banks lending the newly printed money they got from the Fed. Economists study the movement of cash in the system. They call it the velocity of money. When times are good, money moves like a goosed greyhound. Postcrisis, the banks found it a lot easier to sink their money into derivatives and commodities such as gold or corn than to lend it to small businesses and home buyers. So the velocity of money slowed to the speed of an old guy with a cane making his way from the parking lot to the orthopedist's office. Corporations held onto more money than ever before, while joblessness sank into hopelessness. The recovery seemed illusory, a Hollywood set, a trick of the man behind the curtain.

I remember discussing the Big Lie with Pittman in the autumn of 2009, shortly before he died. During the housing boom, the Big Lie was Home Prices Will Always Go Up. (They didn't.) In 2009, the Big Lie, Pittman and I agreed, was We're in Economic Recovery. We clearly weren't.

Nor were we years later. More precisely, the US economy was recovering, but at two speeds. While finance folks and their high-net-worth clients danced on the tables with lampshades on their heads, vast expanses of the country stayed hung over. To most Americans, their wealthiest fellow citizens were in an invisible aristocracy, living in small, mostly gated outposts scattered all over the country. Geographically speaking, though, the vast, hurting America comprised roughly the territory west of Lake Hopatcong, New Jersey, south of the Manassas battlefield in Virginia, and east of Interstate 5 in California.

There was irony in the Fed's attempts to get the economy back on its feet. The lost weekend of 2008 had been caused, in part, by everybody getting drunk on cheap money. The Fed's solution was simple and elegant: make money even cheaper. Clearly the central bank believed the money would make its way to small business owners, cash-strapped students, home buyers, and others in what was charmingly called the "real economy." It didn't. The postcrisis orgy had a hallucinatory feel, as if ZIRP was bankers' LSD. If you weren't already well-off before June 2009, when the longest post–World War II recession ended, the train had left you at the station, Bub. Please move along.

The Fed did all it could, but all it could do was help the banks. It even provided the banks risk-free ways to profit on their free money. Financial institutions could simply sock away their pesky excess lucre at the Fed itself; after years of paying nothing, the central bank in December 2008 had started shelling out 0.25 percent interest on savings accounts the banks kept in its vaults. That rate doesn't sound like much, but consider that in 2012 our old friend Citigroup had $107.2 billion in its Fed account, meaning that it earned $67.7 million just for being beautiful. From the start of 2009 through 2012, I calculated that the six biggest US banks together earned more than $3 billion in interest paid by the Fed. Not shabby. And this was at a time when the banks were paying 0.01 percent on savings accounts. You didn't need an advanced degree in finance to see the play. The bankers could make money risk-free by lending to the US Treasury. So many bankers and so many of their clients opted for this strategy that it drove the returns on Treasury debt to record lows. Bankers had to try very, very hard not to make money after the 2008 financial crisis.

Try they did. That's because most bankers didn't get into the business to make money. They got into the business to rake in truckloads. They weren't satisfied with the $67.7 million they could earn while they visited the Ferrari showroom. The ZIRP effect pushed these go-getters into other trades in order to earn higher returns. Here is where (some of) the money went: sugar prices hit an all-time high in January 2011, silver in April 2011, hogs in July 2011, gold in August 2011, corn (aided by supply-pinching drought) in July 2012, and the Dow Jones Industrial Average in 2013. The surplus of money reshaped how business was transacted. Billy Dunavant, the eighty-year-old patriarch of Memphis-based Dunavant Enterprises, had been the first American to sell cotton to China, in 1975, and had helped invent the cotton futures market, where farmers and other bettors could gamble on the price of cotton months into the future. He told me that he could no longer keep up with the big boys in the industry because the ante was too rich for his blood. His was a family-owned company, and he didn't want to put the entire inheritance at risk on a single trade. So he sold the cotton-trading division of Dunavant Enterprises to a competitor in 2010, just before the price spiked to four times what it had been just a year previous. "You need a huge pile of cash to compete, a billion dollars or more," he told me. "There's more speculation involved."

Folks in the money-flooded zones wondered how the other America could gripe while the prices of stocks and commodities soared. Most Americans weren't benefiting because the cash air-dropped by "Helicopter Ben" Bernanke was only filtering down as far as the penthouses. The folks on the lower floors had lost their small fortunes on their homes and couldn't afford to buy into the bull markets. For many, the bull was short for bullshit. Rising commodity prices didn't make them rich. It only meant they paid more at the supermarket checkout.

That said, ZIRP was terrific for home owners, at least those who didn't owe more on their mortgages than the value of their homes (as many as 12 million at the 2011 peak) or hadn't been booted for nonpayment (7 million). Mortgage rates plummeted to the lowest on record, sparking a refinancing boom in 2012, and that meant monthly bills shrank for millions of borrowers.

ZIRP was horrific for savers, however. In December 2012, for example, JPMorgan Chase, which led US banks with $1.14 trillion in deposits, offered to pay 0.01 percent annual yield on savings accounts of less than $10,000. Bank of America, the second biggest in deposits with $1.06 trillion, offered the same rate on the same deposit amount. It's hard to visualize a smaller number. Factor in inflation, which in the postcrisis years was in the range of just under 1 percent to a little over 2 percent, and customers were essentially paying the banks to take their money at a rate four times what the Fed was paying the banks in interest. Bank of America made it even easier for customers to pay them. Three withdrawals a month were free, but after that, the "bank of opportunity" charged $3 per withdrawal. At 0.01 percent, a fourth withdrawal could wipe out years of interest payments. The low interest rates rendered customer deposits the cheapest source of funding for the banks since the invention of money. Even robbery, with its inevitable lawyers' fees and opportunities lost during jail time, was more expensive.

Few middle-class people live off interest, but a lot of them, mainly retirees, supplement their monthly income that way. I talked to one of them, George Sanchez, a sixty-five-year-old former director of library services at LIM College in Manhattan. Sanchez said that when he first started an annuity in 2005, his interest rate was 5.25 percent. In December 2012, it was 2 percent. That meant that instead of getting a monthly payout of $700, he got $413. It wasn't like he was starving or living in a cardboard refrigerator box on decommissioned subway tracks. But it did mean he had to teach part-time at the Fashion Institute of Technology (FIT) to make ends meet at a time when he would have preferred kicking back.

The job at FIT could have gone to someone else, maybe a recent graduate with student loans to repay. Suppose that recent graduate couldn't find a decent job and, burdened with debt, had to live with her parents. That's one less dwelling rented or sold, with all the furniture, cable charges, and repairs to go with it. You can see how the ZIRP effect rippled out, hurting savers and, mostly, the working and middle classes.

Quantitative easing also profited the banks. In 2013, I calculated what the four biggest lenders had gained just from selling mortgage securities to the Fed, over and above what they would have gotten if they'd sold the same securities in a universe in which the Fed had not embarked on a multi-trillion-dollar orgy of bond buying. Wells Fargo, because it originated nearly one in every three home loans in the country, had reaped additional income of $2.07 billion; Bank of America, $1.16 billion; JPMorgan, $767 billion; and Citigroup, $332 million. Not exactly couch-cushion money.

The architect of this trickle-down style of economic stimulus masquerading as Federal Reserve monetary policy was a soft-spoken, gray-bearded Princeton economics professor who, in his public pronouncements, gave the impression to a bewildered public that he didn't feel as if he had much choice. He was a disciplined man, so he wouldn't say this, but it was clear that with partisan rancor paralyzing lawmakers and an embattled president reluctant to show the leadership the American public expected and deserved, the professor felt compelled to deploy all the tools available to him to single-handedly keep the country from nose-diving back into the gutter. In the process, he remade the US economy into a wholly owned subsidiary of its central bank. He was Ben S. Bernanke, a son of humble Dillon, South Carolina, who rose to become chairman of the Federal Reserve, and for all the money his bank for banks channeled to the largest financial institutions, his greatest gift to them was something altogether different, more lasting, and potentially more damaging to the rest of us.

DERIVATIVES!

Simply reading the word bored you dizzy, didn't it? The weird thing about derivatives (there it is again) is that while most people's eyes glaze over at the mere mention, they're about the most thrilling thing happening in the finance industry.

That's because they're the casino game of the banking world, the equivalent, often, of putting a stack of chips on red and letting Fortuna spin her wheel. Rather than derivatives—four syllables that launched a thousand naps—it might be less soporific to think of them as games of chance.

The idea behind this financial dice game is simple. Think of derivatives as side bets made between two gamblers. Much like two bettors wagering on the outcome of, say, a college football game or whether a housefly will land on a table, the two sides in a derivatives wager are usually betting on whether prices will move up or down. When the bet is made to offset possible losses elsewhere, it's called a hedge. When banks do it to make money for themselves, it's called proprietary trading, or, if you're looking for street cred, call it prop trading.

The daring and resourceful can wager on any number of eventualities:

- *The weather:* Especially useful if you're spilling oil in the Gulf of Mexico or shipping it out of Prince William Sound in a single-hull container ship.
- *Interest rates:* Say you're Jefferson County, Alabama, and you need to borrow money to put in a new sewer system because the old one is so bad that poop winds up in the Cahaba River whenever it rains. You issue a bond with a variable interest rate that could zoom upward because, for now, that's the cheaper option. You'd feel like a sucker if you didn't make a side bet that rates zooming upward would happen. Of course, you'd feel like even more of a sucker if interest rates fell instead and you had to pay off your side of the bet to JPMorgan Chase. In fact, you'd feel like a broke sucker who filed the biggest government bankruptcy in US history up to that time.
- *Future stock prices:* The game to play when you have a hunch or a little bird whispers in your ear.
- *Currency fluctuations:* May I suggest hedging with wheelbarrow futures?
- *The chances of a company defaulting on its loans:* This product is called, for arcane reasons, a credit default swap, or CDS. It's essentially an insurance policy. Say you buy a bond issued by American Airlines. You can also buy a CDS from another bettor that will reimburse you in the event American Airlines stiffs you. The gambler who bets Amer-

ican Airlines will keep paying is said to take the "long" side of the bet, and the one who believes the bank will default is said to go "short." The totally financially innovative thing about CDSs is you don't have to own the bond to take out an insurance policy on it. If you don't own the bond, then it's pure gambling, kind of like off-track betting for the Ivy League. You can hole up in your ancestral McMansion wearing nothing but an ascot and wager that American Airlines will go belly up, then wait for the money to rain o'er you. The more intrepid "investor" can even bet on the performance of a bunch of bonds issued by different companies tossed together into one basket. This is one whale of a wager, and we'll get back to it later.

○ *Home loans:* Wall Street devised a way in 2005 to bet that more and more home owners would quit paying their mortgages. Traders at Deutsche Bank, for instance, made piles of dough betting against subprime borrowers, who lacked any history of being able to repay their debts in a timely way. The traders' "I'm Short Your House" T-shirts remain sought-after souvenirs of this bygone era.

American International Group (AIG), the giant international insurance conglomerate, became a household name by taking the long side of the same bet. More than one company lost heaps providing protection against mortgage defaults in 2008, when borrowers quit paying in Book of Revelation–type numbers, but AIG's lawyers took it one step further. They agreed to reimburse their customers not only when the mortgage bonds defaulted but also when the bonds lost value. This strategy took them—and the American taxpayer—to the lip of a very deep money pit in September 2008.

But all that's ancient history, right? AIG stands as a cautionary tale, a negative example that others would be stupid to emulate, and since financial firms aren't in the business of self-immolation, they would never do anything so idiotic again. Right?

Well, we don't actually know that. Lots of derivatives contracts are private documents, so we have no way of identifying what's in them.

This lack of transparency has haunting implications. The effect of Lehman Brothers's collapse in September 2008 was magnified because the investment bank had made so many secretive derivatives deals with other firms that it proved nearly impossible to untangle them. One estimate pegged the number of transactions at 930,000.

Lehman Brothers was an investment bank. That meant it underwrote and traded securities and advised companies on all sorts of financial matters. It wasn't a commercial bank, the kind with ATMs and pens on leashes that take deposits from customers. And because it didn't take deposits, Lehman Brothers didn't benefit from deposit insurance, issued by the American taxpayer through the auspices of the Federal Deposit Insurance Corporation (FDIC). And because it took no deposits and wasn't covered by deposit insurance, Granny's Christmas Club account and the American taxpayer weren't directly on the hook when Lehman went kaput. Just imagine the peril if Lehman did take deposits. The investment bank might have been tempted, when it started the process of going underwater, slowly and then all at once, to use Granny's insured account to pay off its derivatives bets in order to stay afloat. Or—just picture how bad this could be—to use Granny's deposit money to make the bets in the first place.

Because that would never happen, right? It would just be wrong to risk poor Granny's sleep-at-night money at the roulette wheel. Wouldn't it? What coldhearted villain would help himself to a handful of that sweet little old lady's hard-earned pennies and let them ride on red? American taxpayers, who ultimately back up the FDIC, guarantee those pennies, so it would be a classic case of "heads I win, tails you lose." The depraved gambler, doubtlessly twirling his waxed mustache, could pocket any winnings, but if he lost, his neighbors, the American people, would pick up the tab. Imagine endangering Granny's financial well-being to make a few bucks. Imagine taking advantage of FDIC insurance that way. Imagine letting the money ride on the financial roulette wheel knowing that you could keep the winnings, but if you lost, taxpayers from Maine to Maui would dip into their wallets to save your sorry behind. It was just too sleazy to contemplate. Irresponsible. Adolescent. Sociopathic. There had to be a law against that sort of thing.

Wasn't there?

BRUNO MICHEL IKSIL HAD $1 BILLION RIDING ON RED. His short bet on a basket of corporate bonds would pay off only in the event that one of the companies defaulted before the wager expired on December 20, 2011.

Iksil, who made $6.76 million in 2011, was a trader living in France who commuted to an office in London. He worked in JP-Morgan Chase's investment bank, at a special division called the Chief Investment Office, which managed $350 billion in "excess deposits." According to what Jamie Dimon, the bank's chairman, chief executive officer, and president, told the Senate Banking, Housing, and Urban Affairs Committee, the FDIC insured these excess deposits. In other words, Iksil's job was to take Granny's nest egg to the racetrack.

Iksil helped manage a special section of the Chief Investment Office that the bank referred to as the Synthetic Credit Portfolio. It was "synthetic" because Iksil dealt in derivatives, which aren't, strictly speaking, "real." Though the money they win and lose certainly is.

Just days before the expiration of Iksil's bet, American Airlines declared bankruptcy. Celebration! Iksil made $400 million for JP-Morgan Chase.

A 40 percent payday is winning big, even for Wall Street's high rollers, and after a killing like that, few gamblers fold and head home. The compelling impulse is to keep the winning streak alive and ride that tiger to even greater riches.

In any event, it was Iksil's job to keep the run of luck going. The next month, January 2012, he drew up an "investment" plan for the next few months and presented it to his bosses. (I use quotes around "investment" because calling the choice of red or black an investment doesn't seem accurate.) Iksil's four "trades that make sense" included this: "Go long risk on some belly tranches especially where default may realize." Questioned about it a year later by gum-shoes for the Senate Permanent Subcommittee on Investigations, none of Iksil's bosses could explain what the hell the guy was talking about. (The investigators never spoke to Iksil, who was overseas, so he couldn't help them.) One JPMorgan Chase executive, the guy in charge of monitoring the risks taken by traders in Iksil's office, vol-unteered that Iksil must have meant "buying low and selling high." (You can't make this stuff up.) But the American Airlines score was fresh in the minds of Iksil's bosses, and not understanding the trade was no impediment to providing Iksil with billions of dollars of Granny's cash to execute it.

What followed at the London outpost of the biggest Ameri-can bank was a bacchanalia of buying that swelled the Synthetic Credit Portfolio to $157 billion from $51 billion in less than three months. The pool got so big so fast that Iksil had an $81 billion "investment" in an index that traded an average of only $1.5 bil-lion a day. Even if he'd wanted to sell, it would have been impos-sible. And when he needed to sell, traders from other firms could take advantage by naming their prices. That was not a good situ-ation for Iksil and the JPMorgan Chase folks in London. Traders have a nickname for the special type of sucker who risks tons of money he's bound to lose: whale. Iksil's competitors started blabbing about this whale to Bloomberg reporters, who pretty soon figured out who it was. On April 6, 2012, Iksil's name hit the news. That's when the Office of the Comptroller of the Currency (OCC), the principal regulator in Washington of JPMorgan Chase's deposit-taking bank, heard about Iksil's trades for the first time. The OCC had sixty-five examiners sitting at desks inside the offices of JPMorgan Chase, and anchorwoman Stephanie Ruhle on Bloomberg TV was the one who handed them this important intelligence. All they had to do was turn up the sound and listen. Bruno Michel Iksil took the *nom de finance* "London Whale," and JPMorgan Chase was about to flush an ocean's worth of depositors' dollars out to sea.

FOR YEARS, THE LAW KEPT THE GAMBLERS AWAY FROM GRANNY'S cookie jar. The Glass-Steagall Act of 1933 wouldn't even let them in the same building. It mandated strict separation of deposit banks and securities firms—Wall Street trading houses weren't allowed to run banks that had street-corner branches, and vice versa. Despite some chipping away at that division, the wall between deposit and investment banks kept savings accounts safe from high rollers until 1999, when President Bill Clinton signed the Financial Services Modernization Act. More commonly known as Gramm-Leach-Bliley, it basically said, "Everybody into the pool." It moved the casino into Granny's house, making the creation of financial megamorphs such as Citigroup and JPMorgan Chase possible. The firms formed corporate entities called bank holding companies, which were umbrella companies presiding over the various units of the institution. The only door keeping the bank holding company's gamblers, their muddy boots, their rough language, and their cigarette smoke out of the parlors of the deposit banks was an obscure provision of the Federal Reserve Act of 1933, Section 23A, which limited the movement of money and investments between the deposit banks and the bank holding companies.

The idea of Section 23A was to make sure the bank holding company didn't get its paws on money protected by the government safety net. Section 23A "is among the most important tools that US bank regulators have to protect the safety and soundness of US banks," Scott Alvarez, the Federal Reserve's general counsel, told Congress in March 2008. The problem is, the Federal Reserve, as the chief regulator of the bank holding companies, has the power to issue exemptions to Section 23A. These exemptions allow the bank holding company—let's say Citigroup—to gather its derivatives together and dump them in Citibank, the federally insured deposit-taking division of Citigroup. That way, taxpayers will stand behind losses to the derivatives portfolio. And since Uncle Sam is propping up the deposit-taking bank, it typically has a better credit score than the bank holding company, which does all kinds of secretive things, like cross its fingers that American Airlines will crash. Thus, the bettors on the other side of the banks' derivatives wagers don't require deposit-taking banks to put up as much collateral to guarantee a derivative trade as they do a bank holding company. So it's cheaper for Citibank (the deposit-taking bank) to handle the derivatives contracts than it is for Citigroup (the bank holding company).

If this sounds complicated, that's because it was designed to be.

During the frenzy of the financial crisis, the Fed issued exemption after exemption to Section 23A—to Goldman Sachs, to Morgan Stanley, to JPMorgan Chase, to Citigroup, and to Bank of America. Most of the exemptions allowed the banks to shift assets between the deposit bank and the bank holding company to ensure the firms' survival. They were emergency measures, and the Fed made sure the exemptions expired in 2010.

The 2010 Dodd-Frank Wall Street Reform and Consumer Protection Act gave the FDIC, which provides deposit insurance, veto power over exemptions to Section 23A. Previously the Fed only consulted the FDIC before issuing exemptions. That sounds fine in theory—the FDIC should be vigilant about protecting taxpayers' interests because they align with FDIC interests, even if the Fed and the OCC are more lax—but it's unclear how much fuss the FDIC ever kicked up and whether that fuss ever made a difference. The Fed publishes only exemption letters and doesn't reveal exemptions that have been requested and denied.

In the autumn of 2011, Bank of America's Merrill Lynch division received a downgrade of its credit score. Many of its customers requested that their derivatives contracts with Merrill, the securities firm, be transferred to Bank of America, the deposit bank, which had Uncle Sam backing it up. The Fed, poised to issue an exemption to Section 23A, got an earful from the FDIC. Regulators at the government deposit insurer were weary of being pushed around by the central bank. They said that Fed officials came to them with done deals that benefited bankers but weren't advantageous for taxpayers. There was back-and-forth among bureaucrats, but ultimately it didn't matter. Bank of America's deposit bank took the derivatives. The last barrier had been breached. After the deal was sealed, Bank of America had 69 percent of its derivatives on the books of its deposit-taking division. JPMorgan Chase had 99 percent. Citigroup had 102 percent (the opposite of overdrawn), and Goldman Sachs, a securities firm pretending to be a deposit bank, 92 percent. (I challenge anyone to walk into Goldman Sachs and start a savings account. Good luck.) Congress had passed no laws to trample Section 23A, and none were amended or repealed. No elected official declared Section 23A a detriment to society and called for its emasculation. No votes were taken; no candidate for office was ever asked to weigh in; no national plebiscite or Gallup survey or Iowa straw poll measured public support up or down. Rather, it was simply an order by the Federal Reserve. A few strokes of the metaphorical pen.

The reason for the Fed exemptions is simple: they make it cheaper, and easier, for Wall Street banks to conduct derivatives trading. Why would the central bank make it cheaper and easier for the biggest banks to roll the dice, potentially at the expense of the American taxpayer? One possible explanation is "regulatory capture," meaning that the Fed acts in the interests of the industry it oversees, with less regard for the health of the entire financial system or the common good. Ben Bernanke's central bank was supposed to be the dog guarding the door between Granny's cookie jar and the casino. But the biggest banks had trained the guard dog to roll over and play dead.

JUST HOW MUCH EXPOSURE, AS THE BANKS CALL IT, DOES the American taxpayer have to the derivatives casino? How much of Granny's money is on the hook? The short answer is that we don't really know because, once again, a lot of derivatives deals usually involve two parties, with the details known only to them.

But there is one way to measure the exposure. Every three months, the Office of the Comptroller of the Currency publishes a report that tallies the notional amount of derivatives held by each of the biggest banks. "Notional" doesn't refer to the size of the bet the banks have made. It refers to what's called the referenced amount of the bet. (There's a reason derivatives induce catatonia.) In other words, if I bet ten bucks that a billion dollars' worth of mortgages will fall in value, the notional amount of that bet is $1 billion. The $10 part of the wager is the actual exposure. But due to the lack of transparency in derivatives trading, that number is rarely disclosed.

As of the end of 2012, JPMorgan Chase, where thousands of customers park their savings, had notional derivatives exposure of $69 trillion. That's not a misprint: $69 trillion—roughly the equivalent of the annual economic output of the fifty richest nations. Citibank had $55 trillion. Bank of America had $42 trillion. And Goldman Sachs had $41 trillion.

Together, the four had $208 trillion in notional exposure. All the other deposit banks in the United States combined had $15 trillion. That meant that the Big Four held 93 percent of the outstanding derivatives contracts in 2013.

Again, please keep in mind that this is the notional amount of their derivatives bets and not the actual. But even if the actual amount represented 10 percent of the notional, we're talking $20 trillion. More than the value of everything produced in the United States in 2014.

And if the unimaginable bigness of the number weren't a problem, there would still be the conundrum of concentration. Four banks have deals out worth seventeen times what the rest of the country's banks have. Now do you believe that derivatives can be exciting?

I would argue that the Fed's indulgence on Section 23A did nobody a favor. It has helped the too-big-to-fail banks get bigger and, at least in the case of JPMorgan Chase's London Whale, fail-i-er.

Iksil's belly tranches belly flopped. Just how much money the Synthetic Credit Portfolio lost became a touchy subject, inside and outside the bank. The Senate Permanent Subcommittee on Investigations claimed that JPMorgan Chase's Chief Investment Office had understated the losses in order to hide the extent of the flub. The bank acknowledged miscalculating them and went back to redo the figures after they were first announced. The discrepancy ended up costing the bank more than $1 billion in fines.

Chairman and Chief Executive Officer Jamie Dimon scoffed at the initial media reports about the London Whale. A week after the news broke, on an April 13, 2012, conference call to unveil the bank's financial condition for the first three months of the year, Dimon characterized the kerfuffle over the whale as a "complete tempest in a teapot." He later took that back. Chief Financial Officer Douglas Braunstein told investors, analysts, and reporters on the call that the London Whale trades were "fully transparent" to government regulators. That was, of course, a pile of horse manure. The OCC's examiners didn't know about Iksil's spending spree or the extent of the peril with which he was flirting until they saw it on Bloomberg TV with everyone else. Braunstein said that the trades conformed to firm-wide risk-management rules. In fact, the Senate report said Iksil's deals had violated the bank's risk standards 330 times. Braunstein also said the deals were meant to hedge the risk of other trades the bank was doing, but Dimon acknowledged later that that wasn't true. The asset purchases may have started out as hedges, he said, but "morphed" into something he couldn't publicly defend. When questioned, bank executives couldn't come up with specific trades that Iksil's portfolio was meant to hedge. Clearly, JP-Morgan Chase traders were shooting craps with Granny's money. And their bosses weren't being straight about what had happened, or maybe they didn't even know.

At least no one at the bank blamed Ben Bernanke. It was his zero interest rate policy, after all, that played a role in pushing traders such as Bruno Iksil to make exotic wagers in search of higher returns.

Dimon was invited to discuss the whale trades with the Senate Committee on Banking, Housing, and Urban Affairs in June 2012 and, a week later, the House Financial Services Committee—to face the scrutiny of people who spent half their time calling people such as Dimon to beg them for campaign money. Testifying to both committees in such a short time span had been a pleasure reserved for the Federal Reserve chairman; for a commoner it was the 2010s equivalent of Bruce Springsteen gracing the covers of both *Time* and *Newsweek* in the same week in 1975. Dimon's admirers expected fireworks from the usually quick-tempered *capo di tutti capi*. They'd followed Dimon's rise from a low-rent lender in Baltimore called Commercial Credit to the executive suite at Travelers

Group and then, briefly, Citigroup, where he was ousted by Citi's Sandy Weill for reasons that seem to have something to do with a younger man (Dimon) breathing down the neck of an older man (Weill) whose job he coveted. Dimon had proven his mettle during his subsequent exile from Wall Street, when he revived the fortunes of Chicago-based Bank One, and returned triumphantly to New York when Bank One was bought by JPMorgan Chase. As the one big-bank CEO who'd managed to survive the 2008 financial crisis without so much as a pimple to soil his official hagiography, the financial press lauded Dimon as The Last Man Standing (the title of Duff McDonald's biography), America's Least-Hated Banker (the *New York Times Magazine*'s cover headline), and Wall Street's Indispensable Man (*Businessweek*'s proclamation). Surely he wouldn't suffer the fools of Washington gladly.

The Senate hearing turned out to be, inadvertently, a theatrical primer on the humiliating effects of money on politics, a five-star kabuki. Senator Mike Crapo, an Idaho Republican and future ranking member, skipped the two dozen hard and/or illuminating questions he could have asked and went right to cadging Dimon for advice on crafting financial regulation. Dimon had for years taken the perfectly reasonable position that he favored "smart regulation" as opposed to more regulation. Ever deferential, Crapo didn't acknowledge the irony of being schooled on "smart" anything by a guy whose appearance was occasioned by his having lost billions of dollars of other people's money—nobody could say just how much—in the time it took to play a cricket match. Crapo's compassion for Dimon's predicament was understandable. Securities and investment firms had been the senator's top campaign contributors from 2007 to 2012, giving him $425,000 out of a total $5.3 million he'd raised. JPMorgan Chase was Crapo's number one benefactor from that lavish industry, pitching in nearly $36,000.

By comparison, the $17,900 that Colorado Democrat Michael F. Bennet received from the bank was kind of embarrassing, but

Bennet didn't fire any fastballs at the dimple in Dimon's chin in retaliation for being nickled-and-dimed. In fact, Bennet, in a previous incarnation as the superintendent of Denver Public Schools, had seen firsthand the good intentions of Dimon's bank. He'd been one of the dignitaries attending the ceremony celebrating JPMorgan Chase Foundation's $500,000 donation to assist an underprivileged Denver neighborhood in 2008, and he'd witnessed the bank's largesse two years later when it helped the Denver schools scratch together the matching funds for an English-language program partly subsidized by the federal government. In all, JPMorgan Chase gave $1.3 million to Colorado nonprofit do-gooders in 2010, the year Bennet was first elected, a 65 percent increase from 2009, when Bennet was appointed to the Senate seat vacated by Ken Salazar. Bennet also enjoyed some familiarity with the rarefied world of finance. Previous to his public service, he was a managing director for the investment company run by Colorado billionaire Philip Anschutz, who made killings in oil and railroads before buying stakes in movie theaters, film production, and the Los Angeles sports teams and their arenas. At the Senate hearing, Bennet begged Dimon's indulgence and invited him to pontificate on the state of Europe "and other places," as if back in his old job. Nebraska Republican Mike Johanns had received nothing substantial in campaign funds from the bank, but not to worry: Johanns complained to Dimon that JPMorgan Chase had no presence in his home state and expressed the wish that it had. "We hope to be there one day," Dimon reassured him.

Altogether, the twenty-two members of the Senate Banking Committee received $15 million from securities and investment firms in the 2012 election cycle. That dwarfed what the sixty souls of the House Financial Services Committee got—just $2 million, a relative pittance, which was reflected, one might be forgiven from concluding, in the comparative lack of supportive questioning from members of the House panel.

Matthew Stoller, a Democratic legislative aide, has said that the leaders of his party placed rookie Congress members who'd be facing tough competition in the next election on the Financial Services Committee, regardless of capability or interest, because they knew the Congress member would receive an abundance of campaign gifts from the finance industry, the better to help win a second term. For banks, with their trillion-dollar balance sheets, the investment didn't have to be dear. Spencer Bachus, who represented the bankrupt Jefferson County, Alabama, got $13,000 in campaign funds from JPMorgan Chase—and he was committee chairman. But there was more than one avenue for the financial industry to thank the sympathetic. Direct contributions have limits, so lobbying firms throw fund-raising galas to shower public servants with the positive regard that only multiple check writing can communicate.

Another way to curry favor and spread influence was the phenomenon known as the revolving door. Politicians such as Mel Martinez, once a US senator from Florida, Rick Lazio, an erstwhile New York congressman, and William Daley, former commerce secretary and brother of the longtime mayor of Chicago, along with enough Capitol Hill aides, had landed jobs at JPMorgan Chase to plant the idea among hardworking Washingtonians that pie in the sky might await them too before they died. "The dirty secret of American politics is that, for most politicians, getting elected is just not that important. What matters is post-election employment," Stoller said. (It couldn't have hurt JPMorgan Chase that the revolving door kept spinning, landing Daley in the Obama White House as chief of staff.)

For more accomplished friends of the industry, there was always the promise of speaking fees. For example, one of Bill Clinton's last acts as president was to sign legislation banning any regulation of derivatives; one of his first acts as ex-president was to accept $125,000 from Morgan Stanley for a speaking gig. Clinton went on to reap millions for something that he did all the time, and endlessly, for free: talk. "It's not a coincidence that deregulation accelerated in the late 1990s, as Clinton and his whole team began thinking about their post-presidential prospects," Stoller said. Regulators cashed in too. Deutsche Bank, Germany's biggest bank, received $66 billion in emergency loans from the Federal Reserve on a single day in November 2008; in June 2013, it paid former New York Fed president and Treasury Secretary Timothy Geithner $200,000 for a conference appearance. "We don't call it bribery," Stoller said, "but that's what it is."

There's also something that James Kwak, a University of Connecticut law professor, called "cultural capture." Especially when strapped for time and confronted with complicated issues, lawmakers rely on the ostensible know-how of a Wall Street sage, who may be deemed trustworthy simply because he's amassed a pile of money. Or perhaps he went to the same school they did, or pledged the same fraternity, or attended the same prayer breakfasts, or frequented the same airport men's rooms. Kwak was referring to regulators, but I think the term applies as appropriately to lawmakers, who "are likely to share more social networks with financial institutions and their lawyers and lobbyists than with competing interest groups such as consumers." Besides, Kwak said, "until recently, few people came to Washington to protect ordinary people from banks."

Cultural capture is a cousin of that basest of emotions: envy. The power of money is, of course, not confined to the possibility of getting some. If you score the game of life in dollars, putting the chiefs of the biggest banks in a Senate hearing room is akin to convening the Moolah Mount Olympus. The aroma of money, like cologne, wafts off men such as Dimon every time they swing through the capital. Cultural capture, and envy, can also infect bank customers—who may continue to do business with a firm that rips them off, perhaps in the hopes of one day winning the positive regard of their assassins, much as diners in a fancy restaurant aim to impress their rude waiter—as well as journalists and industry analysts. It can get ugly. At a 2013 public forum, when Dimon ducked a legitimate question from top bank analyst Mike Mayo with a bullying non sequitur—"That's why I'm richer than you"—the room erupted in sycophantic laughter. Money is honey, Thomas Edward Brown told his little sonny, and a rich man's joke is always funny.

Dimon explained to Bachus's congressional panel that Iksil's strategy was "badly vetted, badly implemented, badly tested," but by then everybody already knew that. He said his bank was big enough to absorb the losses, and no customer money had been lost—though, by appearances, it had been. Shareholders watched as nearly one-third of the value of their JPMorgan Chase stock melted away, but by the time of Dimon's Washington appearance, the fever line had begun moving back upward, the investment community apparently satisfied that the bank was taking appropriate steps to do whatever an extremely large ship needs to do to tack into the Sea of Credibility. JPMorgan Chase fired Iksil and clawed back two years of his salary as punishment. The amount Iksil forfeited came to about $14 million, according to the Senate report. The bank also jettisoned three of Iksil's bosses and made them return earnings, bringing the making of amends to Dimon's doorstep. The buck did not, however, stop at the desk of the chairman and chief executive. The bank's board of directors docked Dimon nearly half his 2012 compensation, or about $11 million. That meant that Iksil, a trader in London, paid for his transgressions with his job and 200 percent of his yearly pay while his boss's boss's boss's boss received a 50 percent cut and kept his job. The debate that followed was not whether Dimon should get the boot along with Iksil and his three bosses but rather whether he should continue to serve as both chief executive officer and chairman—in effect, as his own boss.

While the bank had reported record profits in 2012—thanks in some significant measure to Ben Bernanke and the Federal

Reserve—the London Whale wasn't an isolated instance of Dimon's fiddling while parts of his 260,000-employee empire blew up. Independent bank analyst Joshua Rosner calculated that JPMorgan Chase paid $1 to settle various legal and regulatory issues for every $8 in net income it generated in the four years from 2009 through 2012. Indiscretions included bid rigging in the municipal-bond market (resulting in a $228 million fine and an admission of wrong-doing); allegedly debiting savings account withdrawals in a way that made overdrafts more likely ($110 million to settle litigation); accusations of violating sanctions against Cuba, Iran, and Sudan ($88 million fine); allegedly failing to protect British customer funds from a pool of money used to trade derivatives (sound familiar?); allegedly manipulating electricity prices in California and the US Midwest (six-month suspension from trading and $410 million in paybacks and penalties); accusations of bamboozling the city of Milan, Italy (forced return of assets); and allegedly selling unregistered securities to a Florida public employees fund ($25 million fine). JPMorgan Chase's role as lender to three firms in their death throes—securities dealer MF Global, run by former US senator and New Jersey governor Jon Corzine; Iowa-based hedge fund Peregrine Financial Group; and the eponymous investment company run by Ponzi schemer Bernie Madoff—also cast a dark cloud over Dimon's operation as forensic accountants scoured spreadsheets for signs of missing client cash.

In the wake of all this, Dimon faced a May 2013 shareholder vote on whether the job of chairman should be pried from his grip. A corporate good-governance group came out in favor of taking it away, triggering the Jamie-Jamie-You're-So-Fine lobbying machine. Aging titans Warren Buffett, Jack Welch, and Rupert Murdoch were dispatched to wave the flag for Dimon. Not satisfied with a charm offensive, the public relations lightning war leaked the game-changing tidbit that Dimon would quit the bank altogether if asked to relinquish the chairmanship. The man himself—known, like the mono-monikered Madonna before him, merely as Jamie— added plausibility to the rumored threat by buying 2,600 square feet of office space in the Park Avenue building where he lived. Would he operate a hedge fund there? Write his memoirs? Use it as a counting house for counting all his money? Provide shelter for families improperly foreclosed by his bank? I didn't hear any speculation about what the guy with an ego to match his job(s) would do for fun and profit after running the biggest bank in the Western Hemisphere, but some bluffs aren't meant to be called.

Still, JPMorgan Chase couldn't resist putting its thumb on the scale. A few days before the close of the weeks-long process of shareholder balloting, which incidentally was nonbinding, the bank ordered the firm that conducted the tally to report incremental vote numbers only to the bank and to leave the rest of the world in the dark. The governance group and some shareholders cried foul, but Dimon and his cronies were used to winning, and if they had to step on some necks on their way to daylight, even if those necks belonged to shareholders, that was, after all, the only way they knew how to play the game. You'd think that Dimon might recognize hubris in activities such as these, or in his repetitive assertion that the bank had a "fortress balance sheet," or in his blithe and persistent insistence that JPMorgan Chase didn't need a bailout during the crisis, even though the world knew it took as much as $68.6 billion of emergency loans from the Federal Reserve on a single night in October 2008. That said, Dimon had no incentive to tone down his act. He apologized for the London Whale fiasco, took his lumps, and disgorged more of his hard-earned pay than a subway car stuffed with New Yorkers earned in a lifetime—now get off his lawn.

How did the vote end up? Come on. What do you think?

On the other hand, Braunstein, the purveyor of horse manure on the April 2012 conference call, left his job as the bank's chief financial officer. He went to a better place: the vice chairmanship.

By the end of 2012, losses in the Synthetic Credit Portfolio totaled more than $6.2 billion. We may never know the true extent of the debacle because, before the dust had settled, JPMorgan Chase scooped up the London Whale trades and mixed them into its investment bank's portfolio, rendering them impossible to differentiate from any other "hedges." Unjustifiably anonymous and probably still bleeding Granny's money, the belly tranches, where default may realize, now belonged to history. Jamie had said it was a complete tempest in a teapot. What part of that don't you understand?

FOUR

PRIDE

*The Myth of Competence: Deniz Anginer and
Conjectural Government Guarantees*

I N MAY 2013, JAMIE DIMON COULD LAY UNDISPUTED CLAIM
to the mantle of Wall Street's top dog. He'd prevailed in the non-binding shareholder vote to remain his own boss, and his employer, JPMorgan Chase, was in the middle of a streak of record profits despite the London Whale unpleasantness. Dimon's successful defense of his dominion, however, wasn't much heralded outside LinkedIn, of all places. The networking site trumpeted him as the first bank chief executive officer (and chairman) to contribute to its "Influencer" blog series. Dimon's post included a gratuitous Abraham Lincoln quote and declared that Humility, with a capital *H*, was one of the "essential hallmarks of a good leader." Perhaps Dimon had come by that wisdom the hard way. He'd donned the hair shirt for his "complete tempest in a teapot" comment and endured an $11 million scolding from a board of directors that, at least for the time being, held itself blameless. But still, a LinkedIn blog didn't seem like a sufficient way to celebrate vanquishing the good-corporate-governance people and allowing members of the US Senate to roll over for him like kittens. Where was the usual

Dimon chest pounding, the casually tossed-off that's-why-I'm-richer-than-you wisecracks to send a roomful of toadies into croakings of butt-smooching mirth? Where was the victory party with cascades of Cristal, scandalously clad dancers, and first-year MBA students offered as sacrifices to the money gods? It was one thing for Dimon to say that Humility was an essential hallmark and quite another for him to begin, at this late hour, to practice it.

Could it have been the steroids? In the first half of 2013, the world got a glimpse of the metaphorical jar of androstenedione in Dimon's locker in the JPMorgan Chase executive weight room. Wall Street had been benefitting from performance enhancers that boosted the biggest banks' balance sheets and made them look much more ripped than they really were.

In fact, Dimon's conquest reminded me of Barry Bonds's crowning as Major League Baseball's home run king. Bonds made history in 2006 when he slugged the long ball that vaulted him past Henry Aaron on the all-time list, but few people were watching and even fewer celebrated. The common perception was that Bonds's record didn't really count because he cheated by using drugs that made him bigger and stronger. Even though Bonds was arguably the sport's best player in the mid-1990s, the sleek base-stealing power hitter transformed himself into a fortress of a man, larded with muscle, able to blast home runs at a pace that seemed impossible for mere mortals. He must have had chemical help, people said. Critics remarked on his querulousness and his growing cap size, side effects of human growth hormone. Some wanted to put an asterisk in the record book next to Bonds's home run total so that future generations would remember that the feat shouldn't really count, like that of a sprinter aided by a gale. Dimon, like Bonds, was an elite performer in his profession with or without enhancement. And like Bonds, he plied his trade in an era when a variety of factors, aside from prodigious natural gifts, inflated his statistics. Dimon's swelled head may have been merely an idiomatic expression, and his queru-

lousness may have been a congenital character trait and not a phar-
maceutical side effect, but purists would say the records he and his
bank compiled deserved an asterisk too. Sure, Dimon could fortify
a balance sheet, just as Bonds could hit home runs. But after the
2008 crisis, JPMorgan Chase had help. The performance-enhancing
drug wasn't androstenedione or human growth hormone. It was a
dangerously high dosage of "too big to fail."

IN THE EARLY 2010S, NOTHING MAY HAVE BEEN MORE
universally despised than the idea of another round of bank bailouts.
The very notion that taxpayers would once again take the hammer
to their piggybanks to pay for Wall Street's mistakes ranked right
up there in unpopularity with Congress, the media, and mosquitos.
Not an encouraging word was heard on the subject on C-SPAN,
and cursing the bailouts was a guaranteed applause line at political
campaign stops. Even the bailed-out bankers themselves, whose
jobs and ability to stuff reams of money into their own pockets the
American taxpayer and Federal Reserve had safeguarded, trooped
into TV and radio studios to register their enthusiastic opposition
to doing it again. Perhaps the sentiments of the masses had finally
reached the executive suites. The rescues of 2008 had finished the
process set in motion by years of late fees and overdraft fees and
ATM fees and customer service runarounds and fine-print games-
manship and interest-rate baiting and switching. Americans simply
didn't like their banks. After 2008, they didn't trust or respect them
either. Even the most powerful financiers, men who spent their
lives flitting from Park Avenue to Teterboro Airport, from Aspen to
the Hamptons, could smell the disgust in the air. "We have to get
rid of too big to fail," Dimon told CNBC. "Anybody who thinks
there's a political will to rescue failing financial institutions is not
reading the same papers I'm reading," Lloyd Blankfein, the Goldman Sachs chief executive officer, told Politico. "We don't think

there should be too big to fail," Timothy Sloan, the Wells Fargo chief financial officer, told me. "We don't think we should be bailed out." Bailout revulsion was the one issue that united Mother Earth's children. Even Ben Bernanke, chairman of the Federal Reserve, and Congressman Ron Paul, the Texas Libertarian who wanted the Fed abolished, could agree on this single point. When it came to bailouts, the lion could lay down with the lamb, and the lamb might even get some sleep.

Before the dust had settled from the 2008 crisis, committees around the world rolled up their sleeves and went to work trying to prevent another cataclysm that would necessitate the rescue of large financial institutions. Their aim was to erase the option of devoting public money to save the banks. The Switzerland-based Financial Stability Board, established by the countries with the twenty biggest economies, recommended that banks fund their operations with less borrowed money and more equity—the much-debated, poorly understood "capital requirements"—and that the biggest banks use even less borrowed money. The Bank of England floated the idea of forcing the big boys to shrink or break up.

In the United States, lawmakers crafted the Dodd-Frank Wall Street Reform and Consumer Protection Act, with its flow charts detailing the government's response should a financial giant teeter on the brink. Dodd-Frank forced banks to prepare so-called living wills and designated the Treasury secretary to decide whether to take heroic measures to save the patient or let it die. It established an Orderly Liquidation Authority, becoming, in effect, Dr. Death for complicated financial firms. "Because of this reform, the American people will never again be asked to foot the bill for Wall Street's mistakes," President Barack Obama said on July 15, 2010. "There will be no more taxpayer-funded bailouts, period."

Dodd-Frank, Congress, the president—all of them were, of course, full of baloney.

I WASN'T THE ONE CALLING BALONEY ON THE END OF TOO big to fail—it was the investors who put their money on the line. You've heard the expression "money talks, bullshit walks"? Bond buyers, the people who loan money to the largest banks, were so sure that Uncle Sam, or Uncle Ben Bernanke, would toss financial institutions a lifeline should they start to take on water that they charged the biggest banks less to borrow. They figured that, despite the rhetoric, the American taxpayer or the Federal Reserve would pay the big banks' debts in the event the big banks couldn't. So even as the words were passing Obama's lips, the biggest banks—the ones that Dodd-Frank designated as systemically important financial institutions, or SIFIs—were benefitting from bond buyers' perception by borrowing at a cheaper rate. Lenders were actually taking less in returns because of an implied taxpayer bailout. This was profit and loss, bona fide Yankee dollars, cash on the barrelhead. The rest was just talk.

Period. Asterisk.

DENIZ ANGINER EMIGRATED TO CANADA FROM TURKEY WHEN he was a teenager. Like any ambitious young person with a gift for figures and an instinctive understanding of how mathematical formulas could unlock the secrets of money, he was attracted to New York, the place where the magic happens. Anginer landed a job there advising hedge funds on risk. His first day was September 11, 2001.

"We were doing computer training in Midtown when the planes hit," Anginer told me. He'd been with his girlfriend to the top of one of the World Trade Center towers a couple weeks previously. "I watched the tower come down with a colleague whose father was in the building. Luckily, the dad survived." The attack softened the attitudes of his new neighbors, Anginer said. "New Yorkers are known for their eff-you attitude, and coming from Canada I was somewhat taken aback by everyone's rude and selfish behavior," he told me. "But after 9/11, I've never seen a community come together like that before. There was this sense that people had your back if something bad were to happen." Reliving that time with Anginer, I remembered The Onion's post-9/11 headline, "Rest of Country Temporarily Feels Deep Affection for New York." Things were back to normal soon enough.

Anginer left New York to do his PhD work in Ann Arbor, at the University of Michigan's Ross School of Business. His dissertation examined investor behavior and credit risk—calculating the level of danger that particular borrowers will fail repay their debts on time. His research became more practical after he joined the World Bank as an economist. "There was need for empirical work to guide policy decisions," he told me.

He was on leave from the World Bank and teaching at Virginia Tech's business school when he published a paper that caught my attention. He and a Syracuse University law professor, A. Joseph Warburton, had studied the effects of the government's 2009 rescue of Chrysler on the carmaker's borrowing costs, and it seemed like a natural next step—and a myth-busting opportunity—for them to tackle the borrowing costs of the big banks after the bailouts. He knew that the numbers would tell the truth even when words might not. "People at the banks were saying, 'We paid our money back with interest, everything's great,'" Anginer told me, referring to the assertion that the $20 billion in interest the Treasury Department earned from Troubled Asset Relief Program, or TARP, loans meant the bailout program was a success. "No, everything's not great. There are other costs we should be looking at."

Being able to pinpoint the cost of too big to fail, in dollar amounts, felt like a breakthrough. A number, no matter what it was, would put the lie to the main argument for maintaining the status quo: that regulation or any requirement that the too-big-to-fail banks get smaller would be "punishing success." Revealing the "other costs," as Anginer put it, would show that the same institutions whose mismanagement and incompetence had helped push the American economy to the edge of oblivion were now, after the deathbed experience, just as feckless. That it was the American taxpayer, once again, whose help—or, actually, the mere suggestion of whose possible help—lifted Wall Street to profitability. The dice were loaded, and Anginer could provide figures showing just how rigged the game had become.

Anginer, Warburton, and New York University's Viral Acharya set out to calculate the discount the biggest banks got from bond buyers who believed they'd get repaid even if the borrower banks went belly up because the government would bail them out. They set out to see whether Dodd-Frank had ended the perception that the state would swoop in and save the banks from themselves.

There was already ample evidence that investors believed more bailouts were part of the contingency plans, despite the mountain of rhetoric to the contrary. The credit-rating companies sure believed it. While it's true that these companies had been known to make hellacious mistakes in the past—for instance, the raters gave subprime mortgage securities top grades, allowing insurance companies and pension funds to buy them, even as the flow of money was freezing in 2007—their credit scores did play a role in how much it cost companies to borrow money. The higher the score, the cheaper the loans.

In a March 2013 report, Moody's Investors Service, the second-largest US rating company, said that the likelihood of a government bailout boosted the ratings of all six of the biggest banks by at least two grades. In fact, the bank holding companies of Bank of America and Citigroup would have been tagged with junk ratings if not for the implied taxpayer backstop. That meant that bonds issued by the bank holding companies of the two institutions were so sketchy—the chances they'd repay their debts were so iffy—that many pension funds and insurance companies would be forbidden from buying them; only the implied taxpayer rescue made them palatable. Fitch Ratings, the third-biggest US credit-rating company, had similar double grades for the Big Six. Fitch assigned one grade for the bank with the implied government guarantees factored in and another, lower one excluding them.

Anginer and his colleagues collected more than 84,000 data points for 567 financial firms going back to 1990. They looked specifically at the difference between what the banks paid creditors for borrowing money and what investors earned from owning US government debt. They subtracted the big banks' number from the same measurement for smaller banks to determine the value of the implicit government subsidy.

Anginer wanted to make sure there wasn't another reason the bigger banks may have been getting a borrowing discount. Perhaps creditors thought the big boys were acting more responsibly and taking fewer risks and rewarded them for it. To find out if that was true, he and his fellow researchers isolated a series of risk measurements that affected the cost of debt. One was called maturity mismatch, which gauged how much the banks had been able to borrow short term, for which rates were usually lower, while lending long term. That practice helped doom Lehman Brothers when short-term loans dried up in 2008. They also applied a calculation created by Nobel Prize–winning economist Robert Merton known as distance to default, more commonly used to predict bankruptcy. They discovered that there was no difference between the biggest banks and smaller banks when it came to practicing safe finance. In fact, bond buyers had been banking on what Anginer called "conjectural government guarantees" for at least the previous twenty years. The discount for the top 10 percent of banks from 1990 to 2010 was worth, on average, $20 billion annually. In 2009, as lending dried up and the government actually did backstop the big banks, the borrowing discount ballooned to about $100 billion.

I asked Anginer to do bank-by-bank computations of the postcrisis discounts for the Big Six: Bank of America, Citigroup, Goldman Sachs, JPMorgan Chase, Morgan Stanley, and Wells Fargo. To arrive at a final figure, he subtracted the customer deposits of each firm from the interest-bearing liabilities. He told me that this probably undercounted the discount. Not subtracting the deposits probably overcounted it, he said. I told him that a more conservative number would be fine. I didn't want rioting in the streets.

The six biggest banks' borrowing advantage swelled to $37.2 billion in 2009 after Congress authorized spending $700 billion on the TARP bailouts, based on the more conservative tally. The discount decreased to $29.9 billion in 2010 as the economy improved and to $14.6 billion in 2011, Anginer found. The too-big-to-fail discount was shrinking, but it wasn't going away.

Here's the bank-by-bank rundown:

- *Bank of America* enjoyed a borrowing edge of $911 million in 2005—a useful point of comparison. For 2009, 2010, and 2011, its discount totaled $18.65 billion. That was more than three times the bank's total profit during that time. Imagine what would have happened to the economy of Charlotte, North Carolina, home of the bank of opportunity, without those steroids.
- *Citigroup* had an advantage in 2005 of $1.25 billion. From 2009 to 2011, it was $16.21 billion. That's equal to about 80 percent of its net income for those three years.
- *Goldman Sachs* enjoyed an $828 million edge in 2005, which grew to $12.93 billion in the three years from 2009 to 2011—about half of the bank's profit for that period.
- *JPMorgan Chase*'s advantage in 2005 was $723 million. In 2009, 2010, and 2011 it was $16.27 billion, or about a third of the bank's record net income in that span.

○ *Morgan Stanley* had a borrowing edge of $1.27 billion in 2005 and $12.6 billion from 2009 to 2011. That's more than the $10.16 billion profit Morgan Stanley earned in that time.

○ *Wells Fargo*, in 2005, had a $180 million advantage; in 2009, 2010, and 2011, it was $5.04 billion. Its net income for those three years was an all-time high of $40.51 billion.

Altogether, the Big Six got an $81.69 billion discount for the three years from 2009 to 2011, Anginer found. That was more than half their profit of $150.47 billion during that time, courtesy of implied taxpayer guarantees. Now we knew what too big to fail was costing: at least $82 billion in just the first three years after the crisis. And these were the more conservative numbers.

Anginer wasn't the only one calculating implied subsidies for the biggest banks. Other studies came to similar conclusions. Research by economists at the International Monetary Fund used the less conservative number—they included customer deposits in their calculations—and came up with a borrowing advantage of $64 billion per year for the five biggest banks (dropped from the mix was number six, Morgan Stanley). The Federal Deposit Insurance Corporation masticated some numbers in September 2012 and spit out a borrowing advantage of 0.45 percentage points. They called it a "too-big-to-fail subsidy." Bhanu Balasubramnian of the University of Akron and Ken B. Cyree of the University of Mississippi School of Business Administration found in June 2012 that the passage of Dodd-Frank reduced the advantage to 0.61 percentage points. (The pair also published another study showing that the big banks' edge had turned negative after Dodd-Frank, meaning that the biggest banks paid a premium to borrow after the law's passage, but Cyree, in a conversation with me in 2013, said his findings were generally consistent with Anginer's, the difference being the stretch of time each studied. Anginer's, at more than twenty years, was longer.) Even JPMorgan Chase weighed in. Two of its researchers concluded that globally systemically important banks, or G-SIBs—a status conferred by the Bank of International Settlements in Basel, Switzerland, that included our six American gigundos—had a 0.18 percent cost-of-funding advantage relative to non-systemically-important institutions. A spokesman for the bank sent this particular study to me. He may have thought it discounted the findings of Anginer and his colleagues. It didn't. It showed a smaller discount for the big boys but nonetheless joined a growing consensus that such discounts existed, a truth that the banks and their paid public relations minions found inconvenient.

When Mark Whitehouse of Bloomberg View, the opinionated cousin of Bloomberg News, wrote about the International Monetary Fund's calculations, Senator Elizabeth Warren, the Massachusetts Democrat who'd criticized the banks for a business model dependent on "tricks and traps," asked Fed Chairman Ben Bernanke about the never-ending bailouts. Later, at his quarterly press conference in March 2013, the gray-bearded professor affirmed the existence of the discounts and said he was no fan of them. "On the benefits of being 'too big to fail,' no, we don't have an estimate" of the borrowing discounts, Bernanke told reporters. "It's pretty difficult to control for all the factors that go into determining the size of the subsidy. I think there is some evidence that financial markets are, at least to some extent, taking into account the possibility that large financial institutions will fail." He continued, "That being said, I certainly never meant to say to Senator Warren—and I share her concern about 'too big to fail.' I think it's a major issue. I never meant to imply that the problem was solved and gone. It is not solved and gone. It's still here."

Problem? What problem? No problem here!

That was the response of the financial services trade organizations and the banks' lobbying firms to Bernanke's lament. Big banks were a boon, they said. They provided big corporations with big loans (as if they didn't split those very large loans among multiple banks); they were competitive with humongous European and Asian banks (which, if they weren't careful, would also need bailouts from the Federal Reserve because the US central bank had become, in the dark days of the last crisis, the central bank to the world and had indeed sent billions of its bailout loans to banks headquartered overseas); they could cater to multinational corporations ("an argument for being global, not for being big," Mark Whitehouse wrote); and the diversification of their various businesses actually made them safer and sounder than smaller institutions (as if the effects of the hypothetical collapse of little Saigon National Bank in Westminster, California, could be compared with the conflagration that a Citigroup failure would spark). That little banks were riskier than big banks had been a half-truth advanced by, among others, former Treasury secretary Lawrence Summers, whose lobbying efforts on Capitol Hill while he was President Obama's top economic adviser helped kill a 2010 bill that would have mandated shrinkage for the six biggest US banks. While it was true that small banks did fail a lot more often than, say, a bank the size of Citigroup—wait, bad example—the effect on the global financial system of the little-bank failure was minuscule. (Of course, we now know that one reason small banks fail so often relative to the big boys is their higher cost of borrowing.)

The banks themselves, meanwhile, played it smarter in the public relations arena than their rent-a-friends. They denied the existence of bond-market discounts, but not too strenuously, or insisted they didn't want to have anything to do with them. They focused on the added costs of complying with postcrisis regulations, which they said were in the billions. I had some sympathy for this line of defense only because I had little faith in government regulators. They had a habit of rushing to put out fires just as the last ember was blinking out. Witness the Office of the Comptroller of the Currency finding out about the losing London Whale trades by watching Bloomberg

TV. The Obama administration was cuckoo for bureaucracy; it never identified a problem it didn't want to solve by throwing a new committee at it. The banks had to contort themselves to obey every rule, regardless of whether it actually addressed a real trouble spot or not. Still, this would have been a more compelling argument had the banks' blatant profligacy not cost the world trillions of dollars in the last crisis, and if their recklessness were not threatening the loss of trillions more in the next.

I TRACKED DOWN THE ONE GUY IN THE WORLD WHO THOUGHT bank bailouts were a good thing and welcomed more of them—or rather, the one guy who had the guts to say out loud and in public that failing to bail out the big banks would mean disaster. His name was Gabriel Borenstein, and he was managing director of a New York investment firm called Enclave Capital. When I met him for lunch, at a restaurant across the street from the ice-skating rink at Rockefeller Center in Midtown Manhattan, I was struck by how much he looked like the comic actor Jerry Stiller, who played George Costanza's father on *Seinfeld*. Borenstein was born in Poland—his mother was a survivor of the death camps—and he returned there often to advise the Polish central bank on where to invest its money.

"The biggest mistake that could be made would be to allow significant banking institutions to fail," Borenstein told me. "The sequential events that would follow, largely driven by psychology, cannot be quantified." When Borenstein traveled abroad, he said, he was always being reminded of America's place in the world, how it remained a lighthouse of hope for so many people. He was proud of the United States in a way that rubbed off on me. Despite its flaws, he said, it boasted the most resilient financial system in the world, the envy of strivers everywhere. I paraphrased Winston Churchill for him—American capitalism is the worst system except for all the rest—and he agreed. I told him I thought it could be better. I told him I wasn't sure it could survive with too big to fail. I said that I didn't think the financial industry's reliance on "tricks and traps" was a sustainable business model. I told him I feared for democracy because of money's influence on politics and culture. He called me an idealist. I laughed and steered him back to the bailouts. Borenstein couldn't fathom why others hated the thought of them. "Another Lehman Brothers collapse could trigger a potential implosion which the Fed wouldn't be able to address," he said, referring to the investment bank's 2008 bankruptcy, the biggest in US history. In other words, a few hundred billion administered to buck up a dying patient would be cheaper and less messy than chasing an epidemic that not even the world's most powerful financial institution could contain. "What's in place works," Borenstein said. "Let's maintain the status quo."

BORENSTEIN AND I COULDN'T AGREE ON THAT. I SAW THE status quo as broken and the bureaucratic repair as ineffectual. Dodd-Frank had left many of the rule-making details to regulators such as the Federal Reserve, which, as we've seen, was under the spell of the banks it was supposed to oversee. I preferred the solution of breaking the biggest banks into smaller businesses and allowing them to compete on a level playing field for customers' hearts and minds as well as their dollars. It seemed the only way to address both the financial and nonfinancial costs of too big to fail. Borenstein could see my point, but he disagreed. So did bankers, regulators, and politicians, who had told me and the world countless times that breaking up the banks was impossible, that it was punishing success, that it was better to drain them of billions of dollars to comply with thousands of pages of regulatory edicts of varying degrees of dubiousness. Those arguments had carried the day. The biggest banks were flush and growing flusher. The regulators were caving to their charms. We were headed for another dislocation, which is financial jargon for the biggest banks crowing, "Heads I win, tails you lose."

Given this atmosphere, Borenstein and the bond buyers were the only ones who made sense. Would the government and the Federal Reserve really sit on their hands while a bank with a $2 trillion balance sheet sank slowly, then quickly, into oblivion, dragging millions of businesses and jobs and innocent people's nest eggs with it? An orderly liquidation seemed like a child's bedtime story. The wolf eats Grandma, but then the hunter slays the wolf and Grandma pops cheerfully out of the wolf's belly! If one of these whale-sized banks were bleeding money, what would the others be up to? They traded with one another, they copied each other's methods, they loaned to and borrowed from one another, and they invested in the same firms. Surely a scenario in which only one of them went down, without the angel of death also visiting any of the rest of them, was fantasy. What then? The only entities with balance sheets hefty enough to toss out life preservers were the US government and the Federal Reserve. Financial Crisis 2.0, featuring the Son of the Bank Bailouts. Bond buyers were correct to give the biggest banks a discount. It would be Uncle Sam, Uncle Ben, or cover the children's eyes and run, don't walk, to the exits.

Senator Sherrod Brown, the Ohio Democrat, was willing to try again. He'd introduced the SAFE Act with Senator Ted Kaufman in 2010 in an unsuccessful attempt to shrink the big boys. In 2013, he teamed with Senator David Vitter, a Louisiana Republican, to offer a different way. They wanted to incentivize banks to get less risky. Under their proposal, financial institutions with more than $500 billion in assets—the Big Six—would fund themselves with a minimum of 15 percent equity. That meant they'd have to use $1 in cash for every $6.67 they borrowed. (If that sounds ridiculous, keep in mind that the dearly departed Bear Stearns was operating with $1 in cash for every $42 it had borrowed.) The banks found the Brown-Vitter borrowing limit outrageous, and compared with other proposed regulations, both international and national, it certainly was more restrictive. So Brown and Vitter said to the bankers, Okay, you don't like that? Shrink yourselves. If you're able to reduce your holdings below a certain level, you only have to fund yourselves with 8 percent equity, or $1 in cash for every $12.50 you borrow. The Brown-Vitter proposal gave the big boys a choice. They could continue sleeping on your couch like an obese brother-in-law who mooches off you and your spouse while complaining that the world is full of freeloaders, or (take a guess which alternative I favor) they could close, sell, or spin off lines of business that didn't jibe with the boring work of allocating money to foster innovation and growth; in the process they could become leaner, healthier, and less despised.

A happy side effect of that: they'd be off the juice, clean of steroids. They could erase the asterisks attached to the charity that they call profits, amassed thanks to the past and conjectural future generosity of taxpayers. They'd be making money in a novel way: they'd be earning it.

FIVE

LUST

*Complexity: Saule T. Omarova
and the Phantom Waiver*

I N 2005, JPMORGAN CHASE ASKED THE FEDERAL RESERVE
for permission to become a commodities merchant. Granting it
would entail exempting the bank from a law that for half a century
kept banks, whose primary source of funding was guaranteed by
government deposit insurance, far away from unpredictable industries, such as mining and oil exploration, dominated by competitive
firms with special expertise. The Fed had already granted Citigroup
a nearly identical waiver from the Bank Holding Company Act in
2003, so it only seemed fair to do the same for Jamie Dimon's outfit.
The Fed had three conditions: JPMorgan Chase had to stay out of
the business of storing, extracting, or transporting commodities. No
zinc warehouses, no molybdenum mines, no single-hull oil tankers—
they were too risky, the Fed said. Just like that, the Federal Reserve
was once again in the business of flattening fortifications that for
decades had protected taxpayer-guaranteed bank deposits from a
volatile corner of world trade. The only remnants of those protec-
tions were the three prohibitions.

In 2010, JPMorgan Chase bought Henry Bath & Son, one of the oldest and biggest owners of metals warehouses in the world. JPMorgan Chase was now in the business of storing commodities such as copper and aluminum. Why the Fed would allow the bank to violate its own approval order was a mystery. The Fed wouldn't say. I spent a couple weeks beating my head against the wall, looking for an explanation. Why had the Fed changed its mind? If central bankers believed the warehouse business was too crazy for JPMorgan Chase in 2005, what made them believe it was safe in 2010? If a waiver had been granted, the Fed never made it public and wouldn't comment on it. JPMorgan Chase wouldn't say. Other regulatory agencies, such as the Office of the Comptroller of the Currency, which oversees JPMorgan Chase's street corner banks, and the Commodity Futures Trading Commission, which keeps watch over the buying and selling of pork, sugar, cotton, and the rest, professed no knowledge of it.

I grew more vexed by the secrecy around the exemption, if there was one, than by the question of the exemption itself. Possible explanations for the phantom waiver weren't really tough to come up with. The central bank had always done what it wanted, and as the evidence suggested, the Fed never felt disposed to say no to JPMorgan Chase. It was as if the bank had puppy-dog eyes and the Fed was its guilt-ridden divorced dad. *Whatever you want, honey.* The Fed could always locate a rationale to support the waiver somewhere in the labyrinthine banking regulations. But the secrecy gave the issue an allure that it lacked otherwise. I talked to Fed watchers, most of whom had no clue that these transactions had even taken place—it turned out that the number of people who closely followed the Fed's oversight of Wall Street was not that high—and together, in our ignorance, we tried to come up with possible reasons for the concealment. Had the Fed started to care that it looked like a pushover? Were the central bankers simply weary of being second-guessed? Was the waiver some kind of payback to JPMorgan Chase for a special favor that needed to be kept on the down-low?

Into the vacuum of factual information crept weird theories. One analyst I spoke with pointed to a dusty section of the 1934 Securities and Exchange Act, which allowed companies, with the permission of the US president, to conduct secret operations—even to the point of keeping two sets of accounting books, one excluding the secrets for public consumption and one including them for internal record keeping—as long as the operations involved matters of national security. In 2006, President George W. Bush delegated the authority to grant this approval to his national intelligence director, John Negroponte. I thought the analyst was kidding, but he sent me a link to Bush's one-paragraph directive, published in the *Federal Register*, and the single news story about it, which he'd saved. It had been deleted from the media outlet's website. Was it possible that the Fed waiver was classified? Could Henry Bath have served some sort of antiterrorism function? Was JPMorgan Chase playing a role in some covert, Cold War–style jockeying? If so, this gave entirely new context to the bailouts of 2008. The banks had been rescued because they were doing important national security work! The hypothesis conjured a vision of Jason Bourne fighting a battle on a forklift against a Chinese version of Goldfinger's henchmen at a strategic Henry Bath copper warehouse in Singapore.

China had indeed risen quickly as a leading consumer of industrial metals. But the word I heard was that Chinese metal consumers were concerned about certain warehousing companies manipulating the market, fearful that American and European companies would someday deploy in Shanghai the techniques they used to game the system in Detroit and Rotterdam. The tactics allegedly used to control the price and supply of one of the world's most popular industrial metals, not as a buyer or seller but as a warehouser, were supposedly perfected by a firm locked in competition with JPMorgan Chase, one that people said set the example of how to become not only the most profitable securities firm in Wall Street history but also King of the Beer Can: Goldman Sachs.

THE FEDERAL RESERVE, AS THE COUNTRY'S LEAD WATCHDOG over the financial system, screwed up plenty in the first dozen or so years of the twenty-first century. The failures, in fact, were spectacular. The central bank refused to crack down on the proliferation of subprime mortgages, despite warnings from one of its own governors, and acknowledged the existence of predatory lending only when it was too late. It failed to identify the housing bubble, even after the *New York Times* ran stories about it on the front page of its Sunday business section and Bloomberg News published descriptions of liar loans and traders successfully betting against the mortgage market. It did little to counter the public relations campaign waged by the banks and their professional associations and abetted by members of the financial press, who spread the lie that nobody could have possibly known there was a bubble or divined the severity of its popping beforehand. It lined up behind the big banks even after the courts ruled that the public's right to know was more important than using secrecy to protect large financial institutions from what it called "stigma." It allowed the banks to shoot craps in the derivatives market with Grandma's life savings, an indulgence that benefited only the banks and certainly not Grandma. And it allowed the big boys to trample over the boundaries established by the 1956 Bank Holding Company Act, meant to separate banking and commerce for the benefit of both.

By enabling the big banks to rush into the arena of "physical commodities," the Fed wasn't making the task of oversight any easier for itself. Not only did the central bankers supervise the myriad and sometimes bizarre financial activities of firms that employed the smartest lawyers, accountants, and public relations experts to find, exploit, and spin any advantage, but they were now crossing their fingers and hoping that all was well with the proper credentialing of Morgan Stanley's oil tankers chugging through the Gulf of Mexico, worker safety in Goldman Sachs's coal mines in Colombia, and the legality of JPMorgan Chase's energy trading in California. It was the Fed's impossible job to make sure none of these diverse involvements ended badly for the banks and, by extension, the world financial system. The bailouts of 2008 had allowed the biggest banks not only to get bigger but to spread their networks wider, stick their fingers into more pots, forge fresh alliances, and poke a stick at new competitors. The Fed couldn't possibly check the behavior of grain traders in Malaysia, or assess the health of an oil refinery in Nigeria, or make sure slaves weren't employed in a copper mine in Peru, or guarantee that warehouse employees in Dubai weren't feeding the black market with the merchandise. The central bank had to rely on the financial institutions themselves to declare that no conflicts could possibly arise, even though one part of their operation traded oil, another financed it, another bet on the stocks of competitors, and yet another drilled for it, refined it, transported it, and stored it.

Add to all that the inherent unfairness of an institution funded by deposits jumping into the oil patch. Finance was a bank's primary function, but what would compel a firm to bankroll the operations of another company that might compete with it in natural gas production? What would compel it not to quit financing the operations of a firm it identified as a potential competitor? Why couldn't, hypothetically, a big-bank trader in Houston call up a warehouse manager in the Netherlands and tell him, "Hey, we're betting on zinc, keep a bunch of it in storage to squeeze supply and drive up the price"—or "Release a bunch more than you normally would because we're shorting it"? What would prevent the guys in Singapore from letting slip to the traders in New York that they were pulling out of a partnership with a certain petroleum services firm, and the guys in New York get the message and short the stock, add credit protection, and shift their investments elsewhere? Or a tanker in the northern

Pacific springs a leak, and the bank that owns it is the first to hear, enjoying all the advantages of moving its money before anyone else?

I'm sure my examples, theoretical as they are, lack sophistication, and schemes I've never dreamed of are being hatched during early-morning jogs and on barstools and in impromptu, cigarette-fueled strategy confabs on the sidewalks in front of bank headquarters. Sure, the banks could claim—and they did—that one subsidiary functioned independently of another, and also independently of the mother ship, and that there was no coordination between, say, the traders and the warehousemen. But, really, who aside from the banks themselves would even know? So many parts were moving that regulators would never locate that speck of dust among all the space junk—even if they knew approximately where to look.

The Fed's own research highlighted the growing problem: In 1990, the four biggest US bank holding companies had, combined, about 3,000 subsidiaries. By 2011, the top four had more than 11,000. What profit, what joy, what poetry did all those subsidiaries add to the lives of their fellow Americans? The truth was, in commodity markets such as aluminum and electricity, big-bank involvement cost consumers money without any added benefit to anyone but the banks. Why? Because the subtext of the fretting over the Federal Reserve's lack of concern wasn't only that a tragic mishap involving, say, a wrecked oil tanker would trigger a run that would swamp a big bank, creating a Lehman 2.0 moment, but also that a big bank's participation in a market would prove disastrous for the market and, in the end, for the people all over the world who needed the products traded in that market to manufacture cars, build homes, assemble smart phones, cook dinner, wash the dishes, heal, get to work every day, and read at night.

In February 2010—the same month JPMorgan Chase took over the metal warehouser Henry Bath—Goldman Sachs bought

Metro International Trade Services, a worldwide company that by 2013 owned more than two dozen metals warehouses in the Detroit area, convenient to the auto industry. In July 2013, 80 percent of US aluminum inventory monitored by the London Metal Exchange sat collecting rent in those warehouses. A lot of it was also collecting dust.

Talking to plaintiff's attorneys, traders, aluminum consumers, analysts, and my colleagues at Bloomberg News, I was able to piece together the angle. They told me that Goldman Sachs's stratagem depended on three planets coming into perfect alignment. First, during the 2008 financial crisis, prices for industrial metals collapsed due to decreased demand. The economy, especially home building and car manufacturing, had come to a standstill, and buyers for materials such as copper and aluminum were few. Second, future prices—the prices at which traders were buying and selling the metal for delivery in three or fifteen or sixty-three months—were higher than the current price, a situation traders call "contango." And third: thanks to Uncle Ben Bernanke, interest rates were rock bottom.

Goldman Sachs traders could steer supplies of aluminum into Metro warehouses, my sources told me. Flush with metal, Metro could afford to offer incentives for metal owners to stockpile more and collect storage fees for all of it. When end users such as Budweiser or Ford tried to buy palettes of aluminum to provide the world with such useful items as Bud Ice Lite in cans or the newest model of the popular Ford Gigantor, they'd have to outbid others, who would steer the aluminum back into Metro warehouses, to pay more rent.

The traders were able to do this profitably because of low interest rates. They could sell the aluminum in the futures market. Because the price was higher down the road, they could book a profit right out of the chute. Then the metal owner could use the metal, which would sit idle, as collateral for inexpensive loans. The trade would be profitable as long as interest rates stayed low.

The London Metal Exchange, the world's biggest marketplace for the hard stuff, set a minimum for the amount of metal that warehouses had to ship out of their facilities every day, but it had no rules governing how much could go in. Can you say "logjam"? In June 2011, Coca-Cola complained that more than seven months elapsed between the time the company bought aluminum and the time it was delivered. Analysts at Barclays estimated in 2013 that the waiting period for aluminum to leave Detroit-area warehouses was more than four hundred days. All that time Metro was racking up storage fees.

Timothy Weiner, global risk manager for the brewer MillerCoors, had a great analogy for the predicament he and other aluminum consumers were in. Suppose you go to a liquor store for an icy-cold six-pack of MillerCoors. You find it in the refrigerator and take it up to the counter. The cashier takes your money, then takes away the six-pack and says you can pick it up around back—in four hundred days. And during that time you have to pay a storage fee.

The result was higher-priced aluminum for consumers without any added value. Premiums—the amount US aluminum buyers paid for Detroit-area metal over the benchmark London Metal Exchange price—doubled between June 2010 and June 2013. All this was especially galling because, by 2013, there had been a seven-year global glut of aluminum. The laws of supply and demand had been subverted. The Beer Institute, a Washington trade association, estimated that aluminum consumers paid an additional $3 billion annually from 2009 to 2013 because of the mischief. Goldman Sachs wasn't just smart; the firm was lucky too. The hipster chic of beer in cans was making aluminum more popular. Even craft brewers, who'd shunned aluminum for years because of its supposed metallic taste, were getting heavy into metal. The percentage of US beer sold in cans rose from 48 percent in 2004 to 53 percent in 2010 and stayed there through 2012.

Goldman Sachs denied manipulating the US aluminum market. Warehouse companies don't own the metal, the bank said in a statement on its website; they merely store it on behalf of owners. And Goldman Sachs metals traders are separated from the warehouses by "information barriers, the integrity of which is verified through regular independent audits."

Goldman Sachs wasn't the only firm expanding its warehouse system. Switzerland-based Glencore Xstrata, the biggest commodity trader in the world, owned a warehouse company called Pacorini, and Trafigura, a Dutch company, had a formidable network as well. If Goldman Sachs ever got out of the metal warehouse business, by choice or by regulator decree, these players would gain the most.

The good folks at the Federal Reserve, who approved exemption after exemption for the big banks, made Goldman Sachs's involvement possible. For more than fifty years, the Bank Holding Company Act prevented federally guaranteed banks, such as JPMorgan Chase, from direct participation in commodity markets. The prohibition didn't cover Goldman Sachs and Morgan Stanley, which were investment banks, until they became bank holding companies in an emergency shotgun wedding in the most frenzied days of the September 2008 financial meltdown. Some of their commodity activities were grandfathered in, meaning that they had permanent permission to continue doing what they did. The Fed gave the banks three years to sell the rest of their commodities businesses. In those three years, the firms didn't wind down their hands-on activities in commodities, they extended them. Goldman Sachs picked up Metro, of course, in addition to coal mines in Colombia, a stake in the railroad that transported the coal to port, and part of an oil field off the coast of Angola, among other investments. Morgan Stanley's involvement included TransMontaigne, a petroleum and chemical transportation and storage company, and Heidmar Inc., which managed more than one hundred oil tankers. When the three years of their initial exemption was up, Goldman Stanley (or Morgan Sachs, if you prefer) applied for a one-year extension of the exemptions, then one more. They were doing the exemption-extension shuffle. That meant that each of them had five years of profits stapled to their balance sheets at a time when commodity prices, thanks in large part to the largesse of Ben Bernanke, hit all-time highs. Did they even send a thank-you note? Someday I'll submit a Freedom of Information Act request to the Federal Reserve to find out.

The result of the exemptions and the grandfathering was a mess of rules no one I spoke to could untangle. Morgan Stanley went so far as to say in its filings with the Securities and Exchange Commission that even if the Fed forced it to relinquish its ungrandfathered activities—a hypothetical for sure—the subsequent sell-off would have no material impact on its finances. Nobody I talked to could or would tell me which commodity plays were grandfathered, which were exempt, and which the bank would most likely have to give up if the Fed told it to. In fact, in July 2013, when the *Financial Times* reported that Goldman Sachs and JPMorgan Chase were putting their metal warehouses up for sale, the newspaper's first interpretation was, Oh, gee, the Fed must finally be cracking down. But in truth, the London Metal Exchange was considering rule changes that would have made it more difficult to stockpile aluminum and copper. The trade would no longer be as profitable. The confusion over what was really happening was indicative. When smart people can't explain the distinctions in the regulatory regime, perhaps you've trotted off into the high weeds, never to return without an armada of attorneys to translate, interpret, argue, adjudicate, and bill.

This made the secrecy around JPMorgan Chase's acquisition of Henry Bath even more frustrating. I didn't really believe national security implications were at play; nor did I think the biggest bank in the United States would either try to sneak one past its main regulator or live like an outlaw in some Waylon Jennings demimonde. I'm not sure why I wanted to know so badly how the bank was permitted to buy a metal warehouse network, but I definitely wanted to find out before the bank sold it. I made more phone calls, asking people what they knew about this, and still nobody had any idea. So I asked if they knew anybody else who might know. One name, and only one, kept coming up. "You must talk to Professor Omarova! You must talk to Professor Omarova!" So guess what? I talked to Professor Omarova.

FULL DISCLOSURE: I WAS ALREADY ACQUAINTED WITH SAULE T. Omarova, a law professor at the University of North Carolina. Knowing her before most of my sources did made me feel as if I'd discovered the Grateful Dead before Ken Kesey's acid tests. A Washington-based colleague of mine, Phil Mattingly, had sent me her academic paper on the Fed's beat-down of Section 23A of the Federal Reserve Act—number one on the finance geek best-seller list—and in the fall of 2011, when I found myself in Chapel Hill, I invited her to dinner.

Sprite-like, articulate, and irreverent, with a Eurasian accent, she was funnier in conversation than you'd expect an expert on Section 23A of the Federal Reserve Act to be. She told me about her childhood in Uralsk, a provincial town in Kazakhstan, then part of the Soviet Union. Uralsk is on the border between Europe and Asia, she said. She grew up thinking of the United States as materialistic and belligerent—the enemy intent on harming her and her classmates. They practiced diving under their desks in the event of a missile attack, just as millions of American children had executed the "duck and cover" maneuver in the event Omarova's home country attacked them. Her maternal grandparents were the first generation of Soviet-trained native Kazakh medical doctors, a profession shared by both her mother and father, who had special expertise in the treatment of tuberculosis, a scourge in that part of the world. Omarova told me she had no meaningful exposure to politics in

Uralsk. That changed when she went to study philosophy at Moscow State University in 1989.

"Within the first year, my world changed," Omarova said. "I became disillusioned with official Soviet ideology because of Karl Marx." For a class, she was assigned Marx's early writings, which the Soviet regime condemned. She said she found them agreeably humanistic and, also agreeably, pointedly critical of totalitarianism.

While Omarova was on an exchange program at the University of Wisconsin, Madison, where she earned a PhD in political science, the Soviet Union collapsed. "Ronald Reagan had nothing to do with it," she told me. "There were no more true believers left in that country. Its legitimacy was eroded over time. When people share a sense of helplessness, that's a peril. The Soviet Union rotted from within."

I didn't need to prod her about my own alarm at similar problems I sensed developing in the United States. "We need to revive the practice of civic responsibility," she said of her adopted country. "If something does well and makes money, we think it's good for society. Not necessarily."

After getting her law degree at Northwestern, Omarova landed a job at Davis, Polk & Wardwell in New York. Her specialty was financial regulation. In 2006, Secretary John Snow's Treasury Department recruited her for a unique assignment. Because the financial industry had changed so much since most of the regulatory infrastructure had been created in the 1930s, the Treasury Department wanted to reevaluate the entire framework of oversight. Omarova's job was to provide the intellectual foundation for a new way of doing things. She was to start from scratch. She decided that her first step would be to identify all the different kinds of institutions in the market and analyze the risks they posed to the financial system; she would then design a new way to supervise them for the US government based on that.

She didn't get far. Henry Paulson, the raspy-voiced former college-football lineman and ex–Goldman Sachs chief executive officer, took over from Snow a few months into Omarova's exploration and brought a posse of his Goldman homeys with him to Treasury. "They couldn't have cared less about my project," Omarova told me.

Instead, in early 2007 she was asked to help organize a conference bringing together "thought leaders" of business and finance to discuss "global competitiveness"—a euphemism for what amounted to a festival of whining about perceived overregulation. Treasury officials wanted Wall Street chief executives to participate in a confidential roundtable but couldn't invite them all. The Treasury people went through the names. When they got to Richard Fuld, the head of Lehman Brothers, there was laughter.

"People just went, 'Dick Fuld? Pfft!'" Omarova told me. "It was clear he wasn't regarded highly by Paulson and the others. It was a scene that went through my mind when Lehman wasn't saved," resulting in the biggest bankruptcy in US history. It also confirmed for me that there was a personal element to Paulson's rejection of a lifeline for Lehman in September 2008, as if Fuld had stepped on Paulson's foot at a cocktail party in 1993 and not apologized, and Paulson had never forgotten.

Omarova left Treasury for the relative tranquility of the leafy Chapel Hill campus, but her Washington experience had left a deep impression on her thinking. While researching a 2009 paper on derivatives, she came across the Office of the Comptroller of the Currency's okay for banks to engage in derivatives trading and the Federal Reserve's permission for banks to get their hands dirty in the world of physical commodities. She realized that one was the legal rationale for the other. The Bank Holding Company Act mandated that any nonfinancial activity approved by regulators somehow be "closely related" to finance, and in the two approvals she detected a logic loop, a snake eating its tail. Once the banks got involved in derivatives trading, anything they wanted to do in commodities qualified as "closely related" to their financial business, she said. And because the Fed said it approved of the applications of Citigroup and JPMorgan Chase because dealing in physical commodities would improve the banks' understanding of the markets, the physical commodity side of the business was now informing the derivatives trades. But how could banks' physical commodity deals inform their derivatives trades with a wall supposedly placed between them? Wasn't this mishmashing of banking and commerce, this so-called improved understanding, the very thing that gave Wall Street an unfair advantage? The Fed's circular reasoning eviscerated the spirit of the Bank Holding Company Act. It may also have pushed beyond the letter of the law as well.

In early 2012, Omarova began writing a paper she would call "Merchants of Wall Street: Banking, Commerce and Commodities." It pulled together media reports of banks' transgressions in the commodities business, provided an exhaustive history of the expanding limits of the law, and asked the question she encapsulated for me in a later conversation: "How can one banking regulator develop the expertise to know what's going on?" She faulted the lack of transparency in Wall Street's commodity trading: "It is virtually impossible to glean even a broad overall picture of Goldman Sachs's, Morgan Stanley's, or JPMorgan's physical commodities and energy activities from their public filings with the Securities and Exchange Commission and federal bank regulators." She cited the neutering of the Bank Holding Company Act's "explicitly anti-monopoly policy focus" in the Fed exemptions. And she articulated my own concern over the future of American democracy: "When the same banking organizations that control access to money and credit also control access to such universal production inputs as raw materials and energy, they are in a position to exercise outsized control over the entire economic—and by extension, political—system. If there are good reasons to believe that extreme power breeds extreme abuses thereof, this expansion of large financial holding companies into physical commodities and energy business warrants serious concern."

"Merchants of Wall Street" was posted in late 2012. Buzz built slowly. In April 2013, Senators Sherrod Brown and David Vitter introduced their legislation to incentivize the six biggest banks to get smaller. The senators and their staff members had been reading Omarova. In June, four congressional Democrats wrote Federal Reserve Chairman Ben Bernanke with questions obviously generated by Omarova's paper, such as how regulators took into account a possible bank run should a bank-owned oil tanker pull an *Exxon Valdez*, and how the Fed planned to unwind a failing bank when it had to contend with, for example, the ownership stake in a railroad in South America.

In July 2013, Brown asked Omarova to Washington to testify before the Financial Institutions and Consumer Protection Subcommittee of the Senate Banking, Housing, and Urban Affairs Committee. Just a few days before the hearing, Randall Guynn, partner and head of the financial services group at the Davis, Polk law firm, was added to the witness list. In Guynn's view, enough safeguards were in place to ensure the banks didn't do anything bad with "raw materials" and crash the world. He just happened to be Omarova's former boss and mentor, and it unnerved her that he would be there. "It's playing with my head a little," Omarova told me when I called her a few days before the hearing.

Guynn scolded his former protégé in his testimony, telling the senators that, contrary to what Omarova said, history showed plenty of precedent for banks acting as merchants, going back to ancient Egypt. Omarova struck back. "History can prove too much and too little," she told the senators and her mentor. "Just because some banks somewhere in the past did something and it was okay, doesn't mean necessarily that it's okay today. I'm sure sometime some bank has financed slave trade. That doesn't mean JPMorgan should finance human trafficking based on some historical tradition."

For a Senate hearing, it was a rare moment of drama. But it wasn't a fair fight. Guynn was outgunned. Three of the four senators who posed questions to the panel, which also included bank analyst Joshua Rosner and Timothy Weiner of the MillerCoors beer company, were dubious about banks doubling as commodity dealers. Senator Brown seemed to sense this when he vowed to bring in representatives of the Federal Reserve and the biggest banks to offer testimony in a future hearing.

Brown, in his gravel voice, made me feel better about one thing. He told the witnesses that he and his staff had tried to get information about the exemptions from the Federal Reserve. He said the Fed wouldn't give it to him. I didn't feel so alone.

THE FEDERAL RESERVE DID ACKNOWLEDGE, WHEN IT ALLOWED banks to expand their operations, that "undue concentration of resources, decreased or unfair competition, conflicts of interests or unsound banking practices" might be consequences of Wall Street's involvement in physical commodities. The subtext of those disregarded warnings was that, with the banks' track records, scandal was inevitable.

"It isn't surprising given what we know about the character of these organizations. They exploit opportunities," said Frances Hudson, speaking about a couple of, shall we say, unpleasant things the banks had been accused of doing with their newfound clout. Hudson's job title—global thematic strategist at Standard Life Investments in Edinburgh, Scotland—suggested that she looked at the big picture.

Hudson's home city was also the domicile of Royal Bank of Scotland, which, following a government bailout, was asked to sell off its commodities business, RBS Sempra. JPMorgan Chase, which had gotten a jump start in commodities when it bought the rump investment bank Bear Stearns in a 2008 fire sale, exploited the opportunity to complement its US commodity holdings in 2010 by buying RBS Sempra's worldwide oil and metal investments and

European power and gas assets. Henry Bath and its warehouses, once owned by the infamous Enron (cue audience hiss), were part of that deal.

The Bank Holding Company Act drew a bold line on how many physical commodity assets the banks could hold at any one time: 5 percent of their consolidated tier 1 capital, which is finance jargon for "our accountants are better than the government's accountants." In order not to come anywhere near violating this 5 percent rule— an arbitrary-ish number, to be sure—banks created subsidiaries. JPMorgan Chase had one called J.P. Morgan Ventures Energy to continue the pioneering work of Bear Stearns in the California electricity market.

Employees of J.P. Morgan Ventures Energy, according to the federal regulator, were able to wring $125 million in improper payments from electricity regulators in the US Midwest and from California's Independent System Operator (ISO), one of the energy market gatekeepers in America's biggest state. Scarred by the manipulations of one Houston-based trading firm, the villain Enron (hisssss), California had made punishments for rigging the system tougher and the bureaucracy overseeing the industry denser. Enron was once the world's biggest power broker—in the sense of actual turbine-turning power—and after it was exposed as essentially a con, leading to the company's collapse in 2001, a bunch of its former managers either went to prison or, in the case of its founding chief executive, died. Its legacy endures as the apotheosis of a variety of corporate and societal ills: greed (the default transgression), complexity (all those Enron shell companies with names plucked from *Star Wars* that only traded with one another served as a model for Wall Street's crisis-producing mortgage-securitization madness), innocent people harmed (more than 100,000 employees jobless and an accounting firm vaporized), and the ability of an amoral company to boost energy prices and cause electricity shortages for its own fun and profit. In other words, it did everything that Wall Street's defenders said the big banks, in the same position, wouldn't do.

Why, then, did Robert McCullough, an Oregon-based energy-regulation consultant who'd been in the business for four decades, describe the scheme JPMorgan Chase's subsidiary devised in California as "just like Enron"?

Here's how it worked: California's Independent System Operator takes bids from electricity producers every day and chooses the least expensive to provide power to 38 million Californians and some of their neighbors. Actually, the ISO takes two bids—real-time and next-day bids. As Michael Hiltzik explained so well in the *Los Angeles Times*, the ISO gives plant owners incentive to participate by covering the costs of running their generators at a minimum level, even when their bids aren't accepted. That ensures that there will be enough electricity available at all times. "In simplest terms, JPMorgan submitted bids in the day-ahead market that were so low the firm was certain to be accepted onto ISO's roster of potential electricity suppliers," making it eligible for the running-cost guarantees, Hiltzik wrote. "The next step was for JPMorgan to make sure that ISO didn't actually buy its electricity." To do that, the bank's subsidiary priced its electricity so high that the ISO wouldn't touch it. Voila! The bank's subsidiary got the ISO's payments without actually having to provide anything in return.

JPMorgan Chase disagreed with that assessment, saying it always stood ready, able, and willing to fulfill the bids and noted that because the bids were secret, it was impossible for its traders to know whether theirs would be accepted or not. The secrecy also made it harder for the Federal Energy Regulatory Commission, or FERC, to figure out exactly how many times, and for how much money, the system had been gamed. FERC ultimately came up with a figure of $125 million. Tyson Slocum, who kept an eye on energy markets for Public Citizen, a Washington watchdog organization, told me that while $125 million might be nothing more substantial on Wall Street than budget dust, in the California energy market, it was enough to run a red flag up a high pole. Electricity users, after all, were paying every penny of it. JPMorgan Chase bidders could possibly have kept the strategy going indefinitely, Slocum said, if they'd just been less greedy about it.

Wrangling over wrongdoing with government supervisors after getting caught doing something naughty seemed to be the one thing Wall Street excelled at. There were few cases since the financial crisis in which they hadn't prevailed, or at least succeeded in getting punishment reduced to a slap on the wrist with no admission of culpability. But FERC hadn't gotten the memo. Perhaps the pencil pushers there hadn't yet been enchanted by big-bank charisma to the extent that financial-regulation pencil pushers had. In any event, FERC wasn't pleased with JPMorgan Chase's initial response to its inquiries. The *New York Times* got hold of a March 2013 internal FERC document prepared by investigators that accused JPMorgan Chase of "scores of false and misleading statements and material omissions." Investigators said the bank "planned and executed a systematic cover-up" of documents that exposed its strategy. Personally participating in the cover-up, the newspaper quoted the report as saying, was the head of JPMorgan Chase's global commodity division, Blythe Masters.

In the writing of nonfiction, few occasions offer the pleasure of a closed circle. The satisfaction of a well-executed upshot is usually confined to fiction, and in the best fiction, the karmic resolution is both surprising and inevitable. Real life seldom works out that way. The case of Blythe Masters is the exception.

In 1997, Masters, still in her twenties, and a team of JPMorgan Chase colleagues devised a way for investors to offset possible losses when they performed the risky task of lending money to companies. It was credit insurance, side betting that would pay off in the event the borrower was unable to repay the loan. If you guessed that Masters and her coworkers invented the credit default swap, you're right.

Masters rose steadily through the ranks at JPMorgan Chase, becoming the youngest female managing director in the bank's history. She landed the plum gig as head of global commodities in 2007, just as the world was about to blow up, in part due to those tricky weapons of financial mass destruction, as Warren Buffett had once called credit default swaps. Masters disagreed. Blaming the swaps for the crisis was rather like a poor workman blaming his tools, she told the *Guardian* newspaper in her native Britain.

So here was FERC, having nabbed JPMorgan Chase for allegedly manipulating electricity prices in a manner reminiscent of Enron, now getting pissed off at the country's biggest bank and its head of commodities for, as the regulator claimed, impeding its investigation. And the woman behind the scheme, according to FERC, was the same person who'd conjured a way for Wall Street to bet at the credit casino. In its defense, JPMorgan Chase said its electricity-bidding strategy was legal, transparent, and in full compliance with the applicable rules. Masters wasn't sanctioned, JPMorgan Chase kept her in charge, and she insisted to colleagues and to FERC that she'd done nothing wrong.

The JPMorgan Chase brouhaha wasn't typical comportment in the California energy market, Slocum told me. "It was a case of a New York bank coming in and making things more difficult," he said. "It's taken months of wrangling to unwind this when it should have been far more straightforward."

I don't want to leave readers with the impression that JPMorgan Chase and Goldman Sachs, with its alleged aluminum stratagem, are somehow shadier than other big banks, especially those with headquarters outside the land of the free and home of the brave. I've concentrated on American banks in these chapters because I know them best, they provide plenty of cause for concern and outrage, and they played every day with a few of my tax dollars and the money of my family, friends, and neighbors guaranteed by deposit insurance. And because they were the most coddled by their government and central bank. And because their behavior was egregious. And because they were essential cogs in the world's biggest economy. And—okay, I'll stop.

But banks outside the United States caused problems too. The California energy market and its maze of regulations may have proved too tempting for at least a couple of them, namely, London-based Barclays and Deutsche Bank, Germany's biggest bank. FERC ordered both to pay fines for allegedly manipulating prices. Deutsche Bank agreed in January 2013 to pay $1.6 million with no admission of wrongdoing. Barclays was flagged in July 2013 for $488 million in fines and penalties but said it would fight the charges.

Someone please ask Lawrence Summers, the former Treasury secretary who said small banks were a bigger danger to the financial system than large ones, why little Saigon National Bank in Westminster, California, hasn't yet been accused of rigging its home state's electricity prices to its benefit. Ask him if he thinks the financial system is the only pillar of our society vulnerable to too big to fail. Ask him where we ought to draw the line on the expansion of the biggest financial firms. Ask him who's minding this very, very big store. Ask him how long until he's had enough of these transgressions. I'll wait by the phone for the answers.

JPMORGAN CHASE PAID $410 MILLION IN PENALTIES WITHOUT admitting it broke the rules. FERC suspended J.P. Morgan Ventures Energy's right to make bids in US electricity markets for six months for what it called taking improper payments. The punishment began in April 2013. In May 2013, California's Independent System Operator said the bank's traders were evading the ban by entering into "swap contracts" with other energy-trading companies. "There is precedent for firms using swap contracts to secure a portion of the profit stream from a unit, while masking the identity of a party that has some level of control over the bidding," the ISO told FERC. A JPMorgan Chase spokeswoman declined to comment on the allegation, and little has been heard of it since.

If the swaps contracts were really happening, I wasn't surprised. When it came to the biggest banks, the Federal Reserve had spared the rod and spoiled them shamefully. So had the government. Bad behavior had been not only tolerated but rewarded. What did we expect? JPMorgan Chase denied wrongdoing. Of course, I couldn't tell if the banks' traders had really done anything wrong. Perhaps they hadn't transgressed at all; maybe FERC was simply still angry at them for allegedly blocking its earlier investigation. The traders' violation might have been activity permissible under the letter of tangled California regulation, though not its spirit. Or perhaps J.P. Morgan Ventures Energy was simply robbing the state's electricity consumers blind without guns. Maybe all of the above. But had the bank earned the benefit of our doubt?

Saule Omarova said the craziness was avoidable. Bank involvement in electricity trades didn't create any new jobs or generate any economic value, she said. She wasn't buying the argument that large financial institutions, which control so much of the movement of the world's money, must also be in the business of affecting the flow of electricity, coal, oil, and aluminum. "Why are banks in these markets?" she asked. "What roles do they serve? What positive value do they deliver to consumers?"

If you're a FERC investigator or a defense attorney for JPMorgan Chase, plenty.

SLOTH

Impunity: Walter Lacey, Marianne Miller-Lacey, and Slapstick Tragedy

I am concerned that the size of some of these institutions becomes so large that it does become difficult for us to prosecute them. When we are hit with indications that if you do prosecute, if you do bring a criminal charge, it will have a negative impact on the national economy—perhaps even the world economy—and I think that is a function of the fact that some of these institutions have become too large. It has an inhibiting impact on our ability to bring resolutions that I think would be more appropriate. That's something you all need to consider.

—US Attorney General Eric Holder to the
Senate Judiciary Committee, March 6, 2013

ZELMA LACEY, A WIDOW, MOVED INTO THE THREE-STORY brick home in the Charlestown section of Boston in 1963. Her son, Walter, was eleven. The boy could peer out a window and see the Bunker Hill monument, commemorating the Revolutionary War battle won by the British. Forty-seven years later, on September 3, 2010, Walter Lacey peered out the same window to see an auctioneer and twenty hopeful buyers on the sidewalk in front of his home.

Walter Lacey, who'd bought his boyhood home from his mother, had calculated that he was six months away from paying off his $113,000 mortgage. But Bank of America figured his debt differently. The lender had informed Lacey and his wife, Marianne Miller-Lacey, that it had bought the Laceys' loan from another mortgage company, and the Laceys owed $116,000. Their monthly payments were rising to $5,000 from $1,742.

The Laceys thought the error would be resolved quickly. But after dozens of phone calls and countless letters and e-mails, they said Bank of America employees wouldn't even address the discrepancy. The bank had foreclosed and was now selling the home where Walter had grown up and where he and his wife had raised four children.

It was all Walter and Marianne could do to keep Zelma, ninety-four years old and still living in the house, away from the commotion. They didn't want to have to explain. How could they? They didn't understand it themselves. Instead of telling the Laceys how Bank of America had assigned them a debt greater than the original mortgage they'd been paying down for almost fifteen years, the customer service people—different ones each time the Laceys called—kept trying to push them into the federal government's loan-modification program, using their inflated numbers. It was bizarre. The Laceys didn't understand why they needed to change the terms of the mortgage. They thought they only needed someone to fix the accounting mistake.

At the same time, Bank of America employees kept reassuring the Laceys that the bank wouldn't foreclose as long as they were trying to modify the loan. Then the gavel came down. The auctioneer sold their home—for $501,000.

The next day, Walter Lacey suffered what he thought was a heart attack. Marianne wept over him in his hospital bed, wondering if things could get any worse.

IMAGINE A TIMELINE ON A PAGE. IMAGINE FOLDING THE PAGE in half, with August 2007 in the middle. On both sides of the page you have home-loan trouble.

Before August 2007, you had the mortgage mills. You had predatory lending. You had liar loans. You had overzealous appraisals. You had borrowers taking on more than they could pay. You had loan standards so low that all borrowers had to do to qualify was provide evidence of breathing.

After August 2007, you had the foreclosure mills. You had mortgages being bought and sold without proper paperwork. You had bank and law firm employees "robo-signing" thousands of affidavits. You had borrowers who were making payments getting kicked out of their homes.

Morning, noon, and evening, good times and bad, high tide and low, blue skies or rain, Wall Street and Washington kept messing up mortgages. The simple, foundational transaction of lending people money to buy homes had become a way to swindle them coming and going. As suicidally as the mortgage industry and its regulatory overseers had acted before the 2008 crisis, an argument can be made that their behavior got worse afterward. Some of the 7 million home owners who suffered through foreclosure were treated fairly and with the compassion that comes from knowing that, in the time it takes for a truck to run a red and plow into your car or for cancer to loot your health, any of us could have fallen behind and lost our homes too. Any of us, that is, who didn't know the government would rescue us whenever we got into trouble. The endless bailouts that Deniz Anginer identified had created what economists call moral hazard—the idea, even if it's in the back of your head, that you can do anything, take any risk, because you know you'll never have to reap the consequences. In this atmosphere greed thrived like an opportunistic virus. In this environment financial firms could indulge their bottomless desire to exploit any loophole or shortcut. The movements of money—borrowing and lending, buying and selling—are such delicate operations that it takes little to tip the scales. Washington's interventions had been trillions big. We were now into *Lord of the Flies* territory, with lenders holding the conch shell and borrowers dashed on the seaside rocks. There were no longer any grown-ups minding the kids.

There was also ineptitude on an operatic scale. The response of the banks and the government to the waves of foreclosures would read like slapstick comedy—the Keystone Cops coming to the "rescue" of the Five Stooges—if so many lives hadn't been ruined in the process. If there were such a thing as slapstick tragedy, this would be it.

The Laceys, like Franz Kafka's Gregor Samsa, woke up one morning to discover they were bugs. They certainly weren't human anymore, not to Bank of America's customer service representatives. Thinking I'd be clever and identify the Laceys in this chapter by their referral number—the one assigned by the bank so that customers can give it to the customer service representative whenever they call, so the bank employee can access their file—I asked Marianne Miller-Lacey what theirs had been. She said she didn't have one. "They never let you talk to the same person twice, and the person you spoke to was never accountable to what the last person said," Miller-Lacey told me.

Imagine how frustrating, humiliating, infuriating that would be. To be identified by a single number would be dehumanizing, sure, but at least you wouldn't have to repeat your same sad story every time you called. The convenience would be yours as well as the bank's. Not having a number, or a single employee to handle your account, or at least employees with the knowledge of your past dealings with them at their fingertips is a form of erasure. It says, "Your call is not important to us. We're not listening to you. We don't care. You are nothing." This kind of treatment cannot be blamed on ineptitude. It's a symptom of something much worse.

MORTGAGE SERVICING BECAME A SEPARATE LINE OF BUSINESS with the growth of loan securitization. Securitization—the bundling of home loans into bonds for sale to investors—meant that someone had to collect borrowers' monthly payments and distribute them to the funds and individuals who'd bought the bonds. It was also the servicer's job to handle delinquencies, modify the terms of the loan when appropriate, and deal with foreclosures.

Securitization also meant that an increasing number of home loans would be bought and sold like any other asset. During the credit boom of the 2000s, banks always needed more mortgages to stick into their collections of bonds, and the wholesale trading of loans was commonplace. Independent mortgage companies proliferated during the first decade of the twenty-first century because Washington and Wall Street were buying loans from anyone willing to sell.

The big lenders really bungled it with those transactions. They started a company, Mortgage Electronic Registration Systems, that was supposed to track the changing ownership of home loans and create what amounted to a paper trail. As any schoolkid can tell you, private ownership is the foundation of American capitalism, and the system is all about establishing and maintaining the integrity of that ownership. Confusion over true ownership renders useless entire libraries of law books and makes a mockery of our moneymaking machines. But confusion is exactly what the lenders created. They couldn't keep track of who owned the mortgages.

Borrowers who'd taken loans for more than they could pay fell behind, and home prices started their inevitable decline, initiating a vicious cycle. The underwater borrowers couldn't refinance or sell.

If they stopped paying, the law said the mortgage companies could repossess their homes and sell them to pay off the loan—as long as the servicers followed particular legal procedures. Those procedures don't sound tough to follow, but they proved impossible. One involved proving that you owned the mortgage before you seized the property and sold it.

The biggest mortgage servicers, which were units of the biggest banks, were unprepared for the avalanche of foreclosures, and they resisted hiring enough workers to handle the onslaught properly. Heaven knows, plenty of folks with experience in the mortgage business were looking for work after 2008. About half the mortgage companies in the country had gone out of business in the bust. Most were on the origination side of things, but at least they were familiar with home loans.

Early in the debacle, the servicers might have been forgiven for not staffing up sufficiently, and as the foreclosure cases piled up, judges took mercy on overwhelmed servicing companies that claimed they couldn't find the paperwork proving they owned the loans. Instead of requiring them to produce the actual note before they took a home from the borrower, the courts allowed the mortgage companies to submit a lost-note affidavit—a legal document swearing that they owned the mortgages and just couldn't find the documentation. The judges' indulgence wore thin, however, when they discovered that law firms and mortgage servicers had employees sign stacks of these legal documents without even reading them.

Mortgage servicers had been breaking the law for years. A plaintiff's lawyer in Jacksonville, Florida, named Jim Kowalski may have been the first to unearth what came to be called "robo-signing" back in 2003. His client, who was facing foreclosure, claimed he'd paid off the balance of his mortgage with a cashier's check. The mortgage servicer disputed that version of events, saying the borrower had paid with a personal check that was returned for insufficient funds. Kowalski flew to the servicer's Pennsylvania office to depose an employee who'd signed a notarized affidavit saying that she'd seen the personal check that bounced. "What did you look at before you signed the affidavit?" Kowalski asked her early in the deposition. Her reply: *I read a computer screen. I don't know who created the numbers on the computer screen. If the affidavit had the same numbers as the ones I saw on the computer screen and my name was spelled correctly, I signed it. I put it in a pile, and at some later time it went across the office to be notarized.* "The deposition took a complete ninety-degree turn," Kowalski told me. "Every line of the affidavit except her name was false, including the notarization, which is a criminal offense."

Nobody went to jail in that case. And nearly a decade later, the large mortgage servicers were still committing what Kowalski called robo-perjury. "Take out all human elements, and they only have numbers driving the foreclosure, so it can be cost-effective," Kowalski said. "If you want the servicer to actually read the file so she's telling the truth to the judge, it's costly." This worked well when most home owners weren't contesting their foreclosures, he said.

The servicers defended themselves by saying that they were just taking paperwork shortcuts, that the borrowers wouldn't be in the foreclosure process if they hadn't failed to make payments. Kowalski said that in many cases he'd seen, that simply wasn't true. "When you have those types of paperwork problems, you have substantive problems, too," he told me. One of those substantive problems was proceeding with the foreclosure even when the borrowers were making their payments on time. In some instances servicers never bothered to foreclose because the house was more trouble than it was worth. In the Laceys' case, however, the lender was looking at a property worth four times the mortgage.

IT HAPPENED SO FAST.

The Laceys received the letter on February 1, 2010. It was from BAC Home Loans Servicing, a division of Bank of America, the biggest US bank at the time. The letter told them that Bank of America had succeeded Wilshire Credit as the servicer of their loan and announced the Laceys weren't paying enough.

"We wrote a letter to both banks, Bank of America and Wilshire," Marianne Miller-Lacey said. "We told them, we think your accounting is wrong, please review it and get back to us." At first, the Laceys heard nothing but a cool breeze. Then Bank of America started returning their mortgage payments. "They said we weren't making the required payments and they didn't take partial payments," Miller-Lacey said.

Instead of trying to resolve the accounting issue, Bank of America began peppering the Laceys with leaflets touting the federal Home Affordable Modification Program, or HAMP, a way for borrowers to reduce the amount they owed. "It was bizarre," Miller-Lacey said. In March—just five weeks after informing the Laceys that they'd taken over their mortgage—Bank of America sent them a notice saying it intended to foreclose, with the sale date for their home set for April 9, 2010.

The Laceys made a series of phone calls, but it was as if the customer service representatives were speaking a different language. The bank steered their calls to employees associated with HAMP. They never answered questions about the accounting discrepancy. "Everything was HAMP, HAMP, HAMP," Miller-Lacey said.

President Barack Obama launched HAMP to great fanfare in 2009. He vowed that as many as 4 million borrowers who'd gotten mortgages before January 1, 2009, would be able to reduce the amounts they were paying each month and stay in their homes despite their financial difficulties. By the end of March 2013, 1.1 million home owners had gotten permanent loan modifications through HAMP, and about $4.7 billion of the $29 billion allocated for the program had been spent. Even when borrowers got HAMP loan modifications, however, the program wasn't working. More than one-third of home owners had fallen behind again on the new, modified mortgages.

HAMP was snakebit from the start. As a real estate reporter in 2009, I remember being surprised by the attitudes of most people I talked to, both during the course of my reporting and at get-togethers in suburban New Jersey. The refrain went something like, "Those goddamn banks got bailouts; now look who's got their hands out—home owners." People hated the bank bailouts, but they saved their most venomous resentment for neighbors who'd fallen behind on their mortgages and wanted government help to avoid foreclosure. I found this self-defeating. A foreclosure down the street sucked the value out of every house in the neighborhood. When you went to refinance or sell, that deadbeat borrower in a comparable home would drag down your appraisal. Sometimes that was the difference between getting the refi or not or being able to sell. Then there was the empty house and the untended yard. Better to help the borrower than claim that moral hazard was perverting capitalism. It wasn't fair, of course, to people busting their butts to make their payments every month (I counted myself among the faithful payers), but if we wanted to get out from under the millstone of the real estate bust, we had to limit the damage. People buying crap they don't need is the bedrock of the American financial system, and only when home owners felt comfortable meeting their biggest financial obligation would the economy begin to grow again.

The anger about struggling mortgage payers reached a peak on February 19, 2009, when Rick Santelli, reporting from the Chicago Mercantile Exchange for the business news channel CNBC, went berserker over the hypothetical guy who couldn't make ends meet. "In terms of modifications, I tell you what," Santelli told viewers from the exchange's trading floor. "The new administration is big on computers and technology. How about this, Mr. President and new administration? Why don't you put up a website to have people vote on the Internet as a referendum to see if we really want to subsidize the losers' mortgages? Or would they like to at least buy cars, buy a house that is in foreclosure . . . give it to people who might have a chance to actually prosper down the road and reward people that can carry the water instead of drink the water?" At this point, the traders sitting at their terminals around Santelli cheered. Santelli turned to address them, raising both his arms. "This is America! How many people want to pay for your neighbor's mortgages that has an extra bathroom and can't pay their bills? Raise their hand!" Boos. "President Obama, are you listening? You know, Cuba used to have mansions and a relatively decent economy. They moved from the individual to the collective. Now they're driving '54 Chevys." Santelli continued, "It's time for another tea party. What we are doing in this country will make Thomas Jefferson and Benjamin Franklin roll over in their graves." Santelli, mad as hell and refusing to take it anymore, had given birth to a new political movement in the United States—the Tea Party.

A sizeable slice of the American population was simpatico with this viewpoint, so the servicers, with the wind of public sentiment at their backs, naturally ran away from the costly task of reducing the amount that borrowers owed. At Bank of America, HAMP was more like a SWAMP, according to depositions from former bank employees in a different Massachusetts foreclosure case unrelated to the Laceys' legal action.

Simone Gordon, a senior collector for Bank of America in New Jersey from July 2007 to February 2012, swore under oath that her supervisors told her to lie to borrowers who called the customer service line for help. Gordon said in a deposition that supervisors gave out prizes for foreclosures in what sounded like a half-baked sequel to David Mamet's workplace drama *Glengarry Glen Ross*: Get ten or more home owners into foreclosure and receive a $500 bonus and a gift card to Target or Bed Bath & Beyond. Fail to get ten home owners into foreclosure and receive a pink slip.

Erika Brown, a customer service representative for Bank of America in Texas from June 2009 to June 2010, said in sworn testimony that the bank's practice was "to string along borrowers with no apparent intention of providing the permanent loan modifications it promise[d]." That was because many of the applications were cancelled due to the borrowers' failure to make payments, even though the borrowers had indeed made payments, she said in a deposition. She said the bank put hundreds of borrowers into HAMP's trial payment plan but converted none of their loans into permanent modifications.

Theresa Terrelonge, a loan collector for Bank of America in Texas from June 2009 to June 2010, said under oath that she saw managers change or falsify information so borrowers became ineligible for HAMP. William E. Wilson Jr., who worked for Bank of America in its hometown of Charlotte, North Carolina, from June 2010 to August 2012, said under oath that the lender steered home owners to Bank of America refinances instead of government modifications—the bank made more money that way. Steven Cupples, who worked for Bank of America in Texas from 2009 to June 2012, said in a deposition that the bank ran what he called an ad hoc, parallel program that funneled delinquent borrowers to the foreclosure department. "The system Bank of America used either made no sense, or was nothing more than an effort to give a false appearance of complying with HAMP requirements when it was not," Cupples said under oath. "It was well known among Bank of America employees that the numbers Bank of America was reporting to the government and to the public were simply not true."

Bank of America responded to what it called the employees' "wild misrepresentations" by saying that the employees "could not have witnessed what they claim to have witnessed because they were not in a position to do so and would not have witnessed such things in any event because Bank of America's actual practices were diametrically opposite." Bank of America said some of the former workers had been fired for inappropriate behavior. Some were call center employees active in departments not directly related to HAMP, the bank said.

Bank of America's sale date for the Laceys' Charlestown home was extended to July 9, 2010, and on May 1 the Laceys finally gave in and applied for a HAMP loan modification. Guess what? On May 26, a representative told them they needed to send in documents missing from their application. The sale date was postponed again, to July 29, and again, to August 13.

On August 4, a Bank of America employee thanked them for applying for a HAMP modification and listed the possible outcomes from their application, none of which was foreclosure. That was the last they heard from the bank about HAMP, the Laceys said.

"They were telling us all along our house wouldn't be auctioned off," Walter Lacey told me. "They said, 'You're going through HAMP, your paperwork is going up and down the chain, we'll get back to you.'"

"Then we see it published in the newspaper that the foreclosure sale is scheduled for September 3," Marianne Miller-Lacey said. "We were on the phone what seemed like twenty-four hours a day, practically, trying to get to the bottom of it. They told us the auction won't happen, they're working on it."

Then they woke up one morning to see a guy with a gavel on their front steps.

"I threw up a couple of times," Miller-Lacey said.

"We had to keep my mother away from the window because there was commotion outside," Walter Lacey said.

"We're protecting this ninety-four-year-old woman who shouldn't have any of this going on around her—this should be her easy time," Miller-Lacey said. "So you try to behave as if there are no worries, with this over your head."

The stress got the better of Walter Lacey. His wife broke down when she told me that she'd rushed him to the hospital with chest pains. Quietly, Walter confided that he hadn't been the same since.

"I'm in therapy," he told me, "and I need pills to sleep."

From the hospital, the Laceys hired David Baker, a Boston fore-closure attorney, to kick some ass. His job wouldn't be easy. Bank of America had already sold their home.

THE LACEYS WERE FAR FROM ALONE IN THEIR MISERY. TYPE "foreclosure story" into any search engine, and dozens will pop up. They are chilling in their relentless drumbeat of defeat: The guy in California who shot and killed himself in his motor home after he lost his house. The family in Chicago left at the curb with all their possessions. The grandmother in Florida living in a tent with her grandchildren. If we assume four people in each foreclosed home, 28 million people—1 in 11 Americans—had suffered the humiliation of eviction. Each of the 7 million foreclosures was its own tragedy.

Bank of America was far from alone, too, in its behavior. The government signed two agreements with mortgage servicers, one in 2012 and one in 2013, outlining the damage the banks had caused and providing for borrowers' recompense. The first was called the National Mortgage Settlement. It involved the five biggest servicers—Bank of America, Citigroup, JPMorgan Chase, Wells Fargo, and Ally (which had changed its name from GMAC)—as well as the Department of Justice, the Housing and Urban Development Department, and forty-nine states' attorneys general. The other, the Independent Foreclosure Review, involved the Federal Reserve, the Office of the Comptroller of the Currency (OCC), and fourteen servicers, including the five big boys.

The $25 billion National Mortgage Settlement, signed March 12, 2012, was a landmark document. It laid out, in one place, all the monkeyshines the servicers had been up to since the 2008 crisis. In Bank of America's case, those deficiencies filled eleven pages (double-spaced, but still). And it specified, in excruciating legal detail, the remedies required. Plaintiff's attorneys told me it gave the servicers a framework for proper behavior. Just the mere fact that somebody had finally done something about the widespread abuses merited cheers. When I read the settlement, though, my applause died down to a slow clap. It struck me as trying to incentivize the servicers to do what they should have been doing all along: swearing affidavits only when they knew they were true, training and supervising their employees, keeping track of notarizations, communicating honestly with customers, refraining from foreclosing while at the same time pursuing mortgage modifications (a practice known as dual tracking), actually modifying mortgages instead of steering borrowers to foreclosure, and making sure the outside help they hired, such as law firms, weren't a bunch of raving lunatics with rubber stamps and slacker notaries. My favorite part of the settlement was the requirement that the servicers provide a SPOC—a single point of contact—for customers using the companies' call-in lines. It was too late to give the Laceys and millions of troubled borrowers one person to phone, but it was a potential remedy for the frustration and confusion in store for thousands of others.

As for the other agreement, the Independent Foreclosure Review, that turned into what one US senator called "one more farce."

By September 2010, borrowers and their attorneys had reported so many problems with foreclosures that several servicers called a stone-cold halt to them. Only then did the servicers' primary regulators wade into the craziness. In November 2010, the Federal Reserve and the Office of the Comptroller of the Currency faulted the servicers for what they called severe deficiencies in three areas: preparing foreclosure documents, staffing and supervision of the foreclosure process, and oversight of foreclosure attorneys, who committed a lot of the robo-perjury. In a nutshell: they found problems with just about everything having to do with foreclosures.

Five months later—because what's the hurry when thousands of families are facing eviction at any moment?—the Fed and the OCC issued consent orders against the fourteen servicers. These legal documents told the servicers what they were doing wrong and what to do to make things right. Apparently the banks' two main regulators figured that a systematic breaking of the law by lying on sworn affidavits so that credulous judges would order people thrown out of their homes didn't merit referral for criminal prosecution. The orders included a requirement that the servicers go through their foreclosures case by case to see just how badly they'd messed up. If foreclosed home owners had suffered financial injury due to servicer error, the servicer had to identify and compensate those people.

Neither the servicers, already short on staff because they hadn't done enough hiring, nor the regulators, with their smaller-government straitjackets, had the resources to sift through the 4.3 million cases identified as possibly screwed up to root out wrongdoing. So the banks, with the approval of the Fed and the OCC, hired outside contractors to contact borrowers, assess their foreclosures, and determine where any checks ought to be sent. The fourteen servicers hired seven different contractors, including auditing firms Deloitte and PricewaterhouseCoopers, and a bank advisory company, headed by a former head of the OCC, called Promontory Financial Group. The regulators, finally showing a sense of urgency, gave them four months to do the job. In June 2011, the contractors got to work. They decided to send the 4.3 million former home owners postcards urging them to apply for a review on the Internet.

The mailings got a disappointing response. Later, the Government Accountability Office (GAO) ran the texts of the mailings through something called the Gunning Frequency of Gobbledygook Readability Test, or FOG, and something else called the McLaughlin Simplified Measure of Gobbledygook Formula, or SMOG. (I didn't know those things existed either.) The tests showed that while most Americans read at an eighth-grade level, the outreach literature was written at an eleventh-grade level. The elevated language wasn't exactly Shakespeare, however. The GAO faulted the mailings for using too much financial industry jargon.

The GAO also noted that the mailings did a lot of boasting about the wide scope of the foreclosure review but provided no specific information for borrowers about the potential payoffs for filling out the forms and sending them in—essential if they aimed to persuade people to actually do it. Housing activists complained that not enough of the mailings were in languages other than English and that the Spanish version was incomprehensible. This all assumed that borrowers took the time to read the material. My Bloomberg News colleague Hugh Son reported later that many borrowers simply tossed solicitations into the trash. They'd gotten so many communications from mortgage companies over the years, leading to heartbreak and ruin, that they wouldn't waste even three more minutes digesting more bank baloney. Without looking at the material, borrowers couldn't know that they stood to benefit from the review.

The servicers, in their own defense, said they didn't have a lot of time to put together the outreach and that convening focus groups, whose opinions they could have used to fine-tune the mailings, would have taken six to eight weeks. The government had only given them sixteen weeks to complete the entire review.

It seemed to me that the servicers' attempts at outreach had all the characteristics of narcissism. If they'd been able to put themselves in the borrowers' shoes without the benefit of focus groups, they might have communicated better with people who weren't like them.

The mailings were so bad they had to be redone, and the deadline for borrowers to respond was extended twice, ultimately to September 30, 2012. Even then, out of 4.3 million, only 800,000 borrowers responded. To get this less-than-20-percent response, the contractors had already spent an estimated $2 billion, ten times the money expected. Later, PricewaterhouseCoopers itemized the expenses for its three clients: for the US Bank review, $190 million; for Citigroup, $175 million; for SunTrust Bank, $60 million. That was $425 million for just three of the fourteen lenders. Deloitte said it was paid $465 million for JPMorgan Chase. Grand prize went to Promontory, which said it received a total of $927.5 million for reviewing 250,000 loan files, or $3,700 per file, for Bank of America, Wells Fargo, and PNC.

Alarmed at the escalating cost—despite the fact that the banks would be footing the bill—the Fed and the OCC decided to shut down the foreclosure review. They calculated, somehow, that about 6.5 percent of the foreclosed home owners had been victims of wrongdoing. The regulators settled with the fourteen servicers in January 2013 for $8.5 billion, $3.3 billion of it to be paid out in cash compensation to home owners and the rest in "soft dollars," or credits the servicers could earn when they completed loan modifications with borrowers still in their homes.

At an April 11, 2013, Senate hearing, Democratic Senator Elizabeth Warren of Massachusetts, the home state of Walter Lacey and Marianne Miller-Lacey, questioned three contractors on how the Fed and the OCC had arrived at the 6.5 percent figure. None of them could tell her how the regulators had come up with it. It was an important number because the regulators had based the settlement figure on the so-called error rate of the servicers. But the contractors hadn't been thinking of gathering a statistically significant sampling in order to draw any useful conclusions from the foreclosure data they'd collected, and of course they'd quit well before they'd done the impossible and reviewed all the foreclosures.

"Any information based on the Independent Foreclosure Review should be deemed incomplete," Lawrence Evans of the nonpartisan Government Accountability Office told the senators. "The data does not allow us to render any conclusions about error rates at a particular servicer or make comparisons across servicers."

So the 6.5 percent error rate that the Fed and the OCC had calculated was "just a made-up number," Warren said. The $8.5 billion settlement was Seinfeldian—it was based on nothing. None of the three contractors at the hearing disputed Warren on that point.

"It appears that the people who broke the law are the same people now who have determined who will be compensated from that lawbreaking," Warren said at the Senate hearing. "I find this one amazing."

Promontory's review of Bank of America foreclosures drew the attention of Yves Smith, who covered the foreclosure review on her Naked Capitalism blog. Smith wrote that "the dysfunction of the reviews was inevitable given the state of the bank's records. The only course of action possible was a cover-up; the only open question was how much effort would be expended to create the appearance that a thorough investigation was made. Ironically, we've been told by high level insiders that Bank of America made a more serious attempt at performing these reviews than other major servicers did." Smith came to the conclusion that "anyone who buys a house with a mortgage in America is taking a gamble that his servicer will abuse him."

Smith estimated that Bank of America paid Promontory $500 million for the botched review and calculated that it cost $130 million. That left $370 million of what she called "dark matter" in the billing.

Debra Cope, a Promontory spokeswoman, disputed that accounting. "Promontory performed its work carefully and objectively, adhering to the highest professional standards," she wrote in an e-mailed response to my questions. Promontory wouldn't disclose what each bank had paid the company for the foreclosure review, she told me, though PricewaterhouseCoopers had, and Smith's calculation "does not correspond with our own numbers," Cope wrote.

The $5.2 billion part of the $8.5 billion Independent Foreclosure Review settlement—the "soft dollars"—once again rewarded the servicers for doing things they should've been doing all along. And, as Deborah Goldberg of the National Fair Housing Alliance told another Senate hearing on April 17, 2013, the way those credits were set up favored wealthier mortgage borrowers. The servicers got dollar-for-dollar credit for reducing the amount owed on first mortgages, second mortgages, short sales (borrowers selling their homes for less than they owed on the mortgages), and deeds in lieu of foreclosure (handing over the keys and calling it even). But servicers got credit for the full amount of the mortgages rather than for the amounts they forgave. So if they forgave $1 of a $200,000 mortgage, they got credit for $200,000, not $1. That encouraged servicers to work on reducing the biggest loans first to reach their goals faster, Goldberg said. "The communities that experienced the most harm have smaller loans and it will take more of those loans to get to the soft-dollar goal," she said. It also meant that the credits didn't necessarily lead to the objective of keeping borrowers in their homes, Goldberg noted. "It would be possible for a servicer to meet its goal simply from deeds in lieu of foreclosure and short sales," she said.

About two-thirds of the foreclosed home owners received checks for $300, the smallest payout. That accomplished little more than hitting the refresh button on their anger. Fewer than 1,200 got $125,000, the maximum. Most of the rest got between $400 and $7,500.

To recap: Contractors hired and paid by banks accused of widespread wrongdoing sent an incoherent invitation to home owners and former home owners, who were already battling allergies to lender baloney, asking them to take part in a statistically worthless foreclosure-review process that was 20 percent completed, cost ten times more than expected, and yielded a number that was supposed to represent just how widespread the wrongdoing was, but instead was revealed to have been manufactured out of thin air, yet was nevertheless used by government regulators as the basis for a monetary settlement that favored the wealthiest and did little to keep struggling borrowers in their homes.

Oregon Democratic Senator Jeff Merkley put it succinctly: "It seems like one more farce."

As for the National Mortgage Settlement—the 2012 agreement between prosecutors and the five biggest servicing companies—David Baker, the Laceys' lawyer, saw no cure in it for home owners such as his clients. "No teeth to it," was how David Baker put it.

As if to underscore Baker's unhappiness, the National Housing Resource Center, a Washington nonprofit group, surveyed housing counselors across the country in June 2013 to see how distressed borrowers had fared a little over a year after the settlement. The results were stunning in their awfulness: 68 percent of counselors reported problems with servicers "frequently" or "sometimes" losing borrowers' documents, and even though 83 percent of respondents reported having non-English-speaking or limited-English-proficient clients, 76 percent said their clients were "never" or only "sometimes" able to speak with servicers in their native language or through a translator provided by a servicer. Both the settlement and the independent review were supposed to outlaw dual tracking, where homes owned by borrowers such as the Laceys went to foreclosure at the same time the servicer was discussing a modification with the borrowers. Yet 62 percent of housing counselors said servicers persisted in the practice.

Bank of America had already sold the Laceys' Boston home. It seemed the family would have to leave the house they'd lived in for nearly fifty years. "It's a little embarrassing how emotional I get over this," Marianne Miller-Lacey told me. "If we weren't emotionally attached, if my mother-in-law hadn't raised her children under this roof and if I hadn't raised my four children under this roof, maybe we could sell. But this is not what this is about. It's home. Emotion doesn't stand for anything, but you live and breathe it every day. We don't ask for anything we don't deserve."

Baker was able to get the Laceys into Chapter 13 bankruptcy immediately. And two years after the auction on the front steps of the house, Baker convinced the court to disallow the foreclosure sale. The Laceys had been living in the home during those two years at the recommendation of the bankruptcy judge. But they had skipped home repairs and maintenance because they thought they might be dispossessed at any time.

"We never thought that banks and big companies could act like this—illegally," Walter Lacey told me. "I feel bad for all the people they did this to who didn't go to court, didn't get an accounting and lost their houses."

Baker took Bank of America to court over the foreclosure, and a judge refused the bank's request to dismiss the charges. She faulted the servicer for dual tracking, for foreclosing on the Laceys when they weren't in default, and for failing to account for the difference between what the Laceys said they owed and what the lender said they owed.

Punchline: A forensic accountant determined that Bank of America didn't own the Laceys' mortgage.

"We raised four children under this roof," Marianne Miller-Lacey said. "We still live here, and we want to live here forever."

I WOULD BE REMISS IF I DIDN'T ADDRESS THE THORNY ISSUE of Promontory Financial Group, the contractor that Bank of America and two other mortgage servicers hired to conduct their portions of the Independent Foreclosure Review. Promontory was the object of so much innuendo in the yellow press surrounding its dizzying payday from the failed review that I wanted to jump to the firm's defense. Malcontents with whom I've had occasion to speak simply objected to the firm's very existence. They smeared Promontory as the quintessence of the so-called revolving door through which a parade of distinguished government regulators had cycled and, the malcontents claimed, landed cushy jobs in the private sector after years of overseeing the financial industry in what looked, to these critics, like payback for services rendered.

How cynical. Expertise has never been abundant, especially in the banking industry. Where else would Promontory find people better capable of advising banks on confusing regulations than the folks at the federal agencies who made the regulations so confusing in the first place? As Promontory's Debra Cope wrote me, the firm is "proud that many distinguished former government officials see in our practice a way to continue their commitment to keeping the financial system safe and sound, and ensuring that consumers are protected." And what a terrific job they've done! Seven million foreclosures, bank regulatory fines accumulating toward the same magic $1.2 trillion that the banks accepted as emergency loans from the Federal Reserve on a single day in 2008—the numbers are indeed impressive.

Promontory doesn't lobby regulators on what the banking industry wants; it defines for banks what regulators want. Promontory is wise enough to know that regulators usually want the same things as bankers. This might sound hopelessly circular, like a kind of revolving door of rule enforcement, but that's where its brilliance lies. If financial regulators can be compared with parents, Promontory—along with most of the civilized world—takes the very modern view that discipline can erode a child's self-esteem, and there's nothing more important than a bank's self-esteem.

Critics had also assigned Promontory part of the blame for what they characterized as the permissive attitude of the Federal Reserve and the OCC, as well as what they called the leniency with which the Securities and Exchange Commission appeared to have treated alleged Wall Street malefactors under its purview. I say, if true, that's a small price to pay. If on one side of the revolving door, regulators acted with restraint in the hopes of one day landing a job at Promontory, and the folks on the other side of the revolving door, working for Promontory, functioned as living proof that such rewards were graspable, well, wasn't that the kind of incentive-driven striving we want to encourage among our citizens? It's a great country where even a lowly chief counsel for an obscure bank examiner can someday trade the drudgery of punching the government clock for entertaining clients on an expense account at the toniest restaurant on Manhattan's Park Avenue. Forget home ownership. This is the American dream, my friends.

The mischief-makers pointed, too, to Promontory's founder and chief executive officer, the capable and not-bad-looking Eugene Ludwig. They sniffed that he was a kind of hub from which emanated the spokes of what they pejoratively labeled "the old boy network." They have cited, without nuance, Ludwig's connection to law school friend Bill Clinton, who as president of the United States appointed Ludwig to head the OCC in 1993, and Ludwig's partnership at the totally respectable and hugely influential Washington law firm of Covington & Burling. By all accounts the OCC ran like a top under Ludwig's leadership—only later, when it mattered most, did it become a doormat—and Covington & Burling has recently distinguished itself as the wellspring of two prominent servants of the Obama administration: Attorney General Eric Holder Jr. and Lanny Breuer, head of the Justice Department's criminal division from 2009 to 2013. Holder is as candid a top cop as we're ever likely to see, at least judging from his March 2013 assertion that some banks might be, in the unfortunate buzz phrase, "too big to jail." Breuer's own testimony has verified his altruism. He told the New York City Bar Association that he lay awake at night fretting over whether prosecuting allegedly criminal megabanks would cause unwarranted hardship to innocent employees and stakeholders. Such compassion won him few supporters among the dwindling segment of hotheaded Americans clamoring for post–financial-crisis blood (as if that would bring back their trillions!), but it was the sensible thing for Breuer if he wanted to return, after his stint in public service, to doing even greater good at Covington & Burling. (He rejoined the firm in 2013.)

One might think Ludwig could bask in the reflected glow of such prestigious associations, but the *New York Times*, in an April 2013 unskeining of drivel, aimed to tar and feather him with his own achievement: "Mr. Ludwig has occasionally invited Fed governors and other top officials to parties at his 13,000-square-foot Washington home, an $11.5 million estate replete with a tennis court and a modern art collection," the article read. Mr. Ludwig "is also a regular at the Four Seasons restaurant in New York, where he is known by name and salad order." Dinged for healthy eating! Thankfully, the firm quashed any implications of possible conflicts of interest at such social gatherings: "Promontory said that Mr. Ludwig entertains regulators on occasion but that 'there is no discussion of current matters,'" according to the article. Let that put the matter to rest, *New York Times*! Hit pieces such as this one and an *American Banker* article on Promontory that appeared, suspiciously, only three weeks before the *Times*'s story and quoted some of the same sources convinced me that members of the maladjusted commentariat were protesting too much. What would they tell us next? That Gene Ludwig had shot Tupac Shakur, or that Promontory had hidden Saddam Hussein's weapons of mass destruction in the basement at Fort Knox?

When Promontory hired Mary Schapiro in 2013, just weeks after she'd stepped down as chairwoman of Barack Obama's Securities and Exchange Commission, I knew it had to be because of her expertise in whatever it was Promontory determined her to have expertise in. It couldn't have been a reward for services rendered, because Schapiro had already been paid. She'd received a $9 million bonus after leaving her post atop the Financial Industry Regulatory

Authority, Wall Street's watchdog of itself, to go to the SEC in 2009. To pay her like that twice would be an intolerable inefficiency. A more compelling reason for Schapiro to seek employment at Promontory might have been the camaraderie that the firm offered. At her new workplace she joined a roster of former thises and former thats longer than one can fit into a mere book. Among them were another former head of the SEC (perhaps Ludwig collects them), the guy who ran the NASDAQ stock exchange during the dot-com boom and bust (no stock tips, sir, please!), the onetime chief of staff for President Ronald Reagan (the Old Major of deregulation), a former National Football League commissioner (fifty-yard-line tickets, know'm sayin'?), and a former vice chairman of the Federal Reserve named Alan Blinder. Blinder made the unforced error of pitching one of Promontory's businesses to author Nassim Nicholas Taleb, a notorious scold. In his book *Antifragile*, Taleb described what that business does: takes a wealthy person's $1 million, splits it into four chunks of $250,000, and deposits the chunks into different bank accounts. That way, the high-net-worth individual can enjoy deposit insurance from the American taxpayer through the Federal Deposit Insurance Corporation, essentially insuring $1 million while the government guarantee is designed to top out at $250,000. "It would allow the super-rich to scam taxpayers by getting free government-sponsored insurance," Taleb wrote. "With the help of former civil servants who have an insider edge."

Such bitter carping must end. I have a modest proposal. Since Promontory's savvy is beyond challenge—few firms could be paid so well for a foreclosure review done so poorly—and its employees are compensated so much better than government regulators (a lunch salad at the Four Seasons runs $34), why not outsource all US financial regulation, the whole money burrito, to Promontory? This would cause the small-government Santellis to shudder with erotic delight as their eyes alit upon a budget line of zero where megamillions used to be and render speechless the wealth-hating outrage addicts who bleat ceaselessly about capture. It would be impossible for the regulatory community to be captured because it would no longer exist. Just as they did in the Independent Foreclosure Review, banks could grossly overpay, only this time for regulatory oversight. Taxpayers would be off the hook, nothing too drastic in the rules would change, and Promontory's experts would continue providing an excellent service for their fellow Americans, one for which, until now, they have received scant credit—gouging the banks as thoroughly as the banks have gouged their customers.

SEVEN

GREED

Class War: Rebecca Black and the Pneumatic Tube

There's class warfare, all right, but it's my class, the rich class,
that's making war, and we're winning.
—Warren Buffett, quoted in the *New York Times*,
November 26, 2006

R EBECCA BLACK SEARCHED THE FRONT YARD FOR HER
beloved angel's trumpets. It was a muggy, overcast summer day
in 2012, and she was back at 698 Hazelwood Road for the first time
since 2010, when she left the house she lived in with her teenage
sons, Major and Chris. She'd never had a green thumb, she said, not
really, but she'd loved the droopy yellow flowers she inherited from
Willie Mae Young, the woman who sold her the three-bedroom house
in 2005, and she got them to bloom. But Memphis city workers had
run their lawn mowers over the flowers, along with the grass, and
only the stalks were left, slashed two inches from the ground and
mostly hidden by weeds.

The house had been empty since she left. Black pointed to a
dark dent in the wood beneath an eave where water was getting

in. The hedges were overgrown, and thieves had ripped out the air conditioner. The window Major once climbed through because he didn't have his key and the door Chris used to bang shut—plywood was nailed over them now. The workers had spray-painted "698" in black on the board that covered the front entrance.

"I was crazy about this house, so proud," Black said, placing her palm on the number. "I just didn't have enough money."

Black, a sixty-four-year-old Army veteran who worked feeding, bathing, and dressing a man crippled by Lou Gehrig's disease, made $24,000 in 2012, the same amount listed on her 2005 mortgage application.

To those who say that Black never should have gotten a mortgage, that single moms who bamboozled Wall Street into lending them money they would never pay back had brought the financial system to its knees in 2008, consider this: Rebecca Black paid her mortgage for two years. She had a 12.5 annual percentage rate, more than twice what borrowers with better credit histories paid, and she made twenty-four on-time payments of $502. Only when the bill ratcheted up to $637 and, six months after that, to $649 did she struggle. She didn't buy the boys new clothes or take them to the movies, and she served them chicken necks for dinner instead of pork chops. But you know what? She always paid the bank on time. It was the futility she saw stretching out in front of her as far as she could see, the daily sacrifices that would claim more and more of her and her boys as time went on, that finally broke her spirit and became too much for her to bear.

Rebecca Black could afford the house. She couldn't afford the mortgage.

HAZELWOOD ROAD WAS NEVER EDEN, BUT BLACK CHERISHED it when she first moved there in 2005. The neighbors kept the front yards neat and pretty, and they relaxed and barbecued in back. Their children played on the sidewalks and in the street. Black said the residents weren't chummy, but they were friendly enough to greet each other whenever they crossed paths.

When I told Black that in March 2012, a twenty-eight-year-old man was shot and killed while driving a pickup truck on Hazelwood Road, just steps from her old front yard, she blurted, "I didn't know that!" She shielded her eyes from the hazy smudge of sun and looked toward the house, three doors down, marred by gang graffiti. "I can't say I'm surprised," she said softly.

Between 2005 and 2012, Hazelwood Road, never high on the economic totem pole, took a boot to the head. In 2011, the house two doors down from Black's old place sold for $3,000. I wouldn't have paid a nickel for it. It was surrounded by weeds, and as with Black's old house, there was plywood where the windows and doors should have been. The high price of copper had made it attractive for vandals to rip the pipes out of abandoned houses. A neighbor's dog snarled at me when I got out of my car, and the house across the street had a tax-sale notice stapled to a front post. The neighbor's fence was still flattened where, months before, the murder victim's pickup truck, continuing to roll after the driver died from the gunshot wound, ran it over.

As the community's caretakers, Black and her neighbors deserve blame for the decline, but not all of it. Hazelwood Road was plundered. Just about everything of monetary value had been stripped away, and only a husk remained. There wasn't much money there to start with; now there was just about none. How did it happen? Picture a pneumatic tube sucking money out of Hazelwood Road, out of Memphis, out of cities and towns across the country—Durham and Victorville, Kalamazoo and Cape Coral, Oklahoma City and Baltimore, Las Vegas and Cleveland—and sending it to New York, where it showed up in the paychecks of people such as Tom Marano.

Tom Marano was head of mortgages at Bear Stearns, the New York investment bank that was the parent company of EMC Mortgage, where Black got her home loan.

Let's get something straight before we dive too deeply into this: to suggest that Marano was a villain who caused the financial crisis of 2008 would be absurd. On the other hand, to argue that he didn't play a role, as many others did, would be just as outrageous. I've heard it argued that bankers do only what they're incentivized to do, as if they're slack-jawed beasts with no considerations wider than their next kill; that the decisions that created and enabled bankers to profit from the housing boom, then allowed them to turn around and profit again from the wreckage of the bust, simply reflected the path of self-interest anyone would have followed given the same circumstances.

But not everyone did follow that path.

Since the 2008 crisis—since the biggest banks solidified their presence as unmanageable, unprosecutable, and largely unaccountable—the widening of the divide between the rich and the not-so-rich has accelerated. In 2011, the earnings gap between the wealthiest Americans and the rest of the country grew to its broadest point in more than four decades. The 1.2 million households whose incomes ranked them in the top 1 percent saw their pay rise 5.5 percent that year, while incomes fell 1.7 percent for the 96 million households in the bottom 80 percent—those that made less than about $100,000 a year. Corporate profits reached a record at the same time as wages as a percentage of the US economy dipped to their lowest since the statistic was first kept in the 1940s. The schism caused by the housing bust and Washington's response to it created an economic apartheid, with the upper crust enjoying a level of wealth almost unimaginable in places like Hazelwood Road. In Memphis, one in four residents lived below the poverty line.

Predatory lending—the practice of steering racial minorities to loans with higher interest rates and harsher terms, even when they might have qualified for better mortgages—was the means by which the rich picked the pockets of the working class.

Everyone involved in Rebecca Black's mortgage has denied it was a predatory loan, and that may be the case. Maybe she couldn't have qualified for a better loan. Yet they all got a piece of what little the $11-an-hour home health aide possessed. Her mortgage broker, Marcus Lenier Gibbs of Global Finance Services in Memphis, took his cut, and the man who funded the loan, William M. Medley Jr. of BayRock Mortgage Corporation in Alpharetta, Georgia, made out as well. So did HSH Nordbank, based in Hamburg, Germany, which ended up owning Black's mortgage through the magic of securitization. No one broke the law. No one did anything that hadn't been done a million times. They all profited. Until they didn't anymore.

This is how it worked. Willie Mae Young, who sold 698 Hazelwood Road to Black, recommended she get a mortgage from Gibbs, whose company occupied space in a steel-and-glass office building in East Memphis, just off a highway exit ramp. Because Black made so little money, Gibbs says he worked hard to find her a loan. And he succeeded. "I remember how happy she was," Gibbs told me.

Gibbs was rewarded with an origination fee of $3,088 and what was called a yield-spread premium of $1,235. Yield-spread premiums were common in the mid-2000s. Lenders paid them to mortgage brokers who managed to get borrowers to pay higher interest rates.

Black told me in 2012 that she thought her mortgage had a fixed interest rate and that she insisted she wouldn't sign it unless it did. But when I read the paperwork she showed me, it clearly said, "Variable Rate Mortgage Program Disclosure."

"I thought it was a fair loan," Gibbs told me. He advised Black to take what was called a 2–28—a loan that had a fixed rate for two years and then adjusted periodically for the next twenty-eight years—and if she paid her bills on time, she could refinance into a cheaper mortgage. The loan stipulated that Black would have to pay a prohibitive penalty if she refinanced before the first two years were up. "I didn't trick her or anything," Gibbs said. "I didn't say she was getting a fixed loan and she wasn't. I wouldn't do that."

Evidently, he didn't. But Black believed what she wanted to believe. And she believed she'd signed on for a fixed rate.

BayRock, which at its peak had four hundred employees who processed as much as $100 million in mortgages a month, charged a $70 tax service fee, a $725 administration fee, and $95 for something called a "desk review fee." Black's closing costs added up to $6,445, which seems brutal for a $57,483 mortgage. Medley's company typically would fund the loan and after a month or two sell it to a Wall Street bank, which would bundle the mortgage with hundreds of others and sell the resulting securities to investors, such as the Hamburg-based bank, looking for something that paid a bit more than boring US Treasury debt.

The whole world was dancing to the beautiful music of the US housing boom. To Medley, there was little doubt who was calling the tune. "We weren't setting our own market," Medley told me. "We were doing what the big guys wanted." That would be Wall Street.

It was all good. Black got her house, Gibbs made a decent living, Medley had his own company, Marano and his crew socked away millions, and the German bank got higher returns for a supposedly safe investment. When the music stopped, the Germans deployed their lawyers, Medley had to close his doors and let four hundred people go, Gibbs had to find another way to make a living, and Black was demoralized and ruined. In hindsight, the fact that they all profited on the way up became a way to distribute blame for the downturn, just as bundling the mortgages and selling them to investors was supposed to diffuse the risk of making home loans.

"I never made a loan Wall Street wouldn't buy," a mortgage broker named Daniel Sadek once told me. Sadek ran an outfit in Orange County, California, called Quick Loan Funding, which one hedge fund manager claimed may have been the worst subprime lender in the country. Bill Medley of BayRock said he didn't play the same game. "There were a lot of loans I wouldn't do that Wall Street would buy," Medley told me. "I felt they were too risky."

BayRock's number one customer: Bear Stearns.

IN THE 2000S, BEAR STEARNS WAS THE FIFTH-LARGEST US investment bank behind Goldman Sachs, Morgan Stanley, Merrill Lynch, and Lehman Brothers. My Bloomberg colleague Jonathan Weil called them the five families of Wall Street. Each possessed a different personality and was known for particular quirks: Goldman was calculating and ruthless; Morgan Stanley catered to the country club crowd, while Merrill focused on the middle class; Lehman was more freewheeling and improvisational. Bear's blunt, cigar-smoking chief executive, Jimmy Cayne, personified its reputation as pugnacious. Cayne didn't care where his employees had gone to school or who their fathers were. He cared that they'd work ridiculously hard to satisfy a drive to get rich. And one of the surest ways to get rich in the 2000s was the mortgage business.

From 2005 to 2007, Tom Marano's team at Bear Stearns underwrote almost $300 billion of mortgage bonds created without US government backing, making it the second-biggest underwriter of such securities. (Lehman Brothers, rest in peace, was numero uno.) A half dozen legal complaints, filed as the dust settled after the 2008 crisis, claimed that Bear Stearns cut corners to push its totals that high.

Rebecca Black's mortgage wound up with a lot of other home loans in a security called BSABS 2005-HE8. Bear Stearns sold the security to HSH Nordbank. What we know about the fate of this and other mortgage securities is written in a trail of lawsuits. In one, HSH Nordbank, the German bank, said it lost a minimum of $42 million on BSABS 2005-HE8 and other securities it bought from Bear Stearns.

In another complaint, Ambac Assurance, a company that insured mortgage securities, claimed that Bear Stearns "deliberately and secretly" abandoned loan-quality standards in order to churn out securities it could sell to investors. That conduct enabled Marano and his staff to receive "stratospheric compensation," most of which was paid in cash, the complaint said. (Marano was not a defendant in either legal action.)

Ambac said that Marano's team knowingly dumped bunches of bad mortgages on Ambac. Then, convinced that Ambac and other mortgage insurance companies would suffer as a result, Bear Stearns bet against the stock of Ambac and other loan guarantors, making $55 million on the trades, according to the complaint. Ambac filed for Chapter 11 bankruptcy in 2010, harming all those innocent employees and shareholders Lanny Breuer spent sleepless nights worrying about.

Regardless of what it did or didn't do, Bear Stearns reaped the whirlwind. By 2007, subprime mortgages had become a big part of the investment bank's business, and when those borrowers quit paying—when the first mammoth wave of 2–28 mortgage payments clicked upward and millions of subprime home owners realized they couldn't afford to pay, refinance, or sell—Bear's investors and counterparties abandoned both product and peddler in a New York minute. In just twelve trading days in March 2008, Bear Stearns's stock price slid from $87 to less than $5. Alarmed that Bear's demise would trigger a chain reaction, threatening the four other Wall Street families and the wider economy, the Federal Reserve Bank of New York took over $29 billion of Bear Stearns's worst-performing securities and sold the better-quality merchandise to JPMorgan Chase for the price of the Bear Stearns office building.

Marano, whose fellow 1983 Columbia University graduate was a lanky transfer student named Barack Obama, did not go down with the ship. Soon after Bear Stearns crapped out, Cerberus Capital Management hired Marano to run the home-loan division of

GMAC. Cerberus, named for the mythical three-headed dog that guards the gates of hell, was a leveraged-buyout shop that specialized in acquiring gun and ammunition makers. Buyout firms borrow a ton of money to purchase companies, stick the debt on the companies' balance sheets, fire a bunch of employees, then run the companies, sell them, or offer pieces of them to the investing public. Cerberus, headed by the reclusive Stephen Feinberg, was the kind of firm that would close down a profitable, 119-year-old paper mill in Kimberly, Wisconsin, sending almost 10 percent of the town's population into the purgatory of unemployment insurance, in a move that the mill's workers said enabled the company to jack up the price of coated paper so it could make more money elsewhere.

The Cerberus gig was a lucrative reward for Marano, who'd overseen the most profitable part of the Bear Stearns moneymaking machine until it blew up the eighty-five-year-old firm and required a rescue from the angels at the Federal Reserve. Those angels didn't abandon Marano. Not long after he joined GMAC, the US Treasury sank more than $16 billion into the company to keep it solvent, making the government its largest stockholder. In 2010, GMAC changed its name to Ally Financial and began a blitz of TV commercials that portrayed the bank as less full of baloney than its competitors. American taxpayers held a 74 percent stake in Ally through 2013.

Ask Henry Turley Jr. which of the Memphis residential and office buildings he's developed, and he'll take you out on the balcony of his twelfth-floor offices in the old Cotton Exchange on Union Avenue. With the city's famous pyramid shimmering with reflected sunlight and traffic moving along the bridge high over the Mississippi River to the green Arkansas lowlands behind him, Turley will point out the buildings one by one. He admits the list is inexact because he can't always remember them all; suffice it to say that you can see at least a half dozen smack in the middle of downtown, including the building you are standing in.

The seventy-something Turley, skinny to the point of frailty with a slow drawl and the sometimes-profane wit of a guy who doesn't need to censor what he says, is a local real estate celebrity. He even has a gold star with his name on it on the sidewalk a couple blocks east of the Cotton Exchange, just outside the hoity-toity Peabody Hotel, along with other pooh-bahs of Memphis property development. Just about everyone I talked to in town knew Henry Turley or knew of him; at least a half dozen were glad to hear that I'd met him and asked if I thought he would sponsor, contribute to, or completely underwrite their community projects. I didn't tell them this, but in the short time I spent with Turley, we must have crossed paths with another half dozen people with ongoing neighborhood projects whom he'd already given money to. Sometimes Turley needed to be reminded by those people of his generosity because he obviously wasn't keeping close tabs. His wife, Lynne, had starred for years on a local public-television children's show, and she retained the charm and loveliness worthy of a schoolboy crush. Together, the Turleys were the prom king and queen of this close-knit, not-so-big, not-so-small river town. They didn't go out to dinner so much as affably greet well-wishers. Henry and Lynne Turley were rock stars.

From the Cotton Exchange balcony, Turley made sure I saw the birdhouses he'd built. They were meant for armies of purple martins, migratory swallows known for their agility. While he was trying to develop parts of Memphis close to the Mississippi River, Turley kept hearing people object because, they told him, mosquitoes swarmed the area. Turley did research and determined that the mosquito population was no bigger on the muddy banks of the mighty river than anywhere else. The chatter wouldn't die, however, so Turley took a novel approach. He constructed dozens of homes for purple martins, which, the story went, feasted on mosquitoes, and he put them up all over downtown. In fact, purple martins prefer beetles, and an Audubon Society study that examined the stomach contents of purple martins revealed no mosquitoes whatsoever. This was just fine with Turley; he figured if people wanted to spread the falsehood that mosquitoes infested the riverfront, he could tout the tall tale of the purple martin as skeeter devourer. "We responded to a myth with a countermyth," he said slyly. He showed me at least a dozen of the birdhouses dotting the Memphis skyline and quite a few of the purple martins darting to and fro. (I didn't spot any mosquitoes, though I can't say I was seeking them out.)

If Turley had retired to a rum-besotted island or breezy mountaintop after developing a fair percentage of the Memphis skyline, his star on the Peabody Hotel sidewalk would have been assured. But he didn't. He set about fulfilling a mission to resurrect Memphis, down-and-out after years of white flight and urban neglect. Of course, Turley didn't mind making money, but he was also driven by an abiding love for his hometown. His incentive wasn't the next kill; he drew a circle of self-interest wide enough to include his neighbors. His most famous development was Harbor Town, 130 acres on Mud Island, an aptly named heel of land to the west of the city in the Mississippi River. It wasn't much more than snakes and a small airstrip in the 1990s when Turley first brought potential investors there for a look-see. He cajoled his longtime friends at Belz Investment Company to join him and convinced a Wells Fargo banker named Jim Muir to lend them money. "Jim told me recently that his colleagues teased him about this out-of-pattern loan," Turley told me.

Transforming Mud Island was an act of prestidigitation that remained a big part of the Turley mystique. Harbor Town became a living example of what came to be called new urbanism—self-contained, mixed-income, walkable neighborhoods made up of single- and multifamily houses. Most importantly to Turley, it began the Herculean labor of reviving Memphis's diminished downtown. Turley put the same new urbanism principles to work on another residential development, South Bluff, which consists of clusters of condos and freestanding homes on the cliffs overlooking the Mississippi. But he still wanted to make Memphis a decent place to live for the less fortunate.

In his new development, called Uptown, Turley vowed that poor people's ponds were going to be as nice as rich people's ponds. Turley was determined to make his city vibrant again, for the benefit of everyone.

STEVE LOCKWOOD PRIED THE PLYWOOD AWAY FROM THE doorless entrance and stepped into the darkness. I followed him in. The air was cooler inside. Little of the morning's hot sunlight found its way into the living room of the abandoned house in Memphis's Frayser neighborhood. From the street, the working-class community looked like a schizophrenic patchwork: three or four nicely maintained two- and three-bedroom single-family houses followed by two or three with thigh-high grass and plywood for windows. Some were mere shells, open to the weather. One, blackened by the traces of a fire that had eaten half its carcass, reminded me of photos of buildings damaged by artillery. In 2012, Shelby County, where Memphis is located, was adding 350 properties a month to the 3,000 parcels it had already seized for delinquent taxes. The $200,000 the county had set aside for the maintenance of the properties wasn't enough. It had to add another $300,000 to its $363 million budget to cover plywood installation and lawn mowing, some of it done by inmates.

Lockwood, in his early sixties but with the wiry, trim body of a younger man, shined his flashlight through the dark. It found a shapeless jumble of crumbled Sheetrock, busted two-by-fours, and tangled electrical wiring. The room smelled of mold and wet gypsum. Dust danced in the flashlight beam. Lockwood shook his head. The ceiling had collapsed, reducing the prospects for the house's rehabilitation. We kept moving, careful not to step on broken glass or upturned nails, through a wrecked kitchen, toward a glow at the end of a hall. One of the back bedrooms had nothing covering a window. Sunlight poured in. On the floor, hidden under the remnants of another half-demolished wall, was a sleeping bag. Some poor soul had been living there.

Lockwood was checking out the house because its owner had offered to give it to him, free of charge. But Lockwood wasn't going to take it. "I can't afford it," he told me.

Lockwood, executive director of the nonprofit Frayser Community Development Corporation, patrolled the funkier precincts of Memphis, searching for hope. His development organization tried to bolster neighborhoods by buying and fixing up abandoned houses sold or donated by big banks such as Wells Fargo or government agencies like the Department of Housing and Urban Development. Lockwood told me he normally spent about $45,000 to make a house livable. He was able to do that because he received a grant from the Neighborhood Stabilization Program, a federal pool of money administered by the state of Tennessee. His Frayser development group got $3.7 million in 2009, and it was supposed to last four years. He turned down a lot of free and cheap houses. Aside from the expense of rehabbing those that may have been beyond salvaging, he was mindful of a community's character. "If there are gangs and I don't want to put a family on a certain block, I don't want the house," he said.

We got back into his pickup truck. Lockwood was eager to show me a success story. There weren't enough of them, he told me. In the Frayser section of Memphis, population 40,000, Lockwood estimated that nearly half the twenty-five square miles were empty. "I'm a guy who believes that this neighborhood has been relegated to being thrown away," Lockwood told me as we passed an entire block of perfectly kept homes, a couple with rose bushes snaking through the fences in their gardens, then an entire block that looked like the plague had swept through. "It's not a fair fight without people like me fighting for them."

We arrived at a recently renovated home waiting for a buyer or a renter. The yard had landscaping. Lockwood's workers had put in new hardwood floors and repaired and painted the walls. There was carpet in the bedrooms and a new washer-dryer. Lockwood said he preferred finding a family to buy the house because they would have a bigger stake in the community than renters, but it was usually a matter of economics. "A family can pay $650 a month to rent or pay $480 a month to buy with 3 percent down on a $55,000 house," he said. "That's the deal." The problem: it was difficult to find a family in Memphis wealthy enough to take advantage. His customers' average credit score was 540, Lockwood said, and they needed 620 to qualify for a mortgage. The $1,650 down payment was out of reach for many of them.

Meanwhile, the empty houses kept multiplying. Lockwood said that since he started working at the development group in 2002, he'd seen some homes go into foreclosure two or three times. He called it "an ongoing cancer."

"I'm proud of what my people do and what we've accomplished, because we've accomplished a lot," Lockwood told me. "But we're getting our asses kicked. I don't know how else to put it. We're winning a lot of battles but we're losing the war."

His most insidious enemy: predatory lending.

ASIDE FROM THE FACT THAT THE TWO MOST INFLUENTIAL Americans of my lifetime, Martin Luther King Jr. and Elvis Presley, had breathed their last there, predatory lending had brought me to Memphis, the former cotton and timber hub now home to FedEx and AutoZone. In fact, King and The King were appropriate symbols for the widening split in postcrisis American culture. The haves, in many cases, were rewarded for their 2000s profligacy, while the have-nots had to learn to live with having even less.

Memphis and Shelby County had filed a lawsuit against Wells Fargo claiming that the bank was responsible for the disproportionate economic devastation of the black community. All over the country, lenders were 3.5 times more likely to steer blacks to high-interest mortgages than they were whites with comparable credit scores, according to a Center for Responsible Lending study of 27 million loans originated from 2004 to 2008. "It's not hyperbole to say that this is one of the biggest civil rights issues of our time," said Webb A. Brewer, an attorney who helped draw up the Memphis lawsuit.

Wells Fargo and Shelby-Memphis settled in May 2012 for what seemed to me like peanuts, especially after a judge refused the lender's request to have the case dismissed. Wells Fargo, which had become the country's largest mortgage company, admitted no wrongdoing and paid the city and county $3 million to repair homes and businesses—some of which Lockwood hoped to get for the Frayser Community Development Corporation but, alas, was unable to—in addition to committing $4.5 million to help new borrowers with down payments and pledging to make as many as $125 million in mortgage loans to low- and moderate-income buyers in the area through 2017. It seemed to me that Wells Fargo had gotten off easy. The contrast between what Memphis received and the amount the bank had cleared since the crisis was whopping: in 2012, Wells Fargo reported net income of $18.9 billion, a record, after $15.9 billion in 2011 (a record), $12.4 billion in 2010 (a record), and $12.3 billion in 2009 (a record). The legal remedy didn't seem to compute.

Brewer set me straight. In part, cost had pushed the city and county to settle, he told me. Government entities with dwindling resources pitted against a giant bank with, by comparison, a seemingly bottomless legal war chest didn't stand a chance. "The case could have stayed in litigation easily for five more years," Brewer told me. And they had settled partly out of desperation. "I get a lot of calls from people facing foreclosure and hopefully the settlement can help people now," he said.

Lenders capitalized on his constituents' lack of financial sophistication, Memphis mayor A C Wharton Jr. told me when I visited him in his city hall office. That, combined with their compelling desire to buy a house, meant many of the city's 650,000 residents—63 percent of whom were black and almost 27 percent of whom lived below the poverty line—would be paying for their financial mistakes for years to come.

"Many of these folks have a Mayberry view of what a mortgage is all about," Wharton said, referring to the small, cornball North Carolina town in the 1960s TV sitcoms *The Andy Griffith Show* and *Mayberry RFD*. "You go to the Mayberry Savings and Loan, which carried the mortgage for your dad, and your daddy could go down there on a Saturday and tell them the crop didn't come in, and they'd tell him, 'We know you. You're good for the money. As long as you keep paying the interest and double up next year, you'll be okay.' There no longer is a Bank of Mayberry. The lender has sold the note into a pool. There's no more understanding ear."

"What exacerbated the situation were lending practices that took so many who were just about to realize the American dream and snatched that away from them," Wharton continued. "You see rows and rows of single-family homes that have been abandoned, not just in the so-called ghetto, but everywhere in the city. Home ownership was beginning to catch on with people who never dreamed of it. Just when they got their hands on the ladder to pull themselves up, it turned out they bought more house than they could afford, and some had interest rates they didn't know they'd agreed to pay. And it was over."

Wells Fargo wasn't the only lender the city and county could have accused of predatory lending, Wharton told me. But the plaintiffs were able to enlist former Wells Fargo employees to help draft their legal complaint. Among the exhibits filed with the lawsuit was a particularly curious one, I thought. It was a screen shot, taken in January 2006, of a page from what the lender called an "easy order" form, which mortgage salespeople apparently filled out when they signed up customers over the phone. Under "Language"—ostensibly the place where the salespeople noted the language spoken by the prospective borrower—the drop-down menu offered a unique option: "African American."

AFTER BEAR STEARNS COLLAPSED, MOSTLY DUE TO BAD HOME loans, Cerberus hired Tom Marano, the head of Bear Stearns's home-loan unit, to be chief executive officer of GMAC's home-loan division, Residential Capital, or ResCap. In 2009, Marano's first full year at the helm, ResCap lost $7.3 billion, and Marano was paid $5.6 million. In 2010, Marano received a 14 percent raise, to $6.4 million, and in 2011, he got an 8 percent raise, to $8 million, the same amount as he earned in 2012. That meant that if Tom Marano took a late lunch, he made more money in a single morning than Rebecca Black did all year.

In May 2012, ResCap filed for bankruptcy.

I've never met Marano. I've tried to talk to him, but he didn't return my calls and e-mails. I did speak to his attorney, Joel C. Haims, a partner with Morrison & Foerster in New York, and he agreed to make sure Marano responded to a series of questions. I asked him all sorts of things.

I asked whether he or anyone else at Bear Stearns was responsible for funding subprime mortgages (that charged high interest rates or excessive fees) despite the borrowers qualifying for loans with lower rates. I asked him whether he or anyone else at Bear Stearns was responsible for funding subprime mortgages (that charged high interest rates or excessive fees) for black borrowers despite their qualifying for better loans. I told him that I was writing about a black single mom who lost her home to foreclosure and filed for bankruptcy after getting a subprime loan, for more than 12 percent, funded by Bear Stearns, and I asked him what he might say to her if given the chance.

"As these questions relate to Bear Stearns, you should contact JP-Morgan Chase," Marano replied, through his attorney, referring me to the bank that bought Bear Stearns on highly favorable terms, thanks to the Federal Reserve. "In addition, I am not familiar with, nor do I have access to, the loan file you reference. Speaking on my own behalf, during my time at Bear Stearns, I was an early adopter and advocate of loan modifications before they were a more common practice. In addition, Bear Stearns had rigorous compliance policies in place to prevent predatory lending and unfair mortgage practices."

I asked Marano whether he thought his ResCap salary was fair. (Okay, I admit that nobody in the history of the world has ever considered him- or herself overpaid, but still.) I asked why ResCap needed to pay him so much, given that the company filed for bankruptcy after two years in which his compensation totaled more than $15 million.

"I was chosen to lead ResCap because of my depth of knowledge of the mortgage industry and my more than twenty-five years of experience in mortgage-backed securities," Marano replied through his attorney. "I believe that given the challenges and complexities associated with ResCap I have had a significant positive impact on the business and obtained the best result possible for all interested parties."

I asked him what role flawed underwriting played in the financial crisis and the subsequent recession. I asked what lessons he'd learned from the crisis and Bear Stearns's demise and how he might be implementing them. And I asked him how he felt about how well he'd done since the crisis as compared with most Americans, who were still hurting.

He declined to comment.

THE UPTOWN DEVELOPMENT CONSISTS OF 882 UNITS WITHIN winking distance of the Memphis pyramid. It took Henry Turley and his development company years to patch together the vacant lots in the heart of the city in order to put together the land for the project. Alexandra Mobley, Turley's Australia-born manager on the Uptown project, told me that some of the lots had no discernable owners, so it was a challenge cobbling together permission to build. That gives you an idea of how worthless many of the parcels were.

Uptown was truly mixed income, with three hundred public housing units. Lawyers lived next to FedEx forklift operators. The essence of the funding for the project came from the federal government's Hope 6 initiative, which required a stringent screening process and tougher rules than public housing. "We really, really looked for those people who said, 'I want to make a difference,' who said, 'I want to work,'" Mobley told me. When residents lost their jobs, full-time staff members helped them get new ones. The help the home owners received made a huge difference: Mobley and Turley were able to tick off the three instances in the previous four years when residents fell behind on their monthly payments. The mortgage-delinquency rate was 0.9 percent. Compare that with a nationwide delinquency rate of 7.4 percent.

"It takes a significant effort," Mobley said.

Ever the optimist, Turley added: "It took Elvis Presley three years from the time he left the Lauderdale Court public housing project to the time he bought Graceland."

REBECCA BLACK WAS RECEIVING TAX AND MAINTENANCE bills for 698 Hazelwood Road two years after she left the house. That was because she moved out before the foreclosure process was completed. Her lender never took possession of the property. She wasn't making mortgage payments, and the bank wasn't pursuing any legal action. The house was stuck in limbo.

It turned out that her mortgage servicer, the company that collected her monthly payments and was charged with handling the foreclosure process, had sent her a letter stating its intention to evict her for nonpayment. That had been enough to convince Black to move out. It would have been smarter to wait for the foreclosure to proceed, but Black said she couldn't face the humiliation of a sheriff's deputy knocking on her door and ordering her to leave.

One mortgage servicer in Chicago told me that some servicing companies determined whether to take possession of a house or not based on zip code. In some zip codes the neighborhoods were so degraded that it didn't pay to take over the property, he said.

I checked the public records on other vacant homes on Hazelwood Road, and I discovered three more still owned by people who no longer lived there—not by the banks that, had the houses been in a better area, might have taken them over and prepared them for resale. That meant that the mortgage borrowers were still on the hook for the tax and maintenance bills. They were also liable if someone got hurt on the property.

In late 2012 and early 2013, I spoke to housing advocates, real estate salespeople, and public officials in North Carolina, California, Oklahoma, and Michigan, who said they were dealing with this phenomenon too. In Kalamazoo, they called them "orphan homes." The blight manager—that was his informal title—told me the city of 74,000 in southwestern Michigan (and hometown of the Yankees' Derek Jeter) had demolished between sixty and eighty orphan homes a year from 2007 to 2011 at a cost of between $3,500 and $7,500 a piece, depending on volume discounts from contractors. In Oklahoma City, where the city's planning director told me that "abandoned houses eat away at the social structure," they called them "bank walkaways." The Federal Reserve called them "foreclosure walkaways." I preferred "zombie houses."

Whatever you called them, they were an epidemic. In early 2013, roughly 1 million such zombies cluttered the country's neighborhoods, inviting drug dealers, attracting firebugs, and weighing down the sale prices of other homes in their vicinity. A housing advocate in Durham, North Carolina, told me, "When people move out, crime moves in." In Detroit, a realtor told me the banks "never foreclose." She went on to say that shady operators rent out zombie homes and pay the taxes but not the mortgages—that way the city won't kick them out for tax delinquency, and with the mortgage companies not caring, they can be landlords for as long as they want. A foreclosure expert in North Lake Tahoe, California, told me that lenders played what he called "foreclosure roulette": they'd choose one borrower in a neighborhood to boot so they could say they were moving forward and not letting borrowers sit in their houses for free or letting the houses sit empty and idle. "That's the basic dynamics of the market," he said. In Nevada, a judge halted all foreclosures because the lenders couldn't prove they owned the mortgages on the homes they were seizing, among other bad craziness. A realtor I spoke to there just threw her hands up. "It's a mess out here," she told me in late 2012. "Just a mess."

ON THE NIGHT OF MARCH 30, 2012, MEMPHIS POLICE SAID Calvin DeWayne Jefferson, commonly known as Mack Kane, a resident of the nearby Westwood neighborhood, was behind the wheel of a white pickup truck on Hazelwood Road when he was shot. As he died, the truck kept rolling, according to a resident, Katie Greer, who said she heard the gun and peeked out her window. The truck flattened a section of chain-link fence across the street from Rebecca Black's old house and came to a stop in the backyard. Police didn't call the killing gang related, but the friends of Kane I talked to described him as a rapper, a pimp, and a prominent leader in the local Bloods gang.

"He was a straight-to-the point guy, a real good dude," said Bobby Niko, a music producer who recorded Kane. "People looked up to him."

It's impossible to draw a straight line from the zombie houses on Hazelwood Road to Mack Kane's death at the age of twenty-eight, said Kioni Logan, who grew up in the neighborhood and knew Cal, as she called him, for more than a decade. "When you live that kind of life, that's how you die," Logan said. It would be equally wrong to conclude that there was no connection at all, she told me. "Gangs take over empty houses," she said. "They have their meetings there. They have parties. They hold their dope there. They do whatever they want. The houses belong to them."

Richard Janikowski, a criminology and criminal justice professor at the University of Memphis, agreed. "The abandoned house starts the cycle," he told me. "It's part of a process that undermines community confidence and stability. You have clusters of foreclosures, and you start losing the folks who can do something about it because the folks who can move, do move."

About two hundred people, maybe more, attended Kane's funeral, according to two people who said they were there. Logan described her dead friend Cal dressed in red with a red tie and a red bandanna tucked under his leg. The casket was red and black. "Bloods," she explained.

At one point, Kane's twin brother, Buck Jefferson, asked everyone to leave so he could share a last private moment.

The wake was chaotic, with "RIP Mack Kane" T-shirts and people yelling, "They killed my homey," said Cattrice Renee Himes, who rapped under the name Slim Goody. Kane left behind a four-year-old son everyone called Little Kane, she said.

Perhaps we shouldn't mourn a man whose friends proudly called him a pimp and gang leader. Maybe the world is better off without him. Maybe, as Kioni Logan said, what goes around comes around. But I prefer to think that any life lost is a lost opportunity. That the man, regardless of his circumstances, leaves behind an unfillable loss, especially for his brother and son. That violence, wherever it's directed, weakens a community and thickens the distance between neighbors. Mack Kane's killing was a sign that Hazelwood Road was becoming unlivable, relegated, in Steve Lockwood's words, to a forgotten place. Someone in New York asked me about property values on the street, and I just shook my head sadly. The rules of the mainstream middle class no longer applied to Hazelwood Road. It was difficult to be concerned about resale value when the people who lived there were worried about not being killed.

Greer, whose house was three doors down from Rebecca Black's old place, said that Kane's killer fled into the woods along a path in the grass next to her house. On the other side of the path, which she called a "cut," was the house with gang graffiti.

"Along that cut I pick up all kinds of things—drugs, pills, marijuana—so I don't have to see it," Greer told me. "That's where they do their dirty work."

Greer said the graffiti on her neighbor's abandoned house might have been written by members of an upstart gang that challenged the Bloods.

"I try to stay prayed-up, and sometimes that doesn't even work," Greer said.

Tom Marano has owned at least two houses in Madison, New Jersey, where the Main Street commercial district features brick- and masonry-fronted bistros, wine shops, and a holistic veterinarian. Commuters can get on New Jersey Transit at the train station, built in 1916 of rough-hewn gray stones and registered as a historic site, and be in New York City in about an hour.

Marano bought a home on busy Shunpike Road in March 2002 for $580,000 and sold it to Oldpike Associates LLC for less than $100 in November 2002, according to County of Morris Tax Board records. Marano was listed as chief executive officer of Oldpike Associates in public records, and his children were identified as members, or shareholders.

Wealthy people sometimes transfer their assets to limited liability companies so their heirs can avoid paying estate taxes or to protect the assets if they get sued, said Y. David Scharf, a partner with the Morrison Cohen law firm in New York, who was speaking generally and didn't represent Marano.

Marano was a defendant in "five or six" securities lawsuits, said Joel Haims, Marano's attorney.

In 2010, the year Black abandoned her dream home to the tall weeds, Oldpike Associates built a 6,000-square-foot, 4.5-bathroom house on ten acres in Park City, Utah, according to public records. It sat on the top of a hill, surrounded by pine, aspen, and oak, at the end of a winding driveway lined by boulders. Park City, which advertises the "greatest snow on earth" and hosted events of the 2002 Winter Olympics, is perhaps best known to nonskiers as the site of the Sundance Film Festival. The Summit County tax assessor valued the home at $1.69 million.

Marano and his then wife, Amy Ullrich, had bought another home in Madison, in July 1995, for $805,000, public records showed. Marano sold his stake to Ullrich in March 2012 for less than $100. It was listed for sale later that year. Asking price: $1.4 million.

The second house was a ten-minute walk up the hill from Shunpike, at the end of a quiet cul-de-sac. In November 2012, I visited the cul-de-sac. It was just after Superstorm Sandy had swept through. The wind and rain had wiped out beach communities throughout the New York–New Jersey–Connecticut area and cut electrical power for millions of people in a broad inland swath. Fallen trees blocked many of the main roads in Madison. I didn't have a GPS, so I stopped at the local police station to get directions to the house where Tom Marano's ex-wife lived.

The street was quiet, and the neighbors' homes were big but not ostentatious. At the top of a hill, the Marano house sprawled—five bedrooms, and I could see where the indoor swimming pool and sauna had been added, to the right as I faced the house from the road—but it wasn't that much bigger than the other houses on the street.

The neighborhood was hushed by a fresh snowfall. The temperature was rising, and the snow was softening. It was the middle of the day, and not a creature was stirring. After a while, I did manage to find one neighbor to talk to. He was scraping the slushy snow at the end of his driveway with a shovel. I stopped and asked him about the Maranos. He said that as far as he could tell, no one was living in the place.

The house apparently had a generator that switched on automatically when the electricity cut off, he told me. The entire neighborhood lost power during the storm—just for a couple of days, he said, so they didn't have it as bad as lot of people. "The funny thing was, every light in their house was on," he told me. "Every other house on the street was dark, and you had this one house that was all lit up, the generator humming away. And there was nobody in it."

REBECCA BLACK HAD ONE MORE THING TO TELL ME. WE were sitting in her one-bedroom apartment, cluttered with belongings that had once fit neatly into a three-bedroom house, the Cubs game playing softly on the TV in the corner, the faintest smell of cigar smoke from her neighbor across the hall. She'd just shown me her mortgage papers, signed seven years before, in 2005, and I'd pointed out to her where it clearly said that her loan had a variable rate. The papers said she made about $11 an hour, the same amount she was making in 2012. She'd also shown me letters from the company that bought and serviced the note, EMC Mortgage, a division of JPMorgan Chase.

"Do you know who I work for?" she asked me.

A visiting nurse service, right?

"Yes," she replied, a sly smile forming. "But do you know who owns it?"

She showed me. The company she worked for was owned by JPMorgan Chase.

IN NOVEMBER 2012, I RECEIVED AN E-MAIL FROM HENRY Turley. I'd written about Hazelwood Road for Bloomberg News, and he'd read the article. No doubt he spotted a possible reclamation project in a city that provided plenty of them, and he'd joined forces with the head of the Frayser Community Development Corporation and done some reconnaissance.

"Steve Lockwood and I went to Hazelwood today," Turley wrote. "Two schools and a park, all physically excellent, are within a child's walk from Ms. Black's house. Plenty of cheap houses on nice lots."

Ever the optimist, I thought. Go get 'em, Henry. Go get 'em, Steve. Turley's resources and vision and Lockwood's tool-belt pragmatism made for an unbeatable combination. Maybe they could awaken Hazelwood Road from its funk.

Then Turley got real.

"But the neighborhood is failing. We talked strategy. It can be reversed, but it's hard to imagine our doing what's needed. We both enjoyed your visit and hope you'll return to cover the story of our successfully rebuilding Memphis."

CONCLUSIONS

We can either have democracy in this country or we can have great wealth concentrated in the hands of the few, but we can't have both.

         —Louis Brandeis

All animals are equal, but some animals are more equal than others.

      —George Orwell, *Animal Farm*

IF YOU'VE READ THIS FAR, YOU PROBABLY HAVE A GOOD IDEA where I stand on the whole too-big-to-fail thing: Get rid of it. It's anticompetitive and antidemocratic. The Dodd-Frank legislation didn't do away with it. Instead, it mandated years of bickering over arcane details of bank rules that were bound to obscure the big picture. Dodd-Frank never put to rest the chance that, despite the sentiment of lawmakers, the American public, and even the bankers themselves, the big banks would need bailing out. The merest glimmer of that possibility, which gives one group exalted status over all others, poisons democracy. Count the continued confusion over too big to fail as Dodd-Frank's greatest disappointment and one of the most exasperating and potentially costly missed opportunities of our time.

The term means different things to different people. Bankers who advocate an end to too big to fail mean we ought to allow their firms to die without bailouts, should it come to that. They mean ending discounts from bond buyers who lend them money more cheaply because of implied taxpayer rescues. They also mean we should continue to let them do whatever they want. If you think of banks as teenagers, it's the equivalent of "Dad, I don't need your help. Now drive me to Jimmy's."

To me, getting rid of too big to fail means making the biggest banks smaller. Anything else leaves too much room for haggling. (It is, after all, too *big* to fail.) Make the biggest banks small enough that their failure won't threaten the global financial system. Make them small enough so that we can quit relying on unreliable regulators to enforce rules they don't understand concerning activities they don't know about. Make the banks small enough that we can allow them to get into risky deals if they want to, without the possibility that the Treasury secretary or the Federal Reserve chairman will have to convene weekend-long emergency confabs to raise rescue funds from banks' competitors, like they did in 2008. Let's cut regulators out of the equation as much as we can and keep Washington off the backs of the banks. The only safe way to do that is to make the banks small enough that the government and the Fed won't have to choose between covering bankers' losses and having America's ATMs run dry.

The easiest way to make the biggest banks smaller is to separate their dice games from Granny's deposits. Right away you've addressed most of the problems in the existing system. Without taxpayers guaranteeing the bankers' gambling stash, there's instant accountability. If the London Whale, for example, wants to go long and risk some belly tranches especially where default may realize, let him do it in good health—with the firm's own money. Never again will we have to haul his boss into an awkward Capitol Hill hearing that turns into one more Senate fund-raising effort. I know that former Fed chairman

Paul Volcker would like to keep banks from gambling with their own money. But if there were no government guarantees involved, and the banks were small enough that their implosion wouldn't set the world on fire, there would be no reason to stop them.

Get banks out of commercial activities and you've shrunken them again. They ought to be financing oil exploration and coal mining, not doing it.

Another way to shrink them is for ordinary folks to shrink their stakes in them. They can close their savings and checking accounts, transfer their credit cards, refinance their mortgages—and switch them all to credit unions or smaller, community banks.

Well-intentioned people have differing opinions about the details of how to get big banks down to manageable sizes. Some say putting limits on how much money the big banks can borrow will do the trick. Some favor incentives for them to sell off assets. Some want them to match in cash reserves their implied taxpayer subsidies. Still others want to mandate that banks sell parts of themselves to competitors or spin them off into new businesses.

Here's a different approach: Put Sandy Weill in charge of breaking up the biggest banks. Nobody knows the tricks and traps of a financial supermarket better than the Dr. Frankenstein who cobbled together different companies to form the outlaw Citigroup, then pushed Congress and President Bill Clinton in 1999 to make his creation legal by repealing the last remnants of the Glass-Steagall Act. In making his shocking and nauseating 2012 about-face, telling CNBC that he thought the biggest banks ought to be divided up, Weill, the former Citi chief executive officer, was motivated by the second-oldest imperative known to humankind: profit. He understood that the sum of big-bank parts would be worth more than the whole. There's nothing wrong with his taking a percentage for his breakup work—what contrarian would deny Weill a piece of the action, even with his billions?—it's the doing-good-while-also-doing-well part that might prove novel to him.

If Weill won't do it, maybe his partner, John S. Reed, will.

Controversy also dogs discussions of what to do about derivatives. I say that if traders persist in buying credit default swaps for corporate bonds they don't own, then start selling fire insurance on their offices to the general public. I'm not advocating arson or violence. But isn't that an accurate analogy for investors who buy default insurance on companies whose debt they don't own? What exactly are they doing? It's like the plot outline for a Billy Wilder film noir—Fred MacMurray with window-blind shadows across his face, filling his pipe and telling Barbara Stanwyck that all their problems would be solved if they could just kill American Airlines. Don't get me wrong. Speculation is not a bad thing. It helped build America and surely will benefit the country for generations to come. But when speculation means betting on companies to crash and burn— different story. (Shorting stock is different; you're betting that share prices will decline, not rooting—or worse—for the company to go kablooey.) Those dollars would be better invested elsewhere, such as figuring out a way to originate and service mortgages without constantly screwing the whole thing up or attempting to issue annual reports that actually tell the public what your bank is up to.

Let's quit trying to prevent the last financial crisis and focus on preventing the next one. Quarrels over issues such as how much banks can borrow to fund their operations would be less urgent if the banks were smaller.

They would also be less relevant if we prosecuted people who broke the law. Think of the message we send when we allow banks to pay millions of dollars in fines without admitting they have done anything wrong. Wall Street guys spend a million on shoes. Without a mea culpa, where's the incentive to act like adults? Bankers feel as if they can get away with anything because they have. The same goes for prosecuting individuals. The highest up the corporate ladder the Securities and Exchange Commission has ventured has been to prosecute Fabrice Tourre, one of scores of Goldman Sachs vice presidents. You'd think a government lawyer might aim for a more prestigious scalp. The SEC goes after top hedge fund managers for insider trading but can't muster cases against Wall Street chiefs who erode faith in the system. If Blythe Masters, head of JP-Morgan Chase's global commodities division, impeded a federal investigation, she ought to be prosecuted. If Sanjiv Das, former head of Citigroup's mortgage department, misrepresented the quality of home loans when he convinced the government to back them, the government ought to come after him. If lenders engaged in predatory lending—steering racial minorities to high-interest loans when they qualified for better ones—the *federales* ought to crack down. If the law somehow doesn't allow prosecutions, the law ought to be changed. If the law remains unchanged, we ought to vote out the bums who maintain the broken status quo and elect new lawmakers who'll do something about it.

Term limits, anyone?

The alternative, it seems, is a political system owned by banks that have been encouraged—helped, actually—to outgrow the laws that govern them.

Some activities aren't illegal, but they aren't anything to brag about to your mother; nor are they suitable for inscription on your tombstone. Which leads me to my last prescription for what ails America: bring back shame. How else do we punish sin?

It isn't just unchecked greed (by Wall Street) or haywire wealth-envy (Washington's apparent feeling that anything done by people with lots of money has to be okay) that causes us to condone predatory lending, or the eviction of mortgage borrowers who are current on their payments, or the flouting of rules meant to safeguard bank customers, or the circumventing of fifty-year-old laws protecting banks and commodity industries from one another. It's a culture in which unchecked greed and haywire wealth-envy aren't shameful. We live in a world in which it's tolerable to gain a little edge, then a little more, then a lot. Competition is a wonderful thing and one of the essential elements of an economic system responsible for building the wealthiest country in history. But there's also the quaint notion of sportsmanship. The drive to win is healthy; the need to cheat in order to obliterate a crippled rival is pathology. Barry Bonds hasn't been elected to the Baseball Hall of Fame. If we refuse to accept cheating, or even the appearance of cheating, in sports, we certainly ought not abide it in finance either. There's a line between acceptable behavior and performance engendered by excessive pride. The government cannot police this; individuals have to. If enough individuals tolerate only competition that's fair, pretty soon you have a community—a community that knows that committing the sin of gluttony leaves others hungry and that one person's sloth means others have to work harder.

To build this new community, this new country, out of the ashes of the 2008 financial crisis will be our greatest challenge. Ours is a generation of excess, of blurred lines. If we want to bequeath to our children and grandchildren the same opportunities we had, or better ones, we must draw lines between what's right and what's wrong. Cheating is wrong. Exercising undue political influence is wrong. Behaving selfishly is wrong. Rigging markets is wrong. Letting people and companies and banks get away with crime is wrong. Pretending these things don't exist is wrong. The American economic and political systems can be paragons, or at least a bit closer to the ideal we all wish they would be, only if we seek redemption for our sins. Start with these seven.

ACKNOWLEDGMENTS

I'M JEALOUS OF AUTHORS LUCKY ENOUGH TO EMPLOY research assistants who can run down a random fact or recall an obscure, seemingly unrelated quote or anecdote from their college reading that makes the author look cool. I've never had an assistant. Jealousy is enough like envy that I can say, without qualification, that I have committed at least one of the seven deadly sins—needlessly. That's because I've been the beneficiary of something far better than a research assistant or two (or three). I've had colleagues around the world with expertise and grace who've always been happy to help me.

First to thank is Matthew Winkler, whose leadership has pushed Bloomberg News to the top of the international news-gathering heap. Mark Pittman once told me that one day we'd tell our grandchildren we worked for Matt. I hope to do that—my own and Mark's. Thanks to Amanda Bennett, without whose encouragement this book would never have happened. Thanks to Reto Gregori and my editors: John Voskuhl, Rob Urban, Robert Friedman, Jonathan Neumann,

Ronald Henkoff, Robert Blau, Gary Putka, Daniel Hertzberg, Otis Bilodeau, David Scheer, Rick Green, Flynn McRoberts, Chris Wellisz, and Robert Simison, who helped shape the stories and molded the copy. A special thanks to Bradley Keoun, whose only concern is the little people, Phil Kuntz, and David Yanofsky. Thanks to collaborators Jody Shenn, Donal Griffin, Alison Fitzgerald, Craig Torres, Greg Stohr, Dakin Campbell, Christopher Condon, Hugh Son, Caroline Salas Gage, Chloe Whiteaker, Heather Perlberg, Matthew Leising, Catherine Smith, Elliot Blair Smith, and David Mildenberg. For remaining kind to me even after countless nagging questions, thanks to William Selway, Agnieszka Troszkiewicz, Jonathan Weil, Mark Whitehouse, Daniel Kruger, Thomas Golden, Joshua Zumbrun, Scott Lanman, Joe Richter, Chanyaporn Chanjaroen, Mary D. Childs, Phil Mattingly, Shannon D. Harrington, Dawn Kopecki, Pierre Paulden, Martin Z. Braun, Alan Katz, Yalman Onaran, Janet Lorin, Michael J. Moore, Lisa Getter, Nela Richardson, Cady North, Kenneth Hoffman, Anita Kumar, Michael Novatkoski, Michael Weiss, and Nick Tamasi. A special thanks to a special guy, Charles Glasser, for whom I had more questions than anyone. For their inspiration and for helping spread the word: Sharon L. Lynch, Saijel Kishan, Jeff Taylor, Cam Simpson, Emma Moody, Alex Nussbaum, Alexis Leondis, Peggy Collins, Millie Munshi, Patrick McKiernan, Marcia Myers, Julie Bykowicz, David J. Lynch, Melissa Pozsgay, Dune Lawrence, Meghan Womack, Wenxin Fan, Linda Shen, Ty Trippet, Lee Cochran, Jesse Drucker, Frank Bass, Kathleen Hays, Vonnie Quinn, Tom Keene, Michael McKee, Erik Schatzker, Stephanie Ruhle, Deirdre Bolton, Carol Massar, Laura Chapman, Carol Zimmer, and the lovely and talented Gillian Wee. Special shout-outs to Vince Bielski, who helped get me started, and the person who represents the best of Bloomberg News, Christine Harper. In my first conversation with Christine, when I'd just started at the organization, I kept telling myself not to say anything because it was bound to sound dumb and disappoint her. I needn't have been intimidated, but I would still hate to let her down. A smarter, wittier, and more generous colleague would have to be developed in a laboratory, and wouldn't be possible even then.

Thanks to John Mahaney, who edited the book, and Jennifer Kelland, who sanded the rough edges; my agents Glen Hartley and Lynn Chu; and Clive Priddle and Peter Osnos at PublicAffairs, whose support was generous and meaningful.

For looking over early drafts, thank you Paul Oestreicher, Richard Bernstein, Dean Starkman, Maureen Tkacik, Christine Richard, Michael W. Hudson, Howard Levine, David Epstein, and Chris Petrucci, and a special Oyster Bar toast to Laura Farenthold-Pittman and Maggie Pittman, whose friendships are dear to me. I'd also like to thank Paul Colton, Bill Pettit, Andy Herman, and Dan Sullivan, who took a little of the edge off, and Annette Ivry and Marc Ivry.

In Memphis, I'm grateful to Dr. Kimberly Lamar, Kioni Logan, Henry Turley, Steve Lockwood, Charia Jackson, and especially Rebecca Black.

Kudos to folks whose work has inspired me to keep at it: Gretchen Morgenson, Brad Miller, David Reilly, Shahien Nasiripour, Saule Omarova, Joshua Rosner, Simon Johnson, Christopher Whalen, Dennis Kelleher, Daniel Alpert, Jeff Horwitz, Ann Rutledge, Sylvain Raynes, Leslie Cockburn, Andrew Cockburn, Melissa Huelsman, Yves Smith, Andy Felkerson, Matthew Stoller, Francine McKenna, Scott Raab, and "Tyler Durden." Y'all keep up the good work.

To the dozens of sources, those who spoke up on the record and those who whispered to me without wanting their identity revealed, 1.2 trillion thanks. Without you, there would be no us.

I'd like to thank my late father, Bert Ivry, who would have loved this but made sure to tell me about all the typos, and my late mother, Judith Ivry, who gave me the gift of irreverence. Also, thank you to my grandparents, three of whom made the journey from Eastern

Europe to New York City and enabled us to live in a country where a book such as this could be published. Your sacrifices were my boon, and I'll never forget.

To my three children, much has been said about my generation being the first in American history to bequeath fewer opportunities to the ones coming up after us. With the talent and good looks you inherited from your mother, I'm betting you'll beat those odds. I hope this book will become one small hammer beating against the stupidity and the cupidity, so that the future will be better than the past.

And to Janelle: your name and mine, inside a heart, upon a wall. Thank you.

NOTES

Introduction

xi   **"Dad, what's a financial crisis?":** Dimon's testimony to the Financial Crisis Inquiry Commission: "First Public Hearing of the FCIC, Panel 1: Financial Institution Representatives," Financial Crisis Inquiry Commission, Stanford Law School, http://fcic.law.stanford.edu/videos/view/17.

xi   **three-bedroom house at 698 Hazelwood Road:** I visited Memphis twice, in July 2012 and again in August. I gleaned most of the information about Hazelwood Road from talking to Rebecca Black numerous times, in person and on the phone, and former neighbors. Black showed me her mortgage contract. Thanks to Dr. Kimberly Lamar of LeMoyne-Owen College in Memphis and her student Kioni Logan for their generous assistance and companionship.

xii   **On nine of the fifteen parcels:** See Chloe Whiteaker's beautiful graphic accompanying my Bloomberg News article on Hazelwood Road: "A Dying Neighborhood in Memphis," Bloomberg News, November 8, 2012, http://go.bloomberg.com/multimedia/hazelwood-road.

xii   **robust recovery:** Whenever I hear the word "robust," my ears prick up. It's a bureaucratic word and more often than not indicates its opposite.

xii   **Dorothea Lange:** For Lange's iconic photo of the thirty-two-year-old mother with some of her seven hungry children, see "Destitute Pea Pickers in California. Mother of Seven Children. Age Thirty-Two. Nipomo, California," Library of Congress (LOC), www.loc.gov /pictures/resource/fsa.8b29516. The next time the kids complain about something like lack of Wi-Fi coverage, show them this: "Migrant Agricultural Worker's Family. Seven Hungry Children. Mother Aged Thirty-Two. Father Is Native Californian. Nipomo, California," LOC, www.loc.gov/pictures/resource/ppmsca.03054.

xiii   **seven deadly sins:** For more on greed, lust, wrath, sloth, envy, pride, and gluttony, try the 7 Deadly Sins website, which invites the reader to "click on the sin": www.deadlysins.com/sins.

xiv   **Rebecca Black got a bill for $520:** Search for 698 Hazelwood Road at Shelby County Assessor's Office: http://register.shelby.tn.us /imgView.php?imgtype=pdf&&id=100413122010.

xiv   **never took ownership:** Shelby County Assessor's Office.

xiv   **unskiable downward slopes:** Median home prices in the twenty largest US markets fell 33 percent from July 2006 to May 2009, according to the S&P Case-Shiller Home Price Index. The "wormy tail ends" I refer to are the roller coaster of price fluctuations from May 2009 to May 2013, when prices hit a new low and rebounded, but never higher than 26 percent below the peak.

xiv   **One foreclosed borrower, Harry Subers:** Subers refinanced his mortgage with a negative amortization loan, or option ARM, with Countrywide Financial. It turned out to be a mistake. I spoke to him in June 2008. None of the top five originators of option ARMs in 2007—Wachovia, Washington Mutual, Countrywide, IndyMac, and Downey Financial in Southern California—were still in business by the end of 2009. Option ARMs were the worst. One mortgage banker told me he called them "neutron loans—three years later the house is still there but nobody is in it."

xiv   **7 million other mortgage borrowers:** Prashant Gopal and Clea Benson, "American Dream Erased as Homeownership at 18-Year Low," Bloomberg News, July 30, 2013, www.bloomberg.com/news /2013–07–30/american-dream-erased-as-homeownership-at-18 -year-low.html.

xv   **the department had spent $5.5 billion:** Interview with Andrea Risotto, a Treasury Department spokeswoman, October 24, 2012.

xv   **$1.2 trillion of loans from the Federal Reserve:** Bradley Keoun and Phil Kuntz, "Wall Street Aristocracy Got $1.2 Trillion in Secret Loans," Bloomberg News, August 22, 2011, www.bloomberg.com/news/2011–08–21/wall-street-aristocracy-got-1–2-trillion-in-fed-s-secret-loans.html.

xv   **peaked on October 1, 2008, at $68.6 billion:** See David Yanofsky's elegant and groundbreaking data visualization: "The Fed's Secret Liquidity Lifelines," Bloomberg News, http://bloom.bg/pjfxX6.

xv   **ludicrous whining:** Jonathan Alter, "A 'Fat Cat' Strikes Back," *Newsweek*, August 15, 2010, www.thedailybeast.com/newsweek/2010/08/15/schwarzman-it-s-a-war-between-obama-wall-st.html.

xv   **he later apologized:** Mark DeCambre, "Schwarzman Likens Bam to Hitler over Taxes," *New York Post*, August 18, 2010, www.nypost.com/p/news/business/what_the_heil_AB2P3PQKS6F8lPAlW1evIN. In August 2013, Bloomberg News estimated that Schwarzman was worth $8.3 billion.

xvi   **$38 burgers:** See the lunch menu for Manhattan's Four Seasons restaurant here: "Lunch in the Grill Room," Four Seasons Restaurant, www.fourseasonsrestaurant.com/images/menu/PDFs/Four-Seasons-Grill-Lunch.pdf.

xvi   **compete with the $85 billion a month:** Joshua Zumbrun and Jeff Kearns, "Fed Maintains $85 Billion Pace of Monthly Asset Purchases," Bloomberg News, March 20, 2013, www.bloomberg.com/news/2013–03–20/fed-keeps-85-billion-pace-of-bond-buying-as-job-market-improves.html.

xvi   **wealth that would have made Croesus demur:** Croesus was ruler of Lydia, now part of Turkey, in the sixth century BCE. His kingdom was known as the first to mint coins—the king's bling—and Croesus was generally recognized as a very wealthy dude. Nothing in the historical record gives one the impression that he ever demurred for any reason. I claim poetic license here.

xvi   **derivatives trading, was a lot less risky:** Thanks to Richard Bernstein for making this excellent point.

xvii **nine of every ten home loans:** Jody Shenn, Clea Benson, and Heather Perlberg, "Fannie Mae Limiting Loans Helps JPMorgan Mortgage Profits," Bloomberg News, October 22, 2012, www .bloomberg.com/news/2012–10–21/fannie-mae-limiting-loans -helps-jpmorgan-mortgage-profits.html.

xvii **Newport Beach to Birmingham:** I refer to the bankruptcies of Orange County, California, and Jefferson County, Alabama, which was the biggest municipal bankruptcy in the United States until Detroit.

xviii **returned $20 billion in interest:** "Remarks by Treasury Secretary Tim Geithner on the State of Financial Reform," February 2, 2012, US Department of the Treasury, www.treasury.gov/press-center /press-releases/Pages/tg1408.aspx.

xix **I'd been a film critic:** A shout-out to my former employer, the *Record* newspaper, owned by the North Jersey Media Group, based at the time in Hackensack and as of this writing in Woodland Park, New Jersey.

xix **Almost immediately I saw articles:** There were many articles about the housing bubble in the *New York Times* midway through 2005, when I was involved in shopping for and buying a home: Columnist and future Nobel Prize–winning economist Paul Krugman wrote on the subject on more than a few occasions (see "Running Out of Bubbles," May 27, 2005, www .nytimes.com/2005/05/27/opinion/27krugman.html; "That Hissing Sound," August 8, 2005, www.nytimes.com/2005/08/08/opinion /08krugman.html; and "Greenspan and the Bubble," August 29, 2005, www.nytimes.com/2005/08/29/opinion/29krugman.html). David Leonhardt described the concern of another future Nobel Prize winner, Yale professor Robert Shiller, over irrational exuberance in "Be Warned: Mr. Bubble's Worried Again," August 21, 2005, www.nytimes.com/2005/08/21/business/yourmoney/21real .html?pagewanted=all&_r=0. Also see Edmund L. Andrews, "Fed Debates Pricking the U.S. Housing 'Bubble,'" May 31, 2005, www .nytimes.com/2005/05/31/business/31housing.html. The quotes around the word "bubble" in the headline tell you all you need to know about the possibility that Alan Greenspan's Fed would do anything to slow soaring home prices and profligate lending. And from Chris Harris, a TV writer, this amusing observation in "Bubble? What Bubble?" August 23, 2005, www.nytimes.com /2005/08/23/opinion/23harris.html: "We already experienced the Internet bubble. The crash taught us all that a feeling of invincibility can lead to disaster. Now that we've learned this humbling lesson, there's absolutely no possible way it could ever happen again to us."

xx **two Federal Reserve chairmen:** Alan Greenspan and Ben S. Bernanke.

xx **chief executives of the majority of the biggest Wall Street firms:** Lloyd Blankfein of Goldman Sachs obviously knew the end was near because his firm began to bet against American home owners, and Citigroup CEO Charles Prince was aware of a housing bubble, as evidenced by his now famous remark about having to dance as long as the music played—which is ironic, because he lost his job for not doing anything about it. Richard Fuld of Lehman Brothers, Stanley O'Neal of Merrill Lynch, John Mack of Morgan Stanley, and Jimmy Cayne of Bear Stearns were among those caught with their pants down, so to speak.

xx **"Where it impacts regular folks":** This Pittman quote was taken from a short film that Leslie Cockburn put together for Pittman's funeral. Cockburn and her husband, Andrew, produced *American Casino*, a documentary film about the mortgage crisis that starred Pittman and preceded the Oscar-winning *Inside Job* by two years. You can view the short film, "Mark Pittman Remembered," on YouTube at www.youtube.com/watch?v=GZkLXCZRBKY.

xx **middle-class income declined:** Richard Fry and Paul Taylor, "An Uneven Recovery, 2009–2011: A Rise in Wealth for the Wealthy; Declines for the Lower 93 Percent," Pew Research, April 23, 2013, www.pewsocialtrends.org/2013/04/23/a-rise-in-wealth-for-the -wealthydeclines-for-the-lower-93.

xxi **VIP citizenship:** "U.S. Offers PlatinumPlus Preferred Citizenship," The Onion, October 29, 1997, www.theonion.com/articles /us-offers-platinumplus-preferred-citizenship,889.

xxi **growth of the biggest banks:** I used data from regulatory filings.

xxi **Wells Fargo, by itself, wrote:** Source is *Inside Mortgage Finance*, a Bethesda, Maryland, trade publication.

xxii **gave the biggest banks borrowing discounts:** A. Joseph Warburton, Deniz Anginer, and Viral V. Acharya, "The End of Market Discipline? Investor Expectations of Implicit Guarantees," Northern Finance Association, November 2011, http://papers.ssrn.com/sol3/papers.cfm?abstract_id=1961656. More about this in Chapter 4.

Chapter One: Gluttony

1 **were told to drop what they were doing:** Conversations with Sherry Hunt formed the basis of descriptions of work life in O'Fallon.

1 ***Truman Show* landscaping:** I eyeballed the CitiMortgage headquarters myself in 2012. I was struck by the neat yard work that often comes with office complexes plopped incongruously in outer suburbs such as O'Fallon. It reminded me of the phony facades portrayed in the 1998 Jim Carrey film *The Truman Show*.

2 **In 2012, the 3,200 CitiMortgage workers:** Source for worker populations was Mark Rodgers, a Citigroup spokesman, in April 2012.

3 **buying as much as $90 billion a year:** Richard Bowen's written testimony to the Financial Crisis Inquiry Commission, April 7, 2010, http://fcic-static.law.stanford.edu/cdn_media/fcic-docs/2010–04–07%20Richard%20Bowen%20Written%20Testimony.pdf.

4 **number of loans it guaranteed:** Joe Gyourko, "Is FHA the Next Housing Bailout?" American Enterprise Institute, November 2011, www.aei.org/files/2011/11/30/-is-fha-the-next-housing-bailout_133147578809.pdf.

4 **delegated all quality control to the lenders:** Helen Kanovsky, Department of Housing and Urban Development (HUD) general counsel, related this astounding tidbit to me in a phone interview on March 1, 2012. While some anecdotes are too good to check, this one was too astounding to believe, so I asked her again, to make sure. Kanovsky said that for the first three years of the Obama administration, HUD focused on building a case against mortgage servicers, which became the National Mortgage Settlement in 2012. "We have limited resources," Kanovsky told me. "It was a question of what you do first." She added that from the beginning

of 2012, the department would be checking mortgage originations more closely.

4   **CitiMortgage guy tapped a finger:** Meeting at Citigroup headquarters in New York, March 30, 2012.

4   **lost $36 billion:** From the bank's filings with the Securities and Exchange Commission.

4   **a bailout of $45 billion:** Referring to the Troubled Asset Relief Program (TARP).

4   **was promised another $301 billion:** The US Treasury Department was willing to guarantee assets held by Citigroup that were falling in value or had indeterminate value, an offer the bank never accepted. Commentators have cited this above-and-beyond-TARP assistance as evidence of special treatment for Citi.

4   **received dozens of overnight loans:** Citigroup was second to Morgan Stanley in the amount it borrowed from the Federal Reserve on a single day: see Yanofsky, "The Fed's Secret Liquidity Lifelines."

5   **in order to save Citigroup:** Sheila Bair, *Bull by the Horns: Fighting to Save Main Street from Wall Street and Wall Street from Itself* (New York: Free Press, 2012). Bair first makes this assertion on the bottom of p. 115 of the hardcover edition. Reading it, I almost dropped the book. It was a rationale for the bailouts I'd always suspected but could never prove. I called a friend who'd already finished the book to ask her if I'd actually read what I thought I had, and she told me that Bair makes the same assertion twice more in the book. And she does.

5   **Obama told author Ron Suskind:** Ron Suskind, *Confidence Men: Wall Street, Washington, and the Education of a President* (New York: HarperCollins, 2011), 246.

5   **one high-placed man in American finance:** I refer specifically to Mohamed El-Erian, chief executive officer of the biggest US bond-fund manager, Pacific Investment Management Co., who said he phoned his wife on September 15, 2008, and asked her to empty the bank account. Quoted in Bob Ivry, Christine Harper, and Mark Pittman, "Missing Lehman Lesson of Shakeout Means Too Big Banks May Fail," Bloomberg News, September 8, 2009,

www.bloomberg.com/apps/news?pid=newsarchive&sid=aX8D
5utKFuGA. Bank analyst Mike Mayo did the same thing. See his
memoir, *Exile on Wall Street: One Analyst's Fight to Save the Big
Banks from Themselves* (Hoboken, NJ: John Wiley & Sons, 2012).

5   **two hundredth birthday:** Max Abelson, "Thain Wins Best Dad
Award as Charities Honor Bankers," Bloomberg News, June 25,
2012, www.bloomberg.com/news/2012–06–25/thain-wins-best-dad
-award-as-charities-honor-bankers.html.

6   **they were cooked:** Sherry Hunt. Also from the Justice Department's complaint against Citigroup, para. 1: "Among other things,
Citi failed to conduct the required full review of all early payment
defaults (i.e., loans defaulting in the first six months), failed to report to HUD findings of fraud and other serious deficiencies in its
loans, and encouraged its business employees to manipulate the
reports of its quality control department to conceal the number and
severity of deficiencies in Citi's loans." Keep in mind that Citi admitted wrongdoing. The complaint is available for study on the Justice Department website at www.justice.gov/usao/nys/pressreleases
/February12/citi/citimortgageinccomplaint.pdf.

7   **"We're going to stand for . . . responsible finance":** A video
of Pandit touting responsible finance has been removed from the
Citigroup website.

7   **Defaults were down:** Delinquencies of all mortgages fell to 7.4
percent in the first three months of 2012 from 10 percent in the
first three months of 2010, according to the Mortgage Bankers
Association.

7   **She was a country girl:** Hunt related the details of her life to me
in a series of phone interviews and on two visits.

8   **liar loans:** Bob Ivry, "Subprime 'Liar Loans' Fuel Bust with $1
Billion Fraud," Bloomberg News, April 25, 2007, www.bloomberg
.com/apps/news?pid=newsarchive&sid=aN2DPRuRs93M.

9   **Citigroup was paying bonuses:** Hunt, confirmed by CitiMortgage CEO Sanjiv Das.

9   **deeply religious man:** Conversations with Richard Bowen.

9   **Bowen shot off an e-mail:** Bowen's written testimony to the Financial Crisis Inquiry Commission.

10   **The Committee to Save the World:** The *Time* cover can be seen on the *Time* website at www.time.com/time/covers/0,16641 ,19990215,00.html.

10   **work for Citi and then demoted:** This is the version of events related by the Financial Crisis Inquiry Commission's report, p. 19. Available at http://fcic-static.law.stanford.edu/cdn_media/fcic -reports/fcic_final_report_full.pdf.

10   **Citi acted on Bowen's concerns:** Brad S. Karp's letter can be viewed in the Financial Crisis Inquiry Commission's archive at http://fcic-static.law.stanford.edu/cdn_media/fcic-docs/2010 –11–01%20Richard%20Bowen%20Response%20to%20Follow -Up%20Questions.pdf.

11   **City Bank received its charter:** For Citi's history, see Mayo, *Exile on Wall Street*; Phillip L. Zweig, *Wriston: Walter Wriston, Citibank, and the Rise and Fall of American Financial Supremacy* (New York: Crown Business, 1995). For the history of the Fed, see William Greider, *Secrets of the Temple: How the Federal Reserve Runs the Country* (New York: Simon & Schuster, 1987); G. Edward Griffin, *The Creature from Jekyll Island: A Second Look at the Federal Reserve* (New York: American Media, 1994). Someone who wears a figurative tinfoil hat to keep the Central Intelligence Agency from reading his mind recommended Griffin's book to me. That person's paranoid ramblings, as well as the more fanciful flights in Griffin's book, could be more blithely dismissed before the revelations about the National Security Agency provided by Edward Snowden in 2013. Tinfoil hats do not, as far as I know, prevent intelligence agents from reading your e-mails.

14   **cocksure wingman:** Duff McDonald, *Last Man Standing: The Ascent of Jamie Dimon and JPMorgan Chase* (New York: Simon & Schuster, 2009).

15   **Ironically—and Citi's history does not lack:** Zweig, *Wriston*; Griffin, *The Creature from Jekyll Island*.

15   **Clinton said in a statement:** The president's statement in its entirety can be found at William J. Clinton, "Statement on Signing the Gramm-Leach-Bliley Act," American Presidency Project, November 12, 1999, www.presidency.ucsb.edu/ws/?pid=56922#axzz2i4tww5tP.

15 **CitiMortgage executives put together a committee:** *US and Sherry Hunt v. Citigroup*, para. 36: "Citi established 'gatekeeper' personnel in its business units who are given the job of pressuring quality control to downgrade its assessment of loan problems." Note the use of the present tense. The Justice Department goes on to say that this is a violation of Department of Housing and Urban Development rules. The complaint is available on the Justice Department website at www.justice.gov/usao/nys/pressreleases /February12/citi/citimortgageinccomplaint.pdf.

16 **create new categories for loans:** The percentages I use for tier 1 and tier 2 defects are illustrative and don't reflect actual numbers.

16 **Mortgages represent the best of our financial system:** The fixed-rate, thirty-year mortgage doesn't have a long history, but it's mostly been a boon to home owner and lender alike.

17 **felt their faces grow hot:** This behavior at Citigroup is an example of moral hazard, which can be defined as doing idiotic things because you know you won't have to face the consequences. The 2008 bank bailouts and subsequent continuation of favored treatment created moral hazard in O'Fallon and elsewhere.

17 **$2.5 trillion in deposits:** Quarterly regulatory filings.

18 **government made sure you prospered:** Readers will see more examples of this in the coming chapters.

18 **Insider stock trading:** Patricia Hurtado and Bob Van Voris, "Ex-SAC Manager Martoma Faces Nov. 4 Insider-Trading Trial," Bloomberg News, June 6, 2013, www.bloomberg.com/news/2013 –06–05/ex-sac-manager-martoma-faces-nov-4-insider-trading-trial .html.

18 **promised to end the phenomenon of too big to fail:** The intrepid reader may find the Dodd-Frank legislation on the Securities and Exchange Commission website at www.sec.gov/about/laws /wallstreetreform-cpa.pdf.

18 **playing bridge and smoking weed:** Kate Kelly, "Bear CEO's Handling of Crisis Raises Issues," *Wall Street Journal*, November 1, 2007, http://online.wsj.com/article/SB119387369474078336.html. Kelly's article, which covers events that occurred a year before Bear Stearns's demise, created quite a ruckus in the finance world. CEO

Jimmy Cayne answered her charges in William D. Cohan's meticulous re-creations of the investment bank's downfall, *House of Cards: A Tale of Hubris and Wretched Excess on Wall Street* (New York: Anchor Books, 2009). As Bear collapsed in 2008, one coldhearted soul joked that Cayne, if the allegations were true, was losing half a billion dollars in the value of his stock between bong hits.

19   **single-night peak of $1.2 trillion:** See Yanofsky, "The Fed's Secret Liquidity Lifelines."

19   **there was a chain reaction:** The best rundown of those frantic days of 2008 can be found in Cohan's *House of Cards*, especially the chapter on the failure of Lehman Brothers, which remains the go-to account years later.

20   **"talking your book":** Justin Fox, "Phil Gramm Says the Banking Crisis Is (Mostly) Not His Fault," *Time*, January 24, 2009, www.time.com/time/business/article/0,8599,1873833,00.html#ixzz2b1vAZsre. Fox quotes Gramm as saying, "Europe never had Glass-Steagall. So why didn't this happen in Europe rather than here?"

20   **"drive this rate down by brute force":** *US and Sherry Hunt v. Citigroup*, para. 40.

20   **Rascal Flatts's "Stand":** See the "Stand" video on YouTube at www.youtube.com/watch?v=G_Vzpjv_kR4.

21   **"it's your asses on the line":** Interview with Hunt. Also see US complaint against Citigroup, para. 43.

21   **Bowen had landed a job:** Interview with Bowen. Also see "Accounting Prof Testifies on Mortgage Meltdown," University of Texas, Dallas, News Center, May 6, 2010, www.utdallas.edu/news/2010/5/6–3041_Accounting-Prof-Testifies-on-Mortgage-Meltdown_article.html.

21   **"I'm afraid of what I know":** Hunt showed me her letter to the Securities and Exchange Commission, which her initial *qui tam* complaint included as an exhibit.

22   **False claims suits:** The Justice Department explains these types of complaints in "False Claims Act Cases: Government Intervention in Qui Tam (Whistleblower) Suits," Department of Justice, www.justice.gov/usao/pae/Civil_Division/InternetWhistleblower%20update.pdf.

22   **only about one in five of them:** The US Justice Department provides these statistics at "Fraud Statistics—Overview, October 1, 1987–September 30, 2012," Department of Justice, www.justice .gov/civil/docs_forms/C-FRAUDS_FCA_Statistics.pdf.

23   **Citigroup agreed to pay:** Press release is available at "Federal Government Settles Fraud Lawsuit Against CitiMortgage, Inc. for Reckless Mortgage Lending Practices," Department of Housing and Urban Development, http://portal.hud.gov/hudportal/HUD?src =/press/press_releases_media_advisories/2012/HUDNo.12–032.

23   **Bank of America paid $1 billion:** Press release is available at "$1 Billion to Be Paid by the Bank of America to the United States Largest False Claims Act Settlement Relating to Mortgage Fraud," Department of Justice, www.justice.gov/usao/nye/pr/2012/2012feb09.html.

23   **Deutsche Bank, Europe's biggest financial institution:** Press release is available at "HUD, HUD Inspector General and U.S. Attorney Announce $202 Million Settlement with Deutsche Bank and Mortgageit," Department of Housing and Urban Development, http://portal.hud.gov/hudportal/HUD?src=/press/press_releases _media_advisories/2012/HUDNo.12–082.

23   **even up to the day of the settlement:** *US and Sherry Hunt v. Citigroup,* para. 8: "Citi's quality control reports became—and remain—a battleground within Citi."

24   **cut her in for $31 million:** Bob Ivry, "Citigroup 'Defrauded' Fannie, Freddie: Whistle-Blower," Bloomberg News, February 22, 2012, www.bloomberg.com/news/2012–02–22/citigroup-defrauded -fannie-freddie-whistle-blower-claims.html.

24   **They immediately started spinning the news:** This annoyed the hell out of me. The lie seemed gratuitous. I pressed Citigroup public relations people about this. I asked them to send me proof that this settlement was connected somehow to the National Mortgage Settlement. I knew very well it was not because the Justice Department didn't mention it when announcing the settlement and because I talked to people who helped arrange the deal who told me it wasn't. Only Citigroup employees were insisting the two settlements were related in any way. For goodness sake, they were a week apart! To illustrate how disappointing this pantomime got,

I received an e-mail from a Citigroup public relations employee defending the bank's conflation of the two settlements and quoting the Justice Department's press release titled "$25 Billion Mortgage Servicing Agreement Filed in Federal Court." The part the Citi employee quoted read, "The United States also resolved certain Federal Housing Administration (FHA) origination claims with Bank of America and with Citibank *in a separate matter*" (italics mine). Yes, you read that right. In order to support Citi's contention that the two settlements were part of the same matter, a Citi employee quoted a press release that said they were separate.

24 **"The FHA was not defrauded":** Interview with Das, March 30, 2012.

25 **finely tuned bullshit meter:** I may have first heard this term from my old buddy Ernest Hemingway blah blah blah. Then I saw that a German engineer had actually invented one: David Moye, "B.S. Detector Invented by German Computer Expert Bernd Wurm," Huffington Post, July 27, 2011, www.huffingtonpost.com/2011/07/27 /bs-detector-invented-by-german-computer-expert-bernd-wurm _n_909625.html. I assure you that I refer to the figurative bullshit meter, not the literal one.

25 **Wall Street had colonized Midtown Manhattan:** Midtown Manhattan is the chopped-salad capital of the world. No wonder bankers migrated there.

25 **buttonwood-lined:** Buttonwoods are more commonly known as sycamores.

26 **a beautiful tower:** I think it's charming, but *New York Magazine*'s architectural critic did not. "This is a building you wouldn't want to get anywhere near at a cocktail party," wrote Joseph Giovannini. "Dressed nearly head to toe in dour granite, and geometrically proper, it's stiff to the point of pass-out boredom." See Giovannini's excoriation at "Bearish on Mad Ave.," *New York Magazine*, http:// nymag.com/nymetro/arts/architecture/reviews/5815.

26 **The $1 billion estimated price tag:** David Jones, "JPMorgan Could Make Bear Stearns Building Its New HQ," The Real Deal, March 17, 2008, http://therealdeal.com/blog/2008/03/17/jpmorgan -could-make-bear-stearns-building-its-new-hq.

26 **accused of illegally manipulating worldwide interest rates:** Referring to the London Interbank Overnight Rate, or Libor, upon which many consumer rates are based. UBS, RBS, and Barclays were the first banks to be nabbed. See Jonathan Weil, "Where Are the Libor Cases Against U.S. Banks?" Bloomberg View, June 27, 2013, www.bloomberg.com/news/2013–06–27/where-are-the-libor -cases-against-u-s-banks-.html.

27 **even as the settlement was being written:** See US and Sherry Hunt v. Citigroup, para. 8: "Citi's quality control reports became— and remain—a battleground within Citi."

28 **waitresses were serving beer to their underage friends:** Not to mention the beer parties the restaurant workers would throw after the boss went home to bed after working fourteen-hour days. The beer came from the poor guy's kegs.

28 **Cabdrivers who exaggerated their proximity to customers' addresses:** Drivers competed for fares by radio and often told the fast-talking dispatcher they were closer to the fare than they actually were. This was a common practice among Yellow Cab drivers in San Francisco when I worked there in the mid-1980s. It was called "stretching," which was short for "stretching the hood" of the car. I know of at least one fistfight between cabbies triggered by a particularly egregious case of hood stretching.

28 **250,000 employees in 160 countries:** Employee census from data compiled by Bloomberg News. The number of countries is proudly trumpeted on the Citigroup website at www.citigroup.com /citi/about/our_businesses.html.

30 **$15 million for 2011:** Donal Griffin, "Pandit Pay Climbs Toward $53 Million as Citigroup Revenue Slumps," Bloomberg News, March 12, 2012, www.bloomberg.com/news/2012–03–12/pandit -compensation-climbs-toward-53-million-as-citigroup-revenue -slumps.html.

30 **put him in the middle of the pack:** With data compiled by Bloomberg News, I put together a list of bankers' top compensation for 2011. Their numbers rival those of the starting lineup for the New York Yankees:

- Jamie Dimon, JPMorgan Chase, $23 million
- John Stumpf, Wells Fargo, $19.8 million
- Richard Fairbank, Capital One, $18.7 million
- Vikram Pandit, Citigroup, $15 million
- James Gorman, Morgan Stanley, $10.5 million
- Michael Carpenter, Ally, $9.5 million
- Lloyd Blankfein, Goldman Sachs, $9 million plus
- Brian Moynihan, Bank of America, $7 million

30 **$800 million sale of his hedge fund:** Anthony Effinger, Katherine Burton, and Donal Griffin, "Pandit Fast Money with Hedge Funds Proving Citi Dead End," Bloomberg News, February 28, 2012, www.bloomberg.com/news/2012–02–29/pandit-fast-money -with-hedge-funds-proves-citigroup-dead-end-with-spinoffs.html.

30 **90 percent decline in Citigroup stock:** Adjusting for the one-for-ten reverse split, Citi's share price when Pandit took over was $332.30. On April 16, 2012, it was $34.

30 **rejecting his compensation:** Donal Griffin and Bradley Keoun, "Citigroup Investors Reject Management Compensation Plan," Bloomberg News, April 17, 2012, www.bloomberg.com/news/2012–04–17 /citigroup-shareholders-reject-management-s-compensation-plan -1-.html.

30 **he'd written what amounted to a mea culpa:** Reed's letter is available at "Letter; Volcker's Advice," *New York Times*, October 23, 2009, http://query.nytimes.com/gst/fullpage.html?res=9B06E5 D71238F930A15753C1A96F9C8B63&scp=3&sq=%22John +S.+Reed%22&st=nyt.

31 **Dick Parsons intimated:** Kim Chipman and Christine Harper, "Parsons Blames Glass-Steagall Repeal for Crisis," Bloomberg News, April 19, 2012, www.bloomberg.com/news/2012–04–19 /parsons-blames-glass-steagall-repeal-for-crisis.html.

31 **most astonishing about-face was Sandy Weill's:** "Wall Street Legend Sandy Weill: Break Up the Big Banks," CNBC.com, July 25, 2012, www.cnbc.com/id/48315170/Wall_Street_Legend_Sandy _Weill_Break_Up_the_Big_Banks. It's worth quoting from this story:

Former Citigroup Chairman & CEO Sanford I. Weill, the man who invented the financial supermarket, called for the breakup of big banks in an interview on CNBC Wednesday.

"What we should probably do is go and split up investment banking from banking, have banks be deposit takers, have banks make commercial loans and real estate loans, have banks do something that's not going to risk the taxpayer dollars, that's not too big to fail," Weill told CNBC's "Squawk Box." . . .

He essentially called for the return of the Glass-Steagall Act, which imposed banking reforms that split banks from other financial institutions such as insurance companies.

"I'm suggesting that they be broken up so that the taxpayer will never be at risk, the depositors won't be at risk, the leverage of the banks will be something reasonable, and the investment banks can do trading . . . ," Weill said. . . .

Weill said that by breaking up banks, they would be "much" more profitable.

32   **Pandit stepped down:** Zachary Tracer, Noah Buhayar, and Donal Griffin, "Pandit Leaves Citigroup Citing Transformation at Bank: Timeline,"Bloomberg News, October 16, 2012, www.bloomberg.com /news/2012–10–16/pandit-leaves-citigroup-citing-transformation -at-bank-timeline.html.

32   **bank's stock price had still lost 89 percent:** On October 16, 2012, the bank's share price was $37.25.

32   **"It's hard to come up with things":** Erik Schatzker, "Citigroup's Pandit Says He Wouldn't Do Anything Different," Bloomberg News, October 16, 2012, www.bloomberg.com/news/2012–10–16 /citigroup-s-pandit-says-he-wouldn-t-do-anything-differently.html.

32   **Citigroup withheld some of a $40 million:** Donal Griffin, "Citigroup Will Pay Former Chief Pandit $6.7 Million," Bloomberg News,

November 10, 2012, www.bloomberg.com/news/2012–11–09
/citigroup-ex-ceo-pandit-gets-6–7-million-compensation-for-2012
.html.

CHAPTER TWO: WRATH

34 **Mark Pittman, former cattle-ranch hand:** Pittman had told me
stories about his job as a bar bouncer—there was once a fight involving pool cues—but I didn't know he'd been a ranch hand until
I read his February 27, 2009, interview with Ryan Chittum of the
Columbia Journalism Review's "The Audit": www.cjr.org/the_audit
/audit_interview_mark_pittman.php?page=all.

34 **Kansas Piggly Wiggly store manager:** I'm deeply indebted to
Pittman's widow, Laura Farenthold-Pittman, for supplying this and
many other details of Mark's life.

34 **Nobody had ever seen numbers like it:** Delinquency rates for
subprime mortgages averaged just over 12 percent for the seven
years from 1999 through 2005, according to the Mortgage Bankers
Association, a Washington trade group. For the six years from 2007
through 2012, the average rate was more than 21 percent, with a
high of 27.2 percent in 2010. The corresponding numbers for prime
mortgages, given to people with the highest credit scores, were 2.4
percent for the seven years from 1999 through 2005 and 4.9 percent
for 2007 through 2012, with a high of 7.3 percent in 2010.

34 **Mortgage Lender Implode-o-Meter:** The website (http://ml
-implode.com) estimated that 388 mortgage companies bit the dust
from late 2006 to the middle of 2013. David Olson, who was in
the mortgage business for fifty years, told me that he estimated
that about half the country's mortgage companies went kaput in
the credit bust.

34 **anyone who could fog a mirror:** This expression became something of a cliché at the tail end of the housing boom. I first heard it
from a Texas mortgage salesman named Greg Bass in 2007.

34 **20 percent of all mortgages written in 2007:** This statistic
comes from the always helpful Guy Cecala of *Inside Mortgage Finance*, an industry publication in Bethesda, Maryland.

35   **Bernanke had insisted that the subprime mortgage crisis:** Bob Ivry, "Bernanke, Paulson Were Wrong: Subprime Contagion Is Spreading," Bloomberg News, August 10, 2007, www.bloomberg .com/apps/news?pid=newsarchive&sid=aygqZPuV0y14.

36   **ten programs, each designed:** For four years, this handy chart sat on my desk, on or near the top of the pile. It shows all the emergency lending programs the Federal Reserve provided to financial institutions to make sure they were never short of cash. Print and laminate: "Forms of Federal Reserve Lending," Federal Reserve Bank of New York, July 2009, www.newyorkfed.org/markets /Forms_of_Fed_Lending.pdf.

36   **little Saigon National Bank:** The bank took $2 million from TARP on December 23, 2008. (That's million, with an *m*.) Its mission is to serve the needs of the Vietnamese business community in Southern California, according to its website.

36   **seemingly limitless Fed loans:** According to the Federal Reserve Act, the central bank must only lend against appropriate collateral and not to insolvent banks. The empirical definition of solvency has been, shall we say, fluid.

37   **intruded on my daydreaming:** I had the desk at the end of the row, with Pittman to my left, and for a while I had a view out the floor-to-ceiling windows of the corner of Fifty-Eighth Street and Third Avenue. I didn't know how distracting that was until we moved upstairs, where we had the same configuration of desks and windows but a balcony blocked my view of the street.

37   **Fed released its updated balance sheet:** The weekly updates can be viewed on the Federal Reserve website at www.federalreserve .gov/releases/h41.

38   **he chided the credit-ratings companies:** Mark Pittman, "S&P, Moody's Mask $200 Billion of Subprime Bond Risk," Bloomberg News, June 29, 2007, www.bloomberg.com/apps/news ?pid=newsarchive&sid=aIzzx2vC10KI.

38   **the creation of the ABX:** Mark Pittman, "Subprime Securities Market Began as 'Group of 5' over Chinese," Bloomberg News, December 17, 2007, www.bloomberg.com/apps/news?pid=newsarchive &sid=aA6YC1xKUoek.

38   **He pointed out that Hank Paulson:** Mark Pittman, "Paulson's Focus on Subprime 'Excesses' Shows Goldman Gorged," Bloomberg News, November 5, 2007, www.bloomberg.com/apps /news?pid=newsarchive&sid=aUXYrK3i6juc.

38   **Lloyd Blankfein, was in the room:** Mark Pittman, "Goldman, Merrill Collect Billions After Fed's AIG Bailout Loans," Bloomberg News, September 29, 2008, www.bloomberg.com/apps /news?pid=newsarchive&sid=aTzTYtlNHSG8.

39   **It's funded by its member banks:** That's to say, the twelve regional branches of the Federal Reserve sell shares to the community banks within their jurisdictions.

39   **twice a year for a proper grilling:** The Humphrey-Hawkins Act of 1978 mandated that the Federal Reserve chairman appear in front of the relevant committees of the House and Senate in February and July of every year to discuss monetary policy.

39   **that can hit "CTRL+P" whenever it wants:** The Federal Reserve creates money.

39   **The Fed deserves its reputation for secrecy:** Once again, my sources are Greider, *Secrets of the Temple*, and Griffin, *The Creature from Jekyll Island.*

42   **Neither were the banks' official reports:** Frank Partnoy and Jesse Eisinger, "What's Inside America's Banks?" *Atlantic*, January 2, 2013, www.theatlantic.com/magazine/archive/2013/01/whats-inside -americas-banks/309196.

43   **a sham, a fake empire:** One of Pittman's favorite bands was The National, which has a song called "Fake Empire."

43   **a way for Bernanke to cover Geithner's ass:** Pittman was stunned when President-elect Barack Obama chose Geithner as his Treasury secretary. I called it the Obama administration's original sin.

44   **infamous plunge of the stock market:** The Dow Jones Industrial Average lost 7 percent of its value, or about $1.2 trillion, on September 29, 2008, as the House of Representatives defeated the TARP proposal 205–228. Four days later TARP passed.

44   **growing disconnect between ordinary people:** I realize this is a minority sentiment, but later events would show that the stock market and the "real economy" were functioning as if on different planets.

44   **increasing the money supply is bound to cause rising prices:** This is indeed fundamental macroeconomics, but the money that's created needs to flow through the system, and in this case it oozed. More on the velocity of money in Chapter 3.

46   **nine Freedom of Information Act exemptions:** Here they are:

1. Those documents properly classified as secret in the interest of national defense or foreign policy;
2. Related solely to internal personnel rules and practices;
3. Specifically exempted by other statutes;
4. A trade secret or privileged or confidential commercial or financial information obtained from a person;
5. A privileged inter-agency or intra-agency memorandum or letter;
6. A personnel, medical, or similar file the release of which would constitute a clearly unwarranted invasion of personal privacy;
7. Compiled for law enforcement purposes, the release of which
    a. could reasonably be expected to interfere with law enforcement proceedings,
    b. would deprive a person of a right to a fair trial or an impartial adjudication,
    c. could reasonably be expected to constitute an unwarranted invasion of personal privacy,
    d. could reasonably be expected to disclose the identity of a confidential source,
    e. would disclose techniques, procedures, or guidelines for investigations or prosecutions, or
    f. could reasonably be expected to endanger an individual's life or physical safety;
8. Contained in or related to examination, operating, or condition reports about financial institutions that the SEC regulates or supervises; or

9. And those documents containing exempt information about gas or oil wells.

Source: "Freedom of Information Act Exemptions," Securities and Exchange Commission, www.sec.gov/foia/nfoia.htm.

46　**had borrowed $20, $30, even $40 for every dollar:** Cyrus Sanati, "Cayne and Schwartz at Odds over Bear's Leverage," *New York Times*, May 5, 2010, http://dealbook.nytimes.com/2010/05/05 /cayne-and-schwartz-at-odds-over-bears-leverage/?_r=0.

47　**Founder Michael Bloomberg had hired Winkler:** Winkler told this anecdote at a newsroom gathering to commemorate the twentieth anniversary of Bloomberg News. For more on the genesis of Bloomberg News, see Michael R. Bloomberg, *Bloomberg by Bloomberg* (New York: John Wiley & Sons, 1997).

48　**Bloomberg . . . was asked if he was okay with the lawsuit:** Peter Grauer, the Bloomberg LP chairman, asked the company's majority owner for permission to proceed with the lawsuit. The mayor gave it.

48　**one of subpoena envy:** Would you rather (1) be able to fly, (2) possess super strength, or (3) have subpoena power?

49　**broomstick of the Wicked Witch of the West:** Dorothy's quest in Victor Fleming's *The Wizard of Oz*, a film about the gold standard.

49　**Bloomberg LP filed suit:** "to compel the Fed to discharge its obligations under FOIA, so that the public can be informed of how the Fed is safeguarding its money." See *Bloomberg L.P. v. Board of Governors of the Federal Reserve System: Filing: 1*, Case number 1:2008cv09595, Justia.com, http://docs.justia.com/cases/federal /district-courts/new-york/nysdce/1:2008cv09595/335178/1.

50　**stepped on the fingers of the economy:** Hat tip to characters played by Cary Grant and Martin Landau in Alfred Hitchcock's *North by Northwest*.

50　**This is how the FOIA often works:** It is, in fact, how it did work. Though I set up this anecdote as a hypothetical, all the facts are accurate.

51　**Brad Pitt in the movie *Se7en*:** "SE7EN Scene—The Box,'" You Tube, www.youtube.com/watch?v=1giVzxyoclE. Hat tip to Scott Raab.

52 **Joseph Heller's World War II novel *Catch-22*:** For fans of irony, just about the best thing ever. Not the best book. The best *thing* ever.

52 **Federal Reserve processed 857 FOIA requests:** I cite 2010 statistics because that was the year I received 1,000 double-sided pages of redactions from the central bank. See the Fed's annual FOIA reports on the Federal Reserve website at www.federalreserve.gov/foia/annualreports.htm.

53 **Called the Valukas report:** The report by Anton R. Valukas, chairman of the Chicago-based law firm Jenner & Block. A more meticulous account of an investment bank in its death throes has yet to be written. Finance geeks rejoice: "Lehman Brothers Holdings Inc. Chapter 11 Proceedings Examiner Report," Jenner & Block, http://jenner.com/lehman.

53 **Obama promised a new era of transparency:** View the memo at "Freedom of Information Act," White House, www.whitehouse.gov/the_press_office/FreedomofInformationAct.

53 **an exhaustive study of Obama's executive branch:** Jim Snyder and Danielle Ivory, "Obama Fails to Deliver Transparency as Cabinet Defies Requests," Bloomberg News, December 18, 2012, www.bloomberg.com/news/2012–12–18/obama-fails-to-deliver-transparency-as-cabinet-defies-requests.html. It may not need to be said that Danielle Ivory is no relation to me. It does need to be said that I would be proud if she were.

54 **Cabinet agencies used exemptions:** Snyder and Ivory, "Obama Fails to Deliver Transparency."

54 **Preska . . . ruled that looking foolish:** "Bloomberg L.P. v. Board of Governors of the Federal Reserve System: Filing: 31," Case number 1:2008cv09595, Justia.com, http://docs.justia.com/cases/federal/district-courts/new-york/nysdce/1:2008cv09595/335178/31.

54 **Three weeks later, the Clearing House Association:** Visit the Clearing House Association website at www.theclearinghouse.org.

55 **a free market acolyte of Ayn Rand:** Paul named his son after her. The boy grew up to become a US senator from Kentucky.

56 **Grayson had roasted her:** I had no idea the Fed had an inspector general until I saw this video. Grayson slaughters her: "Alan

Grayson: Is Anyone Minding the Store at the Federal Reserve?" YouTube, www.youtube.com/watch?v=PXlxBeAvsB8.

56   **Republican Scott Garrett:** Full disclosure: Garrett was my congressman. He marched in a parade in my hometown in 2010. When he saw me standing on the curb, he waved at me and said, "Hi Bob!" My neighbors were impressed. Their dogs quit pooping on my lawn for a whole week.

56   **appeals court upheld:** David Glovin and Bob Van Voris, "Fed Loses Bid for Review of Disclosure Ruling on U.S. Bank Bailout Records," Bloomberg News, March 19, 2010, www.bloomberg.com /news/2010–03–19/fed-loses-bid-for-review-of-disclosure-ruling-on -u-s-bank-bailout-records.html.

56   **asked the full court of appeals to reconsider . . . Preska's ruling would stand:** Bob Ivry, "Fed Loses Bid for Review of Bailout Disclosure Ruling," Bloomberg News, August 23, 2010, www .bloomberg.com/news/2010–08–23/u-s-appeals-court-refuses-to -review-disclosure-ruling-on-fed-bailouts.html.

57   **The Fed decided not to appeal:** Bob Ivry and Greg Stohr, "Fed Won't Join Supreme Court Appeal on Loan Disclosures," Bloomberg News, October 26, 2010, www.bloomberg.com/news/2010–10–26 /fed-won-t-join-banks-appeal-to-high-court-over-emergency-loan -disclosures.html.

57   **justices should force the Fed to release the lending data:** Greg Stohr and Bob Ivry, "Obama Lawyers Say Ruling on Fed Loan Disclosure Should Stand," Bloomberg News, February 19, 2011, www.bloomberg.com/news/2011–02–18/obama-lawyers-urge -court-to-reject-banks-on-loans.html.

57   **central bank disclosed recipients and loan amounts:** Craig Torres and Scott Lanman, "Fed Names Recipients of $3.3 Trillion in Crisis Aid," Bloomberg News, December 1, 2010, www .bloomberg.com/news/2010–12–01/fed-names-recipients-of-3–3 -trillion-of-aid-during-u-s-financial-crisis.html.

57   **a lot of European banks got a lot of money:** Bradley Keoun and Hugh Son, "Federal Reserve May Be 'Central Bank of the World' After UBS, Barclays Aid," Bloomberg News, December 2, 2010,

www.bloomberg.com/news/2010–12–02/federal-reserve-may-be
-central-bank-of-the-world-after-ubs-barclays-aid.html.

57   **firms such as Fidelity Investments and BlackRock:** Bob
Ivry, Christine Richard, and Christopher Condon, "Fed Loans
Hatched in Bathroom Halted Money-Market Run," Bloomberg
News, December 3, 2010, www.bloomberg.com/news/2010–12–03
/fed-created-conflicts-in-improvising-3–3-trillion-financial-system
-rescue.html.

57   **Fed was accepting mystery collateral:** Caroline Salas and Matthew Leising, "Fed Withholds Collateral Data for $885 Billion in
Financial-Crisis Loans," Bloomberg News, December 2, 2010,
www.bloomberg.com/news/2010–12–01/taxpayer-risk-impossible
-to-know-for-some-fed-financial-crisis-programs.html.

57   **legislation that was pretty simple:** Interviews with Sherrod
Brown, Ted Kaufman, and Jeff Connaughton, Kaufman's chief
of staff and author of the excellent *The Payoff: Why Wall Street
Always Wins* (Prospecta Press, 2012). Also, Suskind, *Confidence
Men*.

58   **former FDIC chairman Sheila Bair pointed out:** Bair, *Bull by
the Horns*.

59   **guys at the Treasury Department:** Bob Ivry, Bradley Keoun,
and Phil Kuntz, "Secret Fed Loans Gave Banks $13 Billion Undis-
closed to Congress," Bloomberg News, November 27, 2011, www
.bloomberg.com/news/2011–11–28/secret-fed-loans-undisclosed
-to-congress-gave-banks-13-billion-in-income.html.

59   **forcing the Federal Reserve to release details:** Greg Stohr and
Bob Ivry, "Fed Will Release Bank Loan Data as Top Court Rejects
Appeal," Bloomberg News, March 21, 2011, www.bloomberg.com
/news/2011–03–21/fed-must-release-bank-loan-data-as-high-court
-rejects-appeal.html.

59   **Ten days later, the avalanche came:** Bob Ivry and Craig Torres,
"Fed's Court-Ordered Transparency Shows Americans 'Have a Right
to Know,'" Bloomberg News, March 22, 2011, www.bloomberg.com
/news/2011–03–22/fed-s-court-ordered-transparency-shows
-americans-have-a-right-to-know-.html.

59   **had loaned money to the Bank of China:** Jody Shenn, "Bank of

China New York Branch Was Second-Largest Fed Borrower in Aug. 2007," Bloomberg News, March 31, 2011, www.bloomberg.com /news/2011–03–31/bank-of-china-s-new-york-unit-deutsche-bank -led-august-2007-fed-borrowers.html.

59   **a bank partly owned by Muammar Ghadafi's Libyan government:** Donal Griffin and Bob Ivry, "Libya-Owned Arab Banking Corp. Drew at Least $5 Billion from Fed in Crisis," Bloomberg News, April 1, 2011, www.bloomberg.com/news/2011–03–31 /libya-owned-arab-banking-corp-drew-at-least-5-billion-from -fed-in-crisis.html.

59   **Japanese fishing collective called Norinchukin Bank:** Bradley Keoun and Craig Torres, "Foreign Banks Tapped Fed's Secret Lifeline Most at Crisis Peak," Bloomberg News, April 1, 2011, www.bloomberg.com/news/2011–04–01/foreign-banks-tapped -fed-s-lifeline-most-as-bernanke-kept-borrowers-secret.html.

60   **a whopping $1.2 trillion in loans:** Yanofsky, "The Fed's Secret Liquidity Lifelines."

60   **the firm's chief executive officer, John Mack:** "Morgan Stanley Granted Federal Bank Holding Company Status by U.S. Federal Reserve Board of Governors," press release, Morgan Stanley, www .morganstanley.com/about/press/articles/6933.html.

60   **Vikram Pandit, Citigroup's chief, said on January 16, 2009:** Transcript of fourth-quarter 2008 earnings conference call, available on the *Wall Street Journal* website at http://online.wsj.com /public/resources/documents/CitiTranscript011609.pdf.

61   **Bank of America's top man, Kenneth Lewis:** Letter to shareholders.

61   **Wells Fargo's chief, John Stumpf:** Conference call with analysts to discuss fourth-quarter 2008 results.

61   **Chief Executive Officer Jamie Dimon was bragging:** "JP Morgan Chase to Reduce Quarterly Dividend to $0.05 per Share—Retaining $5 Billion in Additional Capital per Year," JP-Morgan Chase, February 23, 2009, http://investor.shareholder .com/jpmorganchase/releasedetail.cfm?releaseid=367145.

61   **Lloyd Blankfein's comments about Goldman Sachs's:** Fourth-quarter 2008 results: "Goldman Sachs Reports: Earnings per Common

Share of $4.47 for 2008," Goldman Sachs, www.goldmansachs
.com/media-relations/press-releases/archived/2008/pdfs/2008-q4
-earnings.pdf.

63 **"We put out a press release":** The Fed's March 7, 2008, press
release, available on the Federal Reserve website at www.federal
reserve.gov/newsevents/press/monetary/20080307a.htm.

64 **"I wasn't aware of this program until now":** Bob Ivry, "Fed
Gave Banks Crisis Gains on $80 Billion Secretive Loans as Low
as 0.01%," Bloomberg News, May 26, 2011, www.bloomberg.com
/news/2011–05–26/fed-gave-banks-crisis-gains-on-secretive-loans
-as-low-as-0–01-.html.

64 **We had stumbled on an emergency lending program:** Bob
Ivry and Bradley Keoun, "Goldman Sachs Took Biggest Loan from
Undisclosed 2008 Fed Crisis Program," Bloomberg News, July 6,
2011, www.bloomberg.com/news/2011–07–06/goldman-took-biggest
-loan-in-fed-program.html.

66 **and so did I:** Zero Hedge published my eulogy for Pittman (www
.zerohedge.com/article/bob-ivrys-eulogy-mark-pittman). It includes
Maggie Pittman's note concerning the death of her father..

CHAPTER THREE: ENVY

69 **We came up with $7.77 trillion:** Mark Pittman and Bob Ivry,
"Financial Rescue Nears GDP as Pledges Top $12.8 Trillion,"
Bloomberg News, March 31, 2009, www.bloomberg.com/apps/news
?pid=newsarchive&sid=armOzfkwtCA4.

69 **take the punch bowl away:** In what became known as the "punch
bowl speech," October 19, 1955, Martin credits the expression to
"as one writer put it." So its origin remains mysterious. See "Address
of Wm. McC. Martin, Jr., Chairman, Board of Governors of the
Federal Reserve System Before the New York Group of the Investment Bankers Association of America," Fraser, October 19, 1955,
http://fraser.stlouisfed.org/docs/historical/martin/martin55_1019
.pdf.

70 **Starting in December 2008:** We call it ZIRP, but more accu-
rately, it's CTZIRP—close-to-zero interest rate policy. It's actually
a range of zero to 0.25 percent. See the Fed's December 16, 2008,

press release on the Federal Reserve website at www.federalreserve
.gov/newsevents/press/monetary/20081216b.htm.

70 **As for QE:** Bob Ivry, "No Lehman Moments as Biggest Banks
Deemed Too Big to Fail," Bloomberg News, May 10, 2013, www
.bloomberg.com/news/2013–05–10/no-lehman-moments-as-biggest
-banks-deemed-too-big-to-fail.html.

70 **to the tune of $85 billion a month:** Joshua Zumbrun and Jeff
Kearns, "Fed Maintains $85 Billion Pace of Purchases as Growth
Pauses," Bloomberg News, January 30, 2013, www.bloomberg.com
/news/2013–01–30/fed-maintains-85-billion-pace-of-purchases-as
-growth-pauses.html.

70 **They call it the velocity of money:** The Federal Reserve Bank
of St. Louis defines it as "the number of times one dollar is spent
to buy goods and services per unit of time." Researchers at the
bank track it, and the graph line goes, unskiably, straight down the
mountain during the recession of 2007 to 2009 and then stays at
the chalet on the bottom. See for yourself here: "Velocity of M2
Money Stock (M2V)," FRED Economic Data, September 26,
2013, http://research.stlouisfed.org/fred2/series/M2V.

71 **US economy was recovering:** Fry and Taylor, "An Uneven Recovery, 2009–2011."

71 **longest post–World War II recession:** The National Bureau of
Economic Research compiles recession statistics. It says the 2007–
2009 recession, at eighteen months, beat 1973 to 1975 and 1981
to 1982, which were each sixteen months long. The Great Depression was forty-three months long, followed by one month of growth,
then another thirteen months of contraction. Ouch. But nothing in
American history compares to 1873 to 1879, with sixty-five straight
months of economic contraction. See "US Business Cycle Expan-
sions and Contractions," National Bureau of Economic Research,
www.nber.org/cycles.html.

72 **The Fed did all it could:** Some critics say the Federal Reserve
ought to have sat on its hands and let the free market determine
winners and losers. I prefer to shy away from judgments about the
wisdom of the Fed's policies and concentrate on their effects. But
I will say this: the bailouts of 2008 and 2009 had already tossed

dirt on the corpse of free market capitalism. Postcrisis, we were in untrammeled territory.

72   **0.25 percent interest:** The Federal Reserve's press release is clear as mud: "Interest on Required Balances and Excess Balances," Board of Governors of the Federal Reserve System, www.federalreserve .gov/monetarypolicy/reqresbalances.htm.

72   **Citigroup had $107.2 billion:** The amount banks hold in reserve at the Federal Reserve is tallied on the FDIC website at www2.fdic.gov/IDASP/main.asp. Thanks to Dakin Campbell of Bloomberg News for his guidance.

72   **Here is where (some of) the money went:** All commodity 72 from data compiled by Bloomberg. Thanks to Millie Munshi for help in navigating the terminal.

72   **Billy Dunavant:** Interviewed at his Memphis home in June 2012. His favorite expression was "Is a lady pig made of pork?" He said it every time I asked a dumb question, which was, according to my transcript of the conversation, only two or three times a minute.

73   **"Helicopter Ben" Bernanke:** The Federal Reserve chairman got stuck with this nickname when he advocated the injection of cash into the financial system to combat falling prices indicative of a depression. Economist Milton Friedman coined the phrase "helicopter drop" of money in this context. I would surmise that a crop-dusting airplane would do the trick too, but "Crop-Dusting Airplane Ben" is not a catchy nickname.

73   **7 million (foreclosures):** Gopal and Benson, "American Dream Erased."

73   **ZIRP was terrific for home owners:** The interest rate for a thirty-year fixed-rate home loan fell to 3.31 percent, its lowest ever, in November 2012, according to government-controlled mortgage buyer Freddie Mac.

73   **12 million at the 2011 peak:** Not the most exact of calculations. Estimates from real estate data collectors CoreLogic, RealtyTrac, and Zillow have varied, positing that from one-quarter to one-third of home owners owe more on their mortgages than their homes are worth. See Jordan Weissmann, "Millennial Homeowners Are Especially

Screwed," *Atlantic Cities*, August 27, 2012, www.theatlanticcities.com /housing/2012/08/why-millenial-homeowners-are-underwater/3086.

73 **ZIRP was horrific for savers:** Bob Ivry, "Fed's $4 Trillion Rescue Helps Hedge Fund as Savers Hurt," Bloomberg News, December 20, 2012, www.bloomberg.com/news/2012–12–20/fed-s-4-trillion -rescue-helps-hedge-fund-as-savers-hurt.html.

73 **offered to pay 0.01 percent:** For Chase rates, see "Rates and Fees Insert," Chase.com, Tuesday, August 6, 2013, https://chaseonline .chase.com/resources/RateSheetForCons8021862013.pdf.

74 **George Sanchez:** I spoke to Sanchez in December 2012. Thanks to Sharon L. Lynch for her help.

74 **Not exactly couch-cushion money:** Ivry, "No Lehman Moment."

75 **he remade the US economy:** I may be guilty of underplaying the story here. The Federal Reserve might have remade much of the world's economy into its wholly owned subsidiary. Certainly, one could make such a case.

75 **Think of derivatives as side bets:** The Bloomberg News definition: "Derivatives are contracts whose value is derived from stocks, bonds, loans, currencies and commodities, or linked to specific events such as changes in interest rates or the weather."

76 **a little bird whispers in your ear:** Don't try this at home. Trading on nonpublic information is usually a crime.

77 **Wall Street devised a way:** Pittman, "Subprime Securities Market Began as 'Group of 5' over Chinese."

77 **"I'm Short Your House" T-shirts:** Gretchen Morgenson and Louise Story, "Banks Bundled Bad Debt, Bet Against It and Won," *New York Times*, December 23, 2009, www.nytimes.com/2009/12/24 /business/24trading.html?pagewanted=1&_r=1&hp&adxnnl =1&adxnnlx=1261674018-IGEeZCBp4Snd6EUUuhHdEA. Pittman had this tidbit in November 2007 but agreed not to publish it in exchange for a reclusive trader agreeing to talk to him on the record.

77 **lip of a very deep money pit:** Hugh Son and Erik Holm, "Fed Takes Control of AIG with $85 Billion Bailout," Bloomberg News, September 17, 2008, www.bloomberg.com/apps/news?pid=newsarchive &sid=aBPOapW_kJkM.

78 **One estimate pegged the number of transactions at
    930,000:** Michael Greenberger's testimony to the Financial Cri-
    sis Inquiry Commission, "The Role of Derivatives in the Financial
    Crisis," Stanford Law School, June 30, 2010, http://fcic-static.law
    .stanford.edu/cdn_media/fcic-testimony/2010–0630-Greenberger
    .pdf. Greenberger was a law professor at the University of Mary-
    land and former director of the Division of Trading and Markets at
    the Commodity Futures Trading Commission.

79 **Bruno Michel Iksil had $1 billion:** The report by the Senate
    Permanent Subcommittee on Investigations (PSI) can be down-
    loaded here: "Opening Statement at PSI Hearing on JPMorgan
    Chase Whale Trades: A Case History of Derivatives Risks and
    Abuses," Carl Levin, US Senator Michigan, March 15, 2013, www
    .levin.senate.gov/newsroom/speeches/speech/opening-statement
    -at-psi-hearing-on-jpmorgan-chase-whale-trades-a-case-history-of
    -derivatives-risks-and-abuses.

79 **would pay off only in the event:** PSI report, p. 53.

79 **who made $6.76 million in 2011:** PSI report, p. 58.

79 **which managed $350 billion:** PSI report, p. 21. The $350 billion
    would have made the Chief Investment Office the seventh-largest
    bank in the world.

79 **the FDIC insured these excess deposits:** Representative Sean
    Duffy, a Wisconsin Republican, questioned Dimon. Here's a snip-
    pet from the transcript:

> REP. DUFFY: The 2 to 5 billion-dollar loss that you
> incurred, the dollars that were used to make those trades,
> those were dollars that were backed up by the FDIC?
> MR. DIMON: Yes.

> See also PSI report, p. 21.

79 **made $400 million:** PSI report, p. 54.

80 **"trades that make sense"** . . . **"Go long risk on some belly
    tranches"** . . . **"buying low and selling high":** PSI report, p. 74.

80 **was fresh in the minds:** PSI report, p. 55.

80 **swelled the Synthetic Credit Portfolio:** PSI report, p. 35.

80 **Iksil had an $81 billion "investment":** Dawn Kopecki and Michael J. Moore, "Whale of a Trade Shown at Biggest U.S. Bank with Best Control," Bloomberg News, June 4, 2013, www.bloomberg .com/news/2013–06–03/whale-of-a-trade-revealed-at-biggest-u-s -bank-with-best-control.html.

81 **Iksil's name hit the news:** Stephanie Ruhle, Bradley Keoun, and Mary Childs, "JPMorgan Trader's Positions Said to Distort Credit Indexes," Bloomberg News, April 6, 2012, www.bloomberg.com/news /2012–04–05/jpmorgan-trader-iksil-s-heft-is-said-to-distort-credit -indexes.html.

81 **heard about Iksil's trades for the first time:** PSI report, p. 217. The OCC said it questioned JPMorgan Chase about the whale trades and received "such limited data about the trades and such blanket reassurances from the bank about them that, by the end of April, the OCC considered the matter closed."

81 **sixty-five examiners:** PSI report, p. 218.

81 **obscure provision:** Saule T. Omarova, "From Gramm-Leach-Bliley to Dodd-Frank: The Unfulfilled Promise of Section 23A of the Federal Reserve Act," May 2011, Social Science Research Network, http://papers.ssrn.com/sol3/papers.cfm?abstract_id=1828445. For more on Omarova, a law professor at the University of North Carolina, Chapel Hill, see Chapter 5.

82 **Scott Alvarez:** "Testimony: Scott G. Alvarez, General Counsel: Sovereign Wealth Funds," Board of Governors of the Federal Reserve System, March 5, 2008, www.federalreserve.gov/newsevents /testimony/alvarez20080305a.htm.

82 **Fed issued exemption after exemption:** Exemption letters can be found on the Federal Reserve website at www.federalreserve .gov/boarddocs/legalint/FederalReserveAct/2008.

83 **got an earful from the FDIC:** Bob Ivry, Hugh Son, and Christine Harper, "BofA Said to Split Regulators over Moving Merrill Derivatives to Bank Unit," Bloomberg News, October 18, 2011, www .bloomberg.com/news/2011–10–18/bofa-said-to-split-regulators -over-moving-merrill-derivatives-to-bank-unit.html.

83 **derivatives on the books:** "OCC's Quarterly Report on Bank

Trading and Derivatives Activities, Fourth Quarter 2012," Office of the Comptroller of the Currency, www.occ.gov/topics/capital -markets/financial-markets/trading/derivatives/dq412.pdf.

84   **notional amount of derivatives:** "OCC's Quarterly Report."

85   **redo the figures:** PSI report, p. 6.

85   **a "complete tempest in a teapot":** Transcript of JPMorgan Chase conference call to discuss quarterly earnings with analysts.

86   **trades were "fully transparent":** Transcript of the JPMorgan Chase conference call.

86   **330 times:** PSI report, p. 7.

86   **hedge the risk of other trades:** Transcript of the JPMorgan Chase conference call.

86   **Dimon acknowledged later that that wasn't true:** Dimon told the House Financial Services Committee on June 19, 2012, "I think what it morphed into, I cannot defend. It violated common sense."

86   **bank executives couldn't come up with specific trades:** PSI report, p. 4.

86   **zero interest rate policy:** PSI report, p. 29.

86   **Dimon's rise . . . The Last Man Standing:** McDonald, *Last Man Standing.*

87   **America's Least-Hated Banker:** Roger Lowenstein, "Jamie Dimon: America's Least-Hated Banker," *New York Times Magazine*, December 1, 2010, www.nytimes.com/2010/12/05/magazine/05Dimon -t.html?pagewanted=all&_r=0.

87   **Wall Street's Indispensable Man:** Nick Summers and Max Abelson, "Why JPMorgan's Jamie Dimon Is Wall Street's Indispensable Man," *Bloomberg Businessweek*, May 16, 2013, http:// mobile.businessweek.com/articles/2013–05–16/why-jpmorgans -jamie-dimon-is-wall-streets-indispensable-man.

87   **cadging Dimon for advice:** According to the transcript of the Senate hearing, this is what Crapo asked Dimon: "And again, what should the function of the regulators be? Many people say our primary focus from our perspective in terms of policy is— should be—to make sure that the banks are properly capitalized. Should that be our primary focus? And what other areas of oversight would be the most effective for us in terms of our regulatory structure?"

87 **senator's top campaign contributors:** I am forever in debt to OpenSecrets.org, run by the Center for Responsive Politics, which collects and arranges contribution data in so many interesting ways. See Crapo's intake here: www.opensecrets.org/politicians/summary .php?cid=N00006267&cycle=2012.

87 **$17,900 that Colorado Democrat Michael F. Bennet received:** "Top 100 Contributors: Senator Michael F. Bennet 2009–2014," Open Secrets, www.opensecrets.org/politicians/contrib.php ?cid=N00030608&cycle=2014&type=I&newMem=N&recs=100.

88 **JPMorgan Chase Foundation's $500,000 donation:** "Chase to Donate $500,000 to Help Change Denver's Lincoln La Alma Neighborhood," press release, JPMorgan Chase, November 24, 2008, http://investor.shareholder.com/jpmorganchase/releasedetail .cfm?releaseid=350379.

88 **helped the Denver schools scratch together:** Jeremy P. Meyer, "Denver, St. Vrain Schools Raise Private Funds Needed to Receive $28.8 Million in Federal Grants," *Denver Post*, September 8, 2010, www.denverpost.com/news/ci_16016489.

88 **gave $1.3 million to Colorado nonprofit do-gooders:** "JP-Morgan Chase Donates $1.3M to Colo. Nonprofits," *Denver Business Journal*, January 21, 2011, www.bizjournals.com/denver/print -edition/2011/01/21/jpmorgan-chase-donates-13m.html.

88 **managing director for the investment company:** Bennet's Senate bio: "About Michael," Michael F. Bennet, United States Senator for Colorado, www.bennet.senate.gov/about.

88 **invited him to pontificate on the state of Europe:** According to the transcript of the Senate hearing, Bennet said, "Since you're here, and again, Mr. Chairman, with your indulgence; this is unrelated to the topic at hand. But I think you're well aware of my concern about the fiscal condition of this country. And I wonder if you could take the last couple minutes of this time to talk about how you see our relative position vis-à-vis Europe and other places."

88 **received nothing substantial in campaign funds:** See the Open Secrets website at www.opensecrets.org/usearch/index.php?q =johanns&searchButt_clean.x=-1079&searchButt_clean.y=-57 &searchButt_clean=Submit&cx=010677907462955562473%3 Anlldkv0jvam&cof=FORID%3A11.

88 **Johanns complained to Dimon:** Johanns, from the Senate hearing transcript: "Mr. Dimon, it further occurs to me that a—an enterprise as big and as powerful as yours, you've got a lot of firepower and you're—you're just huge. We'll find a way to navigate what has happened here. What I worry about, though, you're not located in my state and I doubt that you're probably considering locating in my state, although it'd be a great place for you to do business."

88 **twenty-two members of the Senate Banking Committee:** "Member Money: Senate Banking, Housing, and Urban Affairs Committee," Open Secrets, www.opensecrets.org/cmteprofiles /profiles.php?cycle=2012&cmteid=S06&cmte=SBAN&congno =112&chamber=S&indus=F07. Note that Sherrod Brown, the senator who sponsored legislation to break up the biggest banks, received less than a quarter what Michael Bennet did.

88 **sixty souls of the House Financial Services Committee got:** "Member Money: House Financial Services Committee," Open Secrets, www.opensecrets.org/cmteprofiles/profiles.php?cycle=2012 &cmteid=H05&cmte=HFIN&congno=112&chamber=H& indus=F06.

89 **Bachus . . . $13,000 in campaign funds from JPMorgan Chase:** "Top 20 Contributors: Representative Spencer Bachus 2011–2012," Open Secrets, www.opensecrets.org/politicians/contrib .php?cycle=2012&cid=N00008091&type=I&newmem=N.

89 **"The dirty secret of American politics":** Stoller was writing on the Naked Capitalism blog: "Bill Clinton's $80 Million Payday, or Why Politicians Don't Care That Much About Reelection," May 22, 2012, www.nakedcapitalism.com/2012/05/its-not-about-reelection -bill-clintons-80-million-payday.html.

89 **one of his first acts as ex-president:** Open Secrets, http://pfds .opensecrets.org/N00000019_2001.pdf.

90 **former New York Fed president and Treasury Secretary Tim-**

othy Geithner: Henny Sender, "Geithner Joins Top Table of Public Speakers with Lucrative Appearances," *Financial Times*, July 7, 2013, www.ft.com/intl/cms/s/0/3dd59602-e42c-11e2–91a3–00144 feabdc0.html#axzz2YU3oPlCb.

90   **"cultural capture":** James Kwak, "Cultural Capture and the Financial Crisis," in *Preventing Regulatory Capture: Special Interest Influence and How to Limit It*, ed. Daniel Carpenter and David Moss (Cambridge: Cambridge University Press, 2013), www .tobinproject.org/sites/tobinproject.org/files/assets/Kwak 20Cultural%20Capture%20%281.16.13%29.pdf.

91   **"That's why I'm richer than you":** Media coverage of this exchange disappointed me because it was mostly pro-Dimon and usually included the observation that Mayo was an unpopular bank analyst. In the video clip from Bloomberg TV, commentator Adam Johnson at least puts Mayo's supposed lack of popularity into context—if Mayo was indeed unpopular, it was because he told the truth and refused to kowtow to bank brass. This is exactly the type of analyst investors should listen to, imho. See "Jamie Dimon to Analyst: 'That's Why I'm Richer Than You,'" YouTube, www.youtube .com/watch?feature=player_embedded&v=8G871csJS6Q#at=11.

91   **"badly vetted, badly implemented, badly tested":** From a transcript of the hearing.

91   **one-third of the value of their JPMorgan Chase stock melted away:** On April 6, 2012, JPMorgan Chase stock was $44.34 a share; on June 4 it hit a low of $31, a 31 percent drop. Then it rebounded.

91   **JPMorgan Chase fired Iksil:** Dan Fitzpatrick, "J.P. Morgan: 'Whale' Clawbacks About Two Years of Compensation," *Wall Street Journal*, July 13, 2012, http://online.wsj.com/article/SB10 001424052702303740704577524730994899406.html.

91   **The bank also jettisoned three of Iksil's bosses:** Dawn Kopecki, "JPMorgan's Drew Forfeits 2 Years' Pay as Managers Ousted," Bloomberg News, July 13, 2012, www.businessweek .com/news/2012–07–13/dimon-says-ina-drew-offered-to-return-2 -years-of-compensation.

91   **docked Dimon nearly half his 2012 compensation:** Dawn

Kopecki and Hugh Son, "JPMorgan Whale Report Spreads Blame as Dimon's Pay Halved," Bloomberg News, January 16, 2013, www.bloomberg.com/news/2013–01–16/jpmorgan-halves-dimon-pay-says-ceo-responsible-for-lapses-1-.html.

92 **bid rigging:** "JPMorgan Chase Admits to Anticompetitive Conduct by Former Employees in the Municipal Bond Investments Market and Agrees to Pay $228 Million to Federal and State Agencies," press release, Department of Justice, July 7, 2011, www.justice.gov/opa/pr/2011/July/11-at-890.html.

92 **debiting savings account withdrawals:** Jonathan Stempel, "JPMorgan Settles Overdraft Fee Case for $110 Million," Reuters, February 6, 2012, www.reuters.com/article/2012/02/06/us-jpmorgan-overdraft-settlement-idUSTRE8151F520120206.

92 **violating sanctions against Cuba, Iran, and Sudan:** Kevin Roose, "JPMorgan to Pay $88.3 Million for Sanctions Violations," *New York Times*, August 25, 2011, http://dealbook.nytimes.com/2011/08/25/jpmorgan-to-pay-88–3-million-for-sanctions-violations.

92 **allegedly failing to protect British customer funds:** Kirstin Ridley, "U.K. Fines JPMorgan Record $49 Million," Reuters, June 3, 2010, www.reuters.com/article/2010/06/03/us-britain-fine-jpmorgan-idUSTRE6521J520100603.

92 **allegedly manipulating electricity prices in California and the US Midwest:** Brian Wingfield and Dawn Kopecki, "JPMorgan Agrees to Pay $410 Million to Settle U.S. Energy Probe," July 30, 2013, www.bloomberg.com/news/2013–07–30/jpmorgan-agrees-to-pay-410-million-to-settle-u-s-energy-probe.html.

92 **accusations of bamboozling the city of Milan:** Elisa Martinuzzi, "JPMorgan, UBS Tricked Milan in Swaps Case, Judge Says," Bloomberg News, February 4, 2013, www.bloomberg.com/news/2013–02–04/jpmorgan-deutsche-bank-tricked-milan-in-swaps-case-judge-says.html.

92 **allegedly selling unregistered securities:** Jerry Hart, "JPMorgan Agrees to Pay Florida $25 Million for Bond Sales to Muni Fund," Bloomberg News, December 22, 2010, www.bloomberg.com/news/2010–12–22/florida-reports-25-million-settlement-with-jpmorgan-chase.html.

92   **MF Global:** Halah Touryalai, "JPMorgan's Other Messy Problem: MF Global's Missing Money," *Forbes*, June 4, 2012, www.forbes.com/sites/halahtouryalai/2012/06/04/jpmorgans-other-messy-problem-mf-globals-missing-money.

92   **Peregrine Financial:** Mark Gongloff, "In PFG Scandal, JPMorgan Chase Had Surprising Role: It Held Customer Accounts," Huffington Post, July 12, 2012, www.huffingtonpost.com/2012/07/12/pfg-customer-account-jpmorgan-chase_n_1668386.html.

92   **Bernie Madoff:** Adam Shapiro, "Madoff: JPM Had to Know What I Was Doing," FOXBusiness, May 23, 2013, www.foxbusiness.com/industries/2013/05/23/madoff-jpm-had-to-know-what-was-doing.

92   **Aging titans Warren Buffett:** Dawn Kopecki, "JPMorgan Should Replace Most of Board, Glass Lewis Says," Bloomberg News, May 7, 2013, www.bloomberg.com/news/2013–05–07/jpmorgan-should-split-chairman-and-ceo-roles-glass-lewis-says.html.

92   **Jack Welch, and Rupert Murdoch were dispatched:** Joe Weisenthal, "Rupert Murdoch: JPMorgan Would Be 'Up a Creek' Without Jamie Dimon," Business Insider, May 10, 2013, www.businessinsider.com/rupert-murdoch-jpmorgan-would-be-up-a-creek-without-jamie-dimon-2013–5#ixzz2bIxGqEpP.

92   **Dimon would quit the bank altogether:** Kevin Roose, "Will JPMorgan Investors Fall for Jamie Dimon's Big Bluff?" *New York Magazine*, May 13, 2013, http://nymag.com/daily/intelligencer/2013/05/jamie-dimons-big-bluff.html.

93   **buying 2,600 square feet of office space:** Oshrat Carmiel, "JPMorgan's Dimon Buys NYC Office for $2.05 Million," Bloomberg News, April 8, 2013, www.bloomberg.com/news/2013–04–08/jpmorgan-s-dimon-buys-nyc-office-for-2–05-million.html.

93   **leave the rest of the world in the dark:** Susanne Craig and Jessica Silver-Greenberg, "Shareholders Denied Access to JPMorgan Vote Results," *New York Times*, May 15, 2013, http://dealbook.nytimes.com/2013/05/15/jpmorgan-voters-are-denied-access-to-results.

94   **more than $6.2 billion:** Kopecki and Moore, "Whale of a Trade."

94   **mixed them into its investment bank's portfolio:** PSI report, p. 87.

CHAPTER FOUR: PRIDE

95   **He'd prevailed:** Nick Summers, "Jamie Dimon Wins Big in JP-Morgan Shareholder Vote," *Bloomberg Businessweek*, May 21, 2013, www.businessweek.com/articles/2013–05–21/jamie-dimon-wins -big-in-jpmorgan-shareholder-vote.

95   **"Influencer" blog series:** Video clip of LinkedIn chief: "Dimon Joins LinkedIn Influencer Team," *Bloomberg Businessweek*, June 3, 2013, www.businessweek.com/videos/2013–06–03/dimon-joins -linkedin-influencer-team.

95   **"essential hallmarks of a good leader":** "The Essential Hallmarks of a Good Leader," LinkedIn, June 13, 2013, www.linkedin.com /today/post/article/20130613121131–257626722-the-essential -hallmarks-of-a-good-leader?trk=mp-reader-card.

96   **The common perception:** Michael S. Schmidt, "Urine Samples Said to Link Bonds to Steroids," *New York Times*, January 28, 2009, www.nytimes.com/2009/01/29/sports/baseball/29bonds.html. In his first year of eligibility for the Baseball Hall of Fame, the man with more career home runs than anyone got 36.2 percent of the vote with 75 percent needed for enshrinement. Baseball writers clearly didn't think Bonds was the cream of the crop.

97   **register their enthusiastic opposition:** Antonia Matthews, "Dimon: Impact of Greek Default on US Banks Almost Zero," CNBC.com, January 26, 2012, www.cnbc.com/id/46144727.

97   **Lloyd Blankfein, the Goldman Sachs chief executive officer, told Politico:** See 0:20 of this video clip: "Lloyd Blankfein: No Political Will for Big Bank Bailouts," Politico, June 13, 2013, www .politico.com/multimedia/video/2013/06/lloyd-blankfein-no-political -will-for-big-bank-bailouts.html.

98   **Timothy Sloan, the Wells Fargo chief financial officer, told me:** Interviewed April 3, 2013.

98   **lamb might even get some sleep:** Fans of Woody Allen may recognize him as the source for this. Allen said, "The lion will lay down with the lamb, but the lamb won't get much sleep."

98   **less borrowed money and more equity:** The Financial Stability Board proposed additional "loss absorbency" in the form of cap-

ital, bank by bank. The four banks that the board would require to fund themselves with the most cash were Citigroup, HSBC, Deutsche Bank, and JPMorgan Chase. See "Update of Group of Global Systemically Important Banks (G-SIBs)," Financial Stability Board, November 1, 2012, www.financialstabilityboard.org /publications/r_121031ac.pdf.

98   **Bank of England floated the idea:** Philip Aldrick, "Banks Should Be Broken Up, Bank of England Governor Mervyn King Warns," *Telegraph*, October 25, 2010, www.telegraph.co.uk /finance/newsbysector/banksandfinance/8086279/Banks-should -be-broken-up-Bank-of-England-Governor-Mervyn-King-warns .html. King, the former governor, and Andrew G. Haldane, the Bank of England's executive director for financial stability, were ahead of their American counterparts on this issue.

98   **should a financial giant teeter on the brink:** See Title II of Dodd-Frank on the Cornell University Law School website at www. law.cornell.edu/wex/dodd-frank_title_ii.

98   **complicated financial firms:** Relationship status: it's complicated.

98   **"Because of this reform":** "Remarks by the President on the Passage of Financial Regulatory Reform," White House, July 15, 2012, www.whitehouse.gov/the-press-office/remarks-president-passage -financial-regulatory-reform.

99   **they charged the biggest banks less:** Ivry, "No Lehman Moments."

99   **Deniz Anginer emigrated:** Numerous phone and e-mail interviews with Anginer.

100   **Rest of Country Temporarily Feels Deep Affection for New York:** The Onion, September 26, 2001.

100   **bailout program was a success:** Treasury Secretary Timothy Geithner, February 2, 2012 (Groundhog Day): "[W]e have been able to dramatically reduce the expected costs of the financial rescue to levels that were unthinkable in early 2009. The financial assistance we provided to banks through TARP, for example, will result in taxpayer gains of approximately $20 billion." See "Remarks by Treasury Secretary Tim Geithner on the State of Financial Reform."

101   **already ample evidence:** Moody's downgraded the credit rating of Bank of America in September 2011 due to a decreased probability

of the bank getting a bailout: "Rating Action: Moody's Downgrades Bank of America Corp. to Baa1/P-2; Bank of America N.A. to A2, P-1 Affirmed," Moody's, September 21, 2011, www.moodys.com /research/Moodys-downgrades-Bank-of-America-Corp-to-Baa1P-2 -Bank—PR_226511.

101 **even as the flow of money was freezing:** Elliot Blair Smith and Bob Ivry, "S&P Credibility Seen Eroded by Complicity in Soured Deals," Bloomberg News, March 8, 2013, www.bloomberg.com /news/2013–03–05/s-p-credibility-seen-eroded-by-complicity-in -soured-deals.html.

102 **Anginer and his colleagues collected:** Methodology taken from A. Joseph Warburton, Deniz Anginer, and Viral V. Acharya, "The End of Market Discipline? Investor Expectations of Implicit State Guarantees," Social Science Research Network, January 1, 2013, http://ssrn.com/abstract=1961656.

104 **borrowing advantage of $64 billion per year:** Kenichi Ueda and Beatrice Weder di Mauro, "Quantifying Structural Subsidy Values for Systemically Important Financial Institutions," International Monetary Fund, May 2012, www.imf.org/external/pubs/ft /wp/2012/wp12128.pdf. ("Bailout expectation lowers daily funding costs.")

104 **borrowing advantage of 0.45 percentage points:** David J. Lynch, "Banks Seen Dangerous Defying Obama's Too-Big-to-Fail Move," Bloomberg News, April 16, 2012, www.bloomberg.com /news/2012–04–16/obama-bid-to-end-too-big-to-fail-undercut-as -banks-grow.html. ("In 2011, funding costs for banks with more than $10 billion in assets were about one-third less than for the smallest banks, according to the FDIC. That gap was only slightly narrower than the 37 percent advantage the largest banks enjoyed when Dodd-Frank was signed.")

104 **reduced the advantage to 0.61 percentage points:** Bhanu Balasubramnian and Ken B. Cyree, "Has Market Discipline on Banks Improved After the Dodd-Frank Act?" Social Science Research Network, June 8, 2012, http://papers.ssrn.com/sol3/papers .cfm?abstract_id=2089745. ("Using secondary market subordinated debt transactions we find that the DFA has been effective in reducing, but not in eliminating the too-big-to-fail [TBTF] effect on yield spreads.")

104 **Even JPMorgan Chase weighed in:** Michel Araten and Christopher Turner, "Understanding the Funding Cost Differences Between Global Systemically Important Banks (G-SIBs) and Non-G-SIBs in the United States," Social Science Research Network, March 11, 2012, http://papers.ssrn.com/sol3/papers.cfm?abstract_id=2226939.

105 **When Mark Whitehouse of Bloomberg View:** "Why Should Taxpayers Give Big Banks $83 Billion a Year?" Bloomberg View, February 20, 2013, www.bloomberg.com/news/2013–02–20/why -should-taxpayers-give-big-banks-83-billion-a-year-.html.

105 **at his quarterly press conference:** From the transcript of the press conference.

105 **big banks were a boon:** All a reporter has to do to get an avalanche of helpful pro-big-bank information is tell the right person he's writing an article on implied taxpayer subsidies. Financial Services Roundtable sent fast facts: "Fast Facts: Dodd-Frank Cumulative Weight," Financial Services Roundtable, www.fsround.org/fsr /pdfs/fast-facts/ff-2013–03–15-Dodd-Frank-Cumulative-Weight .pdf. Financial Services Forum sent a statement from its chief executive officer, Rob Nichols:

> Thanks to a wide array of legislative, industry and regulatory reforms—including increased capital requirements and Dodd-Frank—the U.S. financial system is more safe, sound and stable that ever before. The financial services industry strongly believes that no institution should be "too big to fail" and taxpayer dollars should not be available to bail out a failed firm. As policymakers implement financial services reforms or suggest additional measures, it is critical that any new policy optimizes economic growth and job creation—as well as maintaining America's position as the global economic leader.

The Clearing House Association made its chief economist, Bob Chakravorti, available for an interview, in which he said, "Many people believe that anything a big bank does can be done by a smaller bank. We don't believe that. Some of the things can be done, but at a much higher cost." Sounds reasonable, but when I asked him where the savings accrued by big banks went, he couldn't answer.

106 added costs of complying with postcrisis regulations: Bank of America estimated the cost of complying with Dodd-Frank at about $2 billion over the first two years.

107 throwing a new committee at it: Dodd-Frank did away with the Office of Thrift Supervision, which oversaw savings and loans (S&Ls)—or at least was supposed to. The two biggest S&Ls in the United States, Washington Mutual and IndyMac, both bit the dust in the financial crisis. But Dodd-Frank also established the Financial Stability Oversight Council, chaired by the Treasury secretary, which has the power to kill a dying institution. Dodd-Frank also left the details of implementation to the various bureaucracies.

109 offer a different way: "Brown, Vitter Unveil Legislation That Would End 'Too Big to Fail' Policies," Sherrod Brown, Senator for Ohio, April 24, 2013, www.brown.senate.gov/newsroom/press /release/brown-vitter-unveil-legislation-that-would-end-too-big-to -fail-policies. Brown, a progressive Democrat, and Vitter, a conservative Republican, offer a great example of how issues around too big to fail cut across party and ideological boundaries.

109 Bear Stearns was operating: Sanati, "Cayne and Schwartz at Odds."

Chapter Five: Lust

111 The Fed had three conditions: "To minimize the exposure of JPM Chase to additional risks, including storage risks, transportation risk, and legal and environmental risks, JPM Chase would not be authorized (i) to own, operate, or invest in facilities for the extraction, storage or transportation of commodities." See the Fed's November 18, 2005, press release at the Federal Reserve website at www.federalreserve.gov/boarddocs/press/orders/2005/20051118.

112 JPMorgan Chase bought Henry Bath & Son: Andrew MacAskill and Elizabeth Hester, "JPMorgan Pays $1.7 Billion for Units

of RBS Sempra," Bloomberg News, February 16, 2010, www.
bloomberg.com/apps/news?pid=newsarchive&sid=aSDKaUvU_
BaA. Henry Bath & Son was part of JPMorgan Chase's acquisition
of RBS Sempra.

112   **Other regulatory agencies:** I spoke to Stephanie Allen, a Com-
modity Futures Trading Commission spokeswoman, and Bryan
Hubbard, her counterpart at the Office of the Comptroller of the
Currency. Both said they had no knowledge of a waiver.

113   **a dusty section of the 1934 Securities and Exchange Act:**
I refer to Section 13(b)(3)(A).

113   **to conduct secret operations:** John C. Coffee, a Columbia University securities law professor, explained what the law could cover
to *Businessweek* reporter Dawn Kopecki: "What you might hide is
investments: You've spent umpteen million dollars that comes out
of your working capital to build a plant in Iraq," which the government wants to keep secret. "That's the kind of scenario that would
be plausible," Coffee said.

113   **President George W. Bush delegated the authority:** The cita-
tion in the *Federal Register* can be seen at "Part III: The President:
Memorandum of May 5, 2006—Assignment of Function Relating
to Granting of Authority for Issuance of Certain Directives," *Federal
Register* 71, no. 92 (May 12, 2006), available at the Federation of
American Scientists website at www.fas.org/irp/dni/wh050506.pdf.

115   **Morgan Stanley's oil tankers:** Bob Ivry, "Wall Street Commodity Trading in Jeopardy amid Fed Review," Bloomberg News,
July 22, 2013, www.bloomberg.com/news/2013–07–22/wall-street
-commodity-trading-in-jeopardy-amid-fed-review.html.

116   **one subsidiary functioned independently of another:** This is,
in fact, exactly what the banks said.

116   **research highlighted the growing problem:** Dafna Avraham,
Patricia Selvaggi, and James Vickery, "Peeling the Onion: A Struc-
tural View of U.S. Bank Holding Companies," Federal Reserve Bank
of New York, July 20, 2012, http://libertystreeteconomics.newyork
fed.org/2012/07/peeling-the-onion-a-structural-view-of-us-bank
-holding-companies.html. Hat tip to Shahien Nasiripour and Zach
Carter, "Beer Brewers Blast Wall Street Banks over Aluminum

Business amid Congressional Scrutiny," Huffington Post, July 16, 2013, www.huffingtonpost.com/2013/07/16/banks-commodities -business_n_3601631.html?utm_hp_ref=tw.

116 **Goldman Sachs bought Metro International Trade Services:** Pratima Desai et al., "Goldman's New Money Machine: Warehouses," Reuters, July 29, 2011, www.reuters.com/article/2011/07 /29/us-lme-warehousing-idUSTRE76R3YZ20110729.

117 **owned more than two dozen metals warehouses:** London Metal Exchange list of licensed warehouses: "Active Listed Warehouses," London Metal Exchange, September 23, 2013, www.lme .com/~/media/Files/Warehousing/Approved%20warehouses/LME %20listed%20warehouses.pdf.

117 **80 percent of US aluminum inventory:** London Metal Exchange.

117 **prices for industrial metals collapsed:** The price of aluminum on the spot market went from $3,271.25 per metric ton on July 11, 2008, to $1,251.75 on February 23, 2009, according to data compiled by Bloomberg News. That's a 62 percent nosedive in seven months.

117 **a situation traders call "contango":** London Metal Exchange prices for aluminum 3, 15, 27, 63, and 123 months into the future were all higher than the spot price in July 2013.

117 **who would steer the aluminum back:** David Kocieniewski, "A Shuffle of Aluminum, but to Banks, Pure Gold," *New York Times*, July 20, 2013, www.goldmansachs.com/media-relations/in -the-news/current/goldman-sachs-physical-commodities-7–23–13 .html.

118 **Coca-Cola complained:** Dustin Walsh, "Aluminum Bottleneck: Coke's Complaint: 12% of Global Stockpile Held Here, Boosting Prices," *Crain's Detroit*, June 26, 2011, www.crainsdetroit.com /article/20110626/FREE/306269994/aluminum-bottleneck-cokes -complaint-12-of-global-stockpile-held-here-boosting-prices#.

118 **Weiner . . . had a great analogy:** Weiner spoke at a Senate subcommittee hearing on July 23, 2013.

119 **percentage of US beer sold in cans:** Data from the Beer Institute.

119 **in addition to coal mines in Colombia:** Juan Pablo Spinetto,

"Vale Sells Colombian Coal Assets to Goldman for $407 Million," Bloomberg News, May 28, 2012, www.bloomberg.com/news /2012–05–28/vale-sells-colombian-coal-assets-to-goldman-for -407-million-3-.html.

119 **off the coast of Angola:** Christine Harper, "Goldman Sachs Profit Estimate Rises 21% at ISI on Cobalt's Angola Oil Find," Bloomberg News, February 13, 2012, www.bloomberg.com/news/2012–02 –13/goldman-sachs-profit-estimate-rises-21-at-isi-on-cobalt-s -angola-oil-find.html.

119 **Morgan Stanley's involvement included TransMontaigne:** "TransMontaigne Accepts Morgan Stanley Offer," *Denver Business Journal*, June 22, 2006, www.bizjournals.com/denver/stories /2006/06/19/daily64.html.

119 **Heidmar Inc., which managed:** Press release heralding Morgan Stanley's imminent purchase of the Connecticut-based marine logistics company: "The Heidmar Group Has Entered Exclusive Negotiations to Be Acquired by Morgan Stanley," Heidmar, June 22, 2006, www.heidmar.com/uploads/images/img/press-pdf/2006-Jun -22-Heidmar-Group-Enters-into-Exclusive-Negotiations-to-be -Acquired-by-Morgan-Stanley.pdf.

120 **Morgan Stanley went so far as to say:** From the bank's second-quarter 2013 regulatory filing: "If the Federal Reserve were to determine that any of the Company's commodities activities did not qualify for the [Bank Holding Company (BHC)] Act grandfather exemption, then the Company would likely be required to divest any such activities that did not otherwise conform to the BHC Act by the end of any extensions of the grace period. At this time, the Company does not believe, based on its interpretation of applicable law, that any such required divestment would have a material adverse impact on its financial condition."

120 **putting their metal warehouses up for sale:** Jack Farchy and Daniel Schäfer, "US Banks Eye Metal Storage Exit," *Financial Times*, July 14, 2013, www.ft.com/intl/cms/s/0/a32adac0-ec7f-11e2 –8096–00144feabdc0.html.

120 **London Metal Exchange was considering rule changes:** Maria Kolesnikova and Agnieszka Troszkiewicz, "LME Seeks to

Shorten 100-Day Withdrawal Times at Warehouses," Bloomberg News, July 1, 2013, www.bloomberg.com/news/2013–07–01/lme -seeks-to-reduce-lines-at-warehouses-where-wait-is-100-days.html.

121 sent me her academic paper: Omarova, "From Gramm-Leach-Bliley to Dodd-Frank."

124 she would call "Merchants of Wall Street": Saule T. Omarova, "The Merchants of Wall Street: Banking, Commerce, and Commodities," *Minnesota Law Review* 98 (2013), available at Social Science Research Network, http://papers.ssrn.com/sol3/papers .cfm?abstract_id=2180647.

125 Sherrod Brown and David Vitter introduced their legislation: "Brown, Vitter Unveil Legislation."

125 four congressional Democrats wrote Federal Reserve Chairman Ben Bernanke: Cheyenne Hopkins, "Lawmakers Cite Risk of Banks in Commodities in Bernanke Letter," Bloomberg News, July 3, 2013, www.bloomberg.com/news/2013–07–03/lawmakers -cite-risk-of-banks-in-commodities-in-bernanke-letter.html.

125 Omarova struck back: Transcript of the Senate subcommittee hearing.

126 The Federal Reserve did acknowledge: The Fed's November 18, 2005, press release announcing the approval order for JPMorgan Chase can be found on the Federal Reserve website at www.federal reserve.gov/boarddocs/press/orders/2005/20051118.

127 5 percent of their consolidated tier 1 capital: Technically speaking, this is 5 percent of their best easy-to-sell assets. I spoke to people who said the banks could easily fudge this, though there are no known instances of their doing so. Then again, they haven't had to.

127 $125 million in improper payments: Wingfield and Kopecki, "JPMorgan Agrees to Pay $410 Million."

128 Here's how it worked: Michael Hiltzik, "Manipulation of California Energy Market Gives Consumers a Jolt," *Los Angeles Times*, July 18, 2012, http://articles.latimes.com/2012/jul/18/business/la-fi -hiltzik-20120718. Hats off to Hiltzik, who took a complicated trade and explained it so plainly that even I understood it.

128 **JPMorgan Chase disagreed:** Hiltzik, "Manipulation of California Energy Market."

129 **Electricity users, after all, were paying every penny of it:** This is the essence of the matter, isn't it?

129 **a March 2013 internal FERC document:** Jessica Silver-Greenberg and Ben Protess, "JPMorgan Caught in Swirl of Regulatory Woes," *New York Times*, May 2, 2013, http://dealbook.nytimes.com/2013/05/02/jpmorgan-caught-in-swirl-of-regulatory-woes.

130 **invented the credit default swap:** Gillian Tett, *Fool's Gold: The Inside Story of J.P. Morgan and How Wall St. Greed Corrupted Its Bold Dream and Created a Financial Catastrophe* (New York: Free Press, 2009).

130 **legal, transparent, and in full compliance:** Silver-Greenberg and Protess, "JPMorgan Caught in Swirl."

130 **she insisted to colleagues:** Paul M. Barrett, "Blythe Masters, JPMorgan's Credit Derivatives Guru, Is Not Sorry," *Bloomberg Businessweek,* September 12, 2013, www.businessweek.com/articles/2013–09–12/blythe-masters-jpmorgans-credit-derivatives-guru-is-not-sorry.

131 **Deutsche Bank agreed in January 2013 to pay $1.6 million:** Brian Wingfield, "Deutsche Bank Pays $1.6 Million to End U.S. Trading Probe," Bloomberg News, January 22, 2013, www.bloomberg.com/news/2013–01–22/deutsche-bank-pays-1-6-million-to-end-u-s-trading-probe.html.

131 **Barclays was flagged:** Brian Wingfield, "Barclays, Traders Fined $487.9 Million by U.S. Regulator," Bloomberg News, July 16, 2013, www.bloomberg.com/news/2013–07–16/barclays-traders-fined-487-9-million-in-u-s-energy-probe.html.

131 **JPMorgan Chase paid $410 million:** Wingfield and Kopecki, "JPMorgan Agrees to Pay $410 Million."

131 **bank's traders were evading the ban:** Lynn Doan, "JPMorgan May Evade Power-Trading Ban with Swaps, ISO Says," Bloomberg News, May 10, 2013, www.bloomberg.com/news/2013–05–10/jpmorgan-may-be-evading-power-trading-ban-with-swaps-iso-says.html.

Chapter Six: Sloth

133 **Zelma Lacey, a widow:** Interview with Walter Lacey and Marianne Miller-Lacey. Details were confirmed with the court document "In re: Walter W. Lacey, Debtor; Walter W. Lacey, Plaintiff, v. BAC Home Loans Servicing and Others," available on Google Scholar, at http://scholar.google.com/scholar_case?case=13373418248947727307&q=lacey+feeney&hl=en&as_sdt=2,22.

134 **It was bizarre:** Yet the pattern was repeated for years all over the country.

135 **As suicidally as the mortgage industry:** They were, to put it indelicately, shitting their own bed. Neighbors directly affect each other's home values.

135 **any of us could have fallen behind:** A lost job or illness causes most mortgage delinquencies. The role of moral turpitude is exaggerated.

136 ***Lord of the Flies* territory:** William Golding, *Lord of the Flies* (1954). British schoolboys survive a plane crash on a remote, uninhabited island and create their own society without adults. Kind of like *Lost* without "Freckles."

136 **Keystone Cops coming to the "rescue":** Named after the film studio for whom they romped, the Keystone Cops were bumbling law enforcement officers played for laughs in silent movies of the 1910s.

136 **Five Stooges:** One representing each of Wall Street's five families of mortgage servicing.

136 **like Franz Kafka's Gregor Samsa:** Franz Kafka, *The Metamorphosis* (1915). The protagonist wakes up one morning as a cockroach.

138 **About half the mortgage companies:** This was the estimate of David Olson, a former director of market research at Freddie Mac who ran his own mortgage consultant shop and had been in the industry for more than fifty years.

139 **The Laceys received the letter:** Details from the court document "In re: Walter W. Lacey, Debtor" on Google Scholar.

140 **launched HAMP to great fanfare:** The initiative came with video testimonials, supportive blogs, and its own website. Just a month into his first term, Obama presented the outlines of the program in a speech in Mesa, Arizona: "Remarks by the President on the Home Mortgage Crisis," White House, February 18, 2009, www.whitehouse.gov/the-press-office/remarks-president-mortgage -crisis.

140 **1.1 million home owners . . . More than one-third of home owners:** Clea Benson, "Treasury Extends HAMP Mortgage-Modification Program Through 2015," Bloomberg News, May 30, 2013, www.bloomberg.com/news/2013–05–30/treasury-extends -hamp-mortgage-modification-program-through-2015.html.

141 **Rick Santelli . . . went berserker:** I overstate for effect. Santelli didn't run amok, tearing the limbs off people and wrecking Bloomberg terminals. But he was sufficiently emotional to spawn a political movement. See the video at "Rick Santelli Rant CNBC," YouTube, www.youtube.com/watch?v=or-EKjfVCoA&NR=1.

142 **A sizeable slice of the American population:** About one-quarter of Americans identified themselves as Tea Party members in April 2010, just after the passage of Obamacare, according to Rasmussen, a national polling company. That figure declined to 8 percent in January 2013 as the outrage faded. "Just 8% Now Say They Are Tea Party Members," *Rasmussen Reports*, January 7, 2013, www.rasmussenreports.com/public_content/politics /general_politics/january_2013/just_8_now_say_they_are_tea _party_members.

142 **different Massachusetts foreclosure case:** That complaint is available on the website of the National Consumer Law Center at www.nclc.org/images/pdf/litigation/complaint-hamp-johnson-boa .pdf. See also Hugh Son and David McLaughlin, "BofA Gave Bonuses to Foreclose on Clients, Lawsuit Claims," Bloomberg News, June 15, 2013, www.bloomberg.com/news/2013–06–14/bofa-gave -bonuses-to-foreclose-on-clients-lawsuit-claims.html.

143 **Bank of America responded to what it called:** Hugh Son and David McLaughlin, "BofA Says Ex-Workers Made Impossible Loan-Program Claims," Bloomberg News, July 12, 2013,

www.bloomberg.com/news/2013–07–12/bofa-says-ex-workers
-made-impossible-loan-program-claims.html.

145 The guy in California who shot and killed himself: Harry
Bradford, "Norman Rousseau, Foreclosure Victim, Commits Suicide
During Wells Fargo Lawsuit," Huffington Post, May 17, 2012, www
.huffingtonpost.com/2012/05/17/norman-rousseau-foreclosure
-victim-suicide-wells-fargo_n_1521743.html.

145 The family in Chicago left at the curb: Ta-Nehisi Coates,
"Manhood Among the Ruins: Notes on an Eviction," *Atlantic*, July
1, 2013, www.theatlantic.com/national/archive/2013/07/manhood
-among-the-ruins/277456.

145 The grandmother in Florida living in a tent: Paul Kiel, Olga
Pierce, and Cora Currier, *The Great American Foreclosure Story:
The Struggle for Justice and a Place to Call Home* (New York:
ProPublica Kindle Book, 2012), available at www.amazon.com
/Great-American-Foreclosure-Story-ebook/dp/B007RQMV5W.

145 The first was called the National Mortgage Settlement: For an
executive summary, see Philip A. Lehman, "Executive Summary of
Multistate/Federal Settlement of Foreclosure Misconduct Claims,"
National Mortgage Settlement, July 23, 2012, https://d9klfgibkcquc
.cloudfront.net/NMS_Executive_Summary-7–23–2012.pdf.

145 those deficiencies filled eleven pages: For the Bank of America consent judgment, see https://d9klfgibkcquc.cloudfront.net
/Consent_Judgment_BoA-4–11–12.pdf.

146 SPOC—a single point of contact: The settlement monitor
believed the SPOC was essential too. From the frequently-asked-
questions section of the National Mortgage Settlement website:

> The banks have agreed to major reforms in how they
> service mortgage loans. These new servicing standards re-
> quire lenders and servicers to adhere to a long list of rights
> for those facing foreclosure. For example, borrowers will
> have the right to see all of their loan documents to make
> sure any potential foreclosure is legal; they will be given
> every opportunity to first modify their loan before facing
> foreclosure; lenders and servicers will be required to have

an appropriate number of well-trained staff members to promptly respond to the needs of distressed borrowers; and finally, borrowers will have the right to deal with a reliable, single point of contact so they have access to a person from whom to obtain information throughout the process. This is very important because, throughout the foreclosure crisis, borrowers have lodged widespread complaints about their frustrations in trying to work with their lenders. They've complained about unresponsive employees, lost documents, and conflicting information. ("Joint State-Federal Mortgage Servicing Settlement FAQ," National Mortgage Settlement, www.nationalmortgagesettlement.com/faq.)

146 faulted the servicers for what they called severe deficiencies: "Foreclosure Review: Opportunities Exist to Further Enhance Borrower Outreach Efforts," US Government Accountability Office, June 2012, www.gao.gov/assets/600/592059.pdf. The optimistic title belies a savaging of the process.

147 Fed and the OCC issued consent orders: Bank of America consent judgment.

147 sift through the 4.3 million cases: "Foreclosure Review: Opportunities Exist."

147 The fourteen servicers hired . . . send the 4.3 million former home owners postcards: "Foreclosure Review: Opportunities Exist."

147 The mailings got a disappointing response: "Foreclosure Review: Opportunities Exist."

148 simply tossed solicitations into the trash: Hugh Son, "BofA Give-Away Has Few Takers Among Homeowners: Mortgages," Bloomberg News, July 11, 2012, www.bloomberg.com/news/2012 –07–11/bofa-give-away-has-few-takers-among-homeowners -mortgages.html. Hugh wrote the article in a somewhat different context—Bank of America was trying to comply with National Mortgage Settlement directives—but the "borrower fatigue" cited by a Bank of America spokesman in Hugh's story is the same issue at work.

148 **they didn't have a lot of time:** "Foreclosure Review: Opportunities Exist."

148 **less-than-20-percent response:** "Foreclosure Review: Lessons Learned Could Enhance Continuing Reviews and Activities Under Amended Consent Orders," US Government Accountability Office, July 13, 2013, http://gao.gov/assets/660/653851.pdf.

149 **PricewaterhouseCoopers itemized the expenses:** Testimony of James F. Flanagan, leader of the US Financial Services Practice at PricewaterhouseCoopers LLP, to the Senate Banking Committee's Financial Institutions and Consumer Protection Subcommittee, April 11, 2013.

149 **Deloitte said it was paid $465 million:** Ben Protess and Jessica Silver-Greenberg, "Senator Criticizes Lack of Supervision for Banks' Consultants," *New York Times*, June 20, 2013, http://dealbook.nytimes.com/2013/06/20/senator-criticizes-lack-of-supervision-for-banks-consultants.

149 **Grand prize went to Promontory:** Debra Cope's statement, e-mailed to me September 19, 2013.

149 **decided to shut down the foreclosure review:** Jesse Hamilton, "Banks' $8.5 Billion Deal Kills Review That Never Saw Results," Bloomberg News, January 8, 2013, www.bloomberg.com/news/2013–01–07/u-s-banks-to-pay-8–5-billion-to-settle-foreclosure-missteps.html.

149 **about 6.5 percent of the foreclosed home owners:** Hamilton, "Banks' $8.5 Billion Deal."

149 **settled with the fourteen servicers:** Federal Reserve and Office of the Comptroller of the Currency, "Independent Foreclosure Review to Provide $3.3 Billion in Payments, $5.2 Billion in Mortgage Assistance," joint press release, Board of Governors of the Federal Reserve System, January 7, 2013, www.federalreserve.gov/newsevents/press/bcreg/20130107a.htm. The agreement included Aurora, Bank of America, Citibank, JPMorgan Chase, MetLife Bank, PNC, Sovereign, SunTrust, US Bank, and Wells Fargo.

149 **At an April 11, 2013, Senate hearing:** From a video of the April 11, 2013, hearing on the US Senate Committee on Bank-

ing, Housing, and Urban Affairs website: www.banking.senate.gov
/public/index.cfm?FuseAction=Hearings.LiveStream&Hearing_id
=a52e1199-bc18–4a54-bbd5–159cc53ab44f. There were two Senate hearings on the foreclosure review that April. Warren's questioning occurred at the April 11, 2013, hearing of the Senate
Banking Committee's Financial Institutions and Consumer Protection Subcommittee, chaired by Sherrod Brown, an Ohio Democrat.
The panel featured executives from three of the foreclosure review
contractors: Promontory, Deloitte, and PricewaterhouseCoopers.

The second hearing, on April 17, 2013, was called by the Housing, Transportation, and Community Development Subcommittee,
chaired by New Jersey Democrat Robert Menendez. Witnesses included Lawrence L. Evans of the US Government Accountability
Office, National Mortgage Settlement monitor Joseph A. Smith Jr.,
and Deborah Goldberg of the National Fair Housing Alliance.

149 **statistically significant sampling:** Testimony of Lawrence L.
Evans of the US Government Accountability Office at the April
17, 2013, Senate hearing: www.banking.senate.gov/public/index
.cfm?FuseAction=Hearings.LiveStream&Hearing_id=6aac2b90
-e6ee-4c5c-b6a0–526ab27c70d2.

150 **The $8.5 billion settlement was Seinfeldian:** April 11, 2013,
hearing video.

150 **"It appears that the people who broke the law":** April 11,
2013, hearing video.

150 **"dysfunction of the reviews was inevitable":** Yves Smith, *Whis-
tleblowers Reveal How Bank of America Defrauded Homeowners and
Paid for a Cover Up—All with the Help of "Regulators"* (New York:
Aurora Advisors Inc., 2013), an e-book based on an investigative
series published at the Naked Capitalism blog, available at www.
scribd.com/doc/134192424/Naked-Capitalism-Whistleblower
-Report-on-Bank-of-America-Foreclosure-Reviews.

150 **Smith estimated that Bank of America paid Promontory:**
Yves Smith, "Bank of America Foreclosure Reviews: Why the
OCC Overlooked 'Independent' Reviewer Promontory's Key-
stone Cops Act (Part VB)," Naked Capitalism, February 11, 2013,

www.nakedcapitalism.com/2013/02/bank-of-america-fore
closure-reviews-why-the-occ-overlooked-independent-reviewer
-promontorys-keystone-cops-act-part-vb.html.

151 **servicers got dollar-for-dollar credit:** Video of the April 17, 2013, hearing.

151 **About two-thirds of the foreclosed home owners:** Julie Schmit, "Foreclosure Settlement a Billion-Dollar Bust," *USA Today*, June 25, 2013, www.usatoday.com/story/money/business/2013/06/24 /independent-foreclosure-review-payments/2390073.

152 **Jeff Merkley put it succinctly:** April 17, 2013, hearing video.

152 **"No teeth to it":** Interviews with David Baker.

152 **As if to underscore Baker's unhappiness:** "National Mortgage Settlement Servicing Standards and Noncompliance: Results of a National Housing Counselor Survey," National Housing Resource Center, June 5, 2013, www.hsgcenter.org/wp-content/uploads/2013 /06/NMS_Findings.pdf.

153 **judge refused the bank's request:** "In re: Walter W. Lacey, Debtor."

153 **Punchline: A forensic accountant determined:** "In re: Walter W. Lacey, Debtor."

153 **I would be remiss:** This section is satirical.

153 **Malcontents with whom I've had occasion to speak:** You know who you are.

154 **Expertise has never been abundant:** Please see the rest of this book.

155 **capable and not-bad-looking Eugene Ludwig:** "Eugene Ludwig," Promontory, www.promontory.com/Bios.aspx?id=1022.

155 **too big to jail:** For Attorney General Eric Holder Jr. testifying to the Senate Judiciary Committee, in response to a question by Senator Charles Grassley, on March 6, 2013, see "Holder: Big Banks' Clout 'Has an Inhibiting Impact' on Prosecutions," *Frontline*, March 6, 2013, www.pbs.org/wgbh/pages/frontline/business -economy-financial-crisis/untouchables/holder-big-banks-clout -has-an-inhibiting-impact-on-prosecutions.

155 **He told the New York City Bar Association:** Lanny Breuer addressed the New York City Bar Association on September 13, 2012. This is the relevant section from his speech:

The decision whether to indict a corporation, defer prosecution or decline altogether is not one that I . . . [take] lightly. We are frequently on the receiving end of presentations from defense counsel, CEOs and economists . . . who argue that the collateral consequences of an indictment would be devastating, just devastating for their client. In my conference room over these past years, I've heard sober predictions that a company or bank might fail if we indict. That innocent employees could lose their jobs. That entire industries could be affected, and that even global markets will feel the effects. Sometimes, but let me stress not always, these presentations are compelling. In reaching every charging decision we must take into account the effect of an indictment on innocent employees and shareholders, just as we must take into account the nature of the crimes committed and the pervasiveness of the misconduct.

I personally feel that it's my duty to consider whether individual employees with no responsibility for or knowledge of misconduct committed by others in the same company are going to lose their livelihoods if we indict the corporation. In large multinational companies, the jobs of ten of thousands of employees can literally be at stake, and in some cases the health of an industry or the markets are a very real factor. Those are the kinds of considerations in white-collar cases that literally keep me awake at night, and which must—must—play a role in responsible enforcement. ("The Role of Deferred Prosecution Agreements in White Collar Criminal Law Enforcement," YouTube, www.youtube.com /watch?v=1gbcB5BRzXo)

As far as I can tell, Breuer made no mention of any sleeplessness due to the results of the suspicious behavior of large multinational companies, which can also harm people who are innocent.

Thanks to Martin Smith and the staff at *Frontline* for the tip.

156 **He rejoined the firm in 2013:** Catherine Ho, "Lanny Breuer, Chief of DOJ's Criminal Division, Returns to Covington & Burling," *Washington Post*, March 28, 2013, www.washingtonpost.com /blogs/capital-business/post/lanny-breuer-chief-of-dojs-criminal -division-returns-to-covington-and-burling/2013/03/27/3b27d7a6 –9703–11e2-b68f-dc5c4b47e519_blog.html.

156 **an April 2013 unskeining of drivel:** Ben Protess and Jessica Silver-Greenberg, "Former Regulators Find a Home with a Powerful Firm," *New York Times*, April 9, 2013, http://dealbook .nytimes.com/2013/04/09/for-former-regulators-a-home-on -wall-street/?_r=0.

156 **an *American Banker* article on Promontory:** Jeff Horwitz and Maria Aspan, "How Promontory Financial Became Banking's Shadow Regulator," *American Banker*, March 15, 2013, www.americanbanker.com/magazine/123_4/how-promontory -financial-became-banking-s-shadow-regulator-1057480–1.html.

156 **When Promontory hired Mary Schapiro:** Jean Eaglesham, "SEC Ex-Chief Lands at Consultant; Schapiro Is Latest Former U.S. Regulator to Join Promontory Financial; 'No Revolving Door,'" *Wall Street Journal*, April 2, 2013, http://online.wsj.com/article /SB10001424127887324883604578396973470835516.html. Juiciest quote: "In my case, there's no revolving door. . . . I won't ever be going back to government," Schapiro said in an interview.

156 **Schapiro had already been paid:** William D. Cohan, "Regulators Follow Golden Road to Promontory," Bloomberg View, April 8, 2013, www.bloomberg.com/news/2013–04–07/where-bank-regulators -go-to-get-rich.html.

157 **former thises and former thats:** Horwitz and Aspan, "How Promontory Financial Became Banking's Shadow Regulator."

157 **Blinder made the unforced error:** Nassim Nicholas Taleb, *Antifragile: Things That Gain from Disorder* (New York: Random House, 2012). Taleb recounts his encounter with Blinder on pp. 412–413. Thanks to William D. Cohan for alerting me to this.

157 **a lunch salad at the Four Seasons:** To be exact, wagyu tataki, red shiso–scallion salad, yuzu-ginger sauce, $34. See the latest menu for

yourself at "Lunch in the Grill Room," Four Seasons Restaurant, www
.fourseasonsrestaurant.com/images/menu/PDFs/Four-Seasons
-Grill-Lunch.pdf.

157 **the small-government Santellis:** Dibs on this as the name of a
rock band or softball team.

157 **wealth-hating outrage addicts who bleat ceaselessly about
capture:** You know who you are.

CHAPTER SEVEN: GREED

159 **Rebecca Black searched the front yard:** Interviews with Rebecca
Black.

160 **listed on her 2005 mortgage application:** Black's mortgage.

160 **She couldn't afford the mortgage:** Housing advocates and
plaintiff's attorneys have pointed out this distinction to me more
than once. Thanks to Melissa Huelsman, a Seattle lawyer, who was
the first.

161 **man was shot and killed while driving a pickup truck:**
Scott Carroll, "Police Identify Man Found Shot to Death in
Southwest Memphis," *Commercial Appeal*, April 1, 2012, www
.commercialappeal.com/news/2012/apr/01/police-identify-man
-found-shot-death-southwest-mem. A big thank you to Sergeant
Alyssa Macon-Moore of the Memphis Police Department for her
graciousness in responding to my many questions.

161 **Black's old place sold for $3,000:** Shelby County Assessor's Office.

162 **Tom Marano was head of mortgages:** *Businessweek* provides
a short biography at "Bns Split Corp Ii (Bsc: Toronto Stock Exchange)," *Bloomberg Businessweek*, http://investing.businessweek
.com/research/stocks/people/person.asp?personId=26536972
&ticker=BSC:CN.

162 **saw their pay rise 5.5 percent:** Bob Ivry, "Wall Street Kept Winning on Mortgages Upending U.S. Homeowners," Bloomberg News,
November 19, 2012, www.bloomberg.com/news/2012–11–19/wall
-street-kept-winning-on-mortgages-upending-homeowners.html.

162 **Corporate profits reached a record:** Corporate profits reached
a record $1.67 trillion in the first quarter of 2012, according to

the Federal Reserve Bank of St. Louis. "Corporate Profits After Tax (without IVA and CCAdj) (CP)," FRED Economic Data, updated September 26, 2013, http://research.stlouisfed.org/fred2/series/CP.

162 **wages as a percentage of the US economy:** Federal Reserve Bank of St. Louis. The percentage was the lowest since the statistic began being calculated after World War II, before ticking upward slightly. "Graph: Compensation of Employees: Wages & Salary Accruals (WASCUR)/Gross Domestic Product (GDP)," FRED Economic Data, http://research.stlouisfed.org/fred2/graph/?g=2Xa.

162 **one in four residents lived below the poverty line:** In Memphis, 27.2 percent of people lived below the federal poverty line in 2011, compared with a national poverty rate of 15 percent, according to the US Census Bureau. In 2010, the poverty threshold was $22,314 for a family of four. A few more poverty statistics: 15.1 percent—just over 46 million Americans—were officially in poverty in 2010. This is an increase from 12.5 percent in 2007. Among racial and ethnic groups, African Americans had the highest poverty rate, 27.4 percent, followed by Hispanics at 26.6 percent and whites at 9.9 percent; 45.8 percent of young black children (under age six) lived in poverty, compared to 14.5 percent of white children.

163 **which ended up owning Black's mortgage:** The security that included Black's mortgage, Bear Stearns Asset Backed Securities I Trust 2005-HE8 (or BSABS 2005-HE8, for short), was mentioned as a money loser in an August 31, 2011, complaint filed by HSH Nordbank against JPMorgan Chase, which bought Bear Stearns. *HSH Nordbank AG and HSH Nordbank Securities SA v. JPMorgan Chase Bank NA and Others*, Orrick, http://www.orrick.com /Events-and-Publications/Documents/3989.pdf.

163 **who sold 698 Hazelwood Road to Black:** Shelby County Assessor's Office. Verified by Black.

163 **occupied space in a steel-and-glass office building:** I visited there in August 2012. The suites were empty.

163 **Gibbs says he worked hard:** Phone interview with Marcus Gibbs.

163 **Gibbs was rewarded with an origination fee:** All fees and information from Black's mortgage papers.

164 **BayRock, which at its peak had four hundred employees:** Phone interview with William Medley.

164 **"I never made a loan Wall Street wouldn't buy":** Bob Ivry, "'Deal with Devil' Funded Carrera Crash Before Bust," Bloomberg News, December 18, 2007, www.bloomberg.com/apps /news?pid=newsarchive&sid=awOhpZQuyd6k.

164 **worst subprime lender in the country:** Mark Pittman, "Bass Shorted 'God I Hope You're Wrong' Wall Street," Bloomberg News, December 19, 2007, www.bloomberg.com/apps/news?pid =newsarchive&sid=aC5bZpU8S6f4.

165 **five families of Wall Street:** Jonathan Weil, "Morgan Stanley's Bonuses Get Saved by You and Me," Bloomberg News, October 21, 2008, www.bloomberg.com/apps/news?pid=newsarchive&sid=azo 7aySdpFHw&refer=columnist_weil.

165 **$300 billion of mortgage bonds:** Financial Crisis Inquiry Commission report, p. 155.

165 **it lost a minimum of $42 million:** *HSH v. JPMorgan Chase.*

166 **Bear Stearns "deliberately and secretly" abandoned:** *Ambac Assurance Corp. v. EMC Mortgage LLC and Others*, Ambac, July 18, 2011, www.ambac.com/pdfs/NYS_Ambac_v_EMC_First _Amended_Complaint_2011–07–18.pdf, para. 1.

166 **to receive "stratospheric compensation":** *Ambac Assurance Corp. v. EMC Mortgage LLC and Others*, para. 75.

166 **Bear Stearns bet against the stock:** *Ambac Assurance Corp. v. EMC Mortgage LLC and Others*, para. 24.

166 **Bear Stearns's worst-performing securities:** "Statement on Financing Arrangement of JPMorgan Chase's Acquisition of Bear Stearns," press release, Federal Reserve Bank of New York, March 24, 2008, www.newyorkfed.org/newsevents/news/markets/2008 /rp080324.html.

166 **1983 Columbia University graduate:** "Five Alumni Presented with John Jay Awards," *Columbia College TODAY*, May/June 2009, www.college.columbia.edu/cct/may_jun09/features0.

167 **paper mill in Kimberly, Wisconsin:** Bob Ivry, "Feinberg Despised in Wisconsin Where Cerberus Lives Up to Name," Bloomberg News,

December 23, 2008, www.bloomberg.com/apps/news?sid=alpMxTz
KUbbg&pid=newsarchive.

167 **sank more than $16 billion into the company:** Through the
Troubled Asset Relief Program; data compiled by Bloomberg News.

167 **blitz of TV commercials:** Ally aimed to showcase what it called
its "exceptional customer service." In one commercial, it replaced
an employee at a dry cleaner with a blender—and customers didn't
like it! They wanted to talk to a person, not a blender! Older commercials showed an actor being indulgent to one child and mean
to another. The indulgent treatment was ostensibly how Ally dealt
with its customers; the mean way, presumably, was its competitors' method. The December 12, 2011, announcement about the
new batch of commercials is at "Ally Bank Launches Two New
'People Sense' Commercials," Ally, http://media.ally.com/index
.php?s=20295&item=122855. The blender commercial is at "Ally
Bank TV Spot, 'Dry Cleaner Test: Blender,'" iSpot.tv, www.ispot.tv
/ad/7wtI/ally-bank-dry-cleaner-test-blender.

167 **74 percent stake in Ally:** Data compiled by Bloomberg News.

168 **purple martins prefer beetles:** Herbert W. Kale II, "The Relationship of Purple Martins to Mosquito Control," Florida Audubon
Society, 1968, http://purplemartin.org/update/MosCont.html. The
study concluded that

> mosquitoes appear to be a negligible item in the diet
> of the purple martin. . . . None of the published state-
> ments appearing in the popular or ethnological literature
> that attribute a mosquito-feeding habit to the purple
> martin are based on a factual study; the oft-quoted state-
> ment 'a martin eats 2,000 mosquitoes per day' has no
> evident means of support. . . . The purple martin is one
> of our most beautiful and friendly birds. It daily con-
> sumes a large number of insects. Its aesthetic qualities
> alone recommend it highly to man. There is no need to
> ascribe to the martin abilities greater than those it al-
> ready possesses in order to encourage its protection and
> propagation.

170 **Shelby County . . . was adding 350 properties a month:** Interview with Shelby County mayor Mark H. Luttrell Jr.

171 **Frayser, . . . population 40,000:** US Census Bureau.

171 **nearly half the twenty-five square miles were empty:** Lockwood's organization put together these statistics from the census.

172 **Martin Luther King Jr. and Elvis Presley:** King was from Atlanta, of course. He was thirty-nine years old when he was shot and killed on the balcony of the Lorraine Motel in Memphis on April 4, 1968. The motel has been converted into a spellbinding civil rights museum. At the end of the self-guided tour, visitors find themselves outside the room where King stayed and just a few yards from the concrete slab where he died. I found it very moving. After that, visitors are ushered across the parking lot, through a short tunnel and into an apartment building, where a couple flights up they're standing at the door of the bathroom where James Earl Ray took his shot. After that experience, I was speechless for hours.

   Presley was born in Tupelo, Mississippi, but lived most of his life in Memphis. He was forty-two when he died at his Memphis home, Graceland, on August 16, 1977. The family's apartment in Lauderdale Court, a formerly segregated public housing project, is now owned and managed by Henry Turley's company.

172 **now home to FedEx and AutoZone:** FedEx is Memphis's largest employer. Its chief executive officer, Fred Smith, is a graduate of the Memphis University School, where the headmaster, Ellis Haguewood, told me, "Without Fred Smith I don't know where Memphis would be." AutoZone's chief, Pitt Hyde, is also a graduate of Memphis University School (as is Henry Turley).

173 **Memphis and Shelby County had filed a lawsuit:** Complaint filed April 7, 2010; available at http://media.commercialappeal.com/media/static/Final_Complaint.pdf.

173 **3.5 times more likely:** Debbie Gruenstein Bocian, Wei Li, and Carolina Reid, "Lost Ground, 2011, Disparities in Mortgage Lending and Foreclosures," Center for Responsible Lending, November 2011, www.responsiblelending.org/mortgage-lending/research-analysis/Lost-Ground-2011.pdf.

173 **"It's not hyperbole to say":** Interview with Webb Brewer.

173 **Wells Fargo and Shelby-Memphis settled:** Ted Evanoff, "Leaders Say City Got Best Deal Possible from Bank," *Commercial Appeal*, June 3, 2012, www.commercialappeal.com/news/2012 /jun/03/wells-fargo-goes-from-foe-to-partner/?print=1. A Wells Fargo spokeswoman sent me these comments:

> Wells Fargo strictly prohibits discrimination based on race, age or other demographic factors. We have practices and advocated for responsible home lending and responsible loan servicing for a very long time.
>
> According to the 2011 Home Mortgage Disclosure Act report (the most recently available report), Wells Fargo maintained its leadership in fair mortgage lending. We were the No. 1 lender in the market overall, and in lending to all racial and ethnic groups.
>
> Wells Fargo was the No. 1 originator of home loans across the board in all key categories, including loans to African-Americans, Asians, Hispanics, Native Americans, low- and moderate-income borrowers, and residents of low- and moderate-income neighborhoods.
>
> Here are a few points related to the agreement Wells Fargo has with Memphis and Shelby County.
>
> Earlier this year (2012), Wells Fargo and the City of Memphis and Shelby County all agreed that it was in the best interest of all parties to end the litigation. The City of Memphis and Shelby County agreed to drop their lawsuit against Wells so that we could enter into a collaborative agreement for the benefit of the community. In effect, allowing us to work together to help communities in the area recover from the housing crisis. Memphis and Shelby County are markets where our local bank officials are active partners in the community.
>
> Some of the details of the agreement are:
>
> ○ Wells Fargo will provide $4.5 million for a home own-

ership program that will provide down payment and renovation grants as well as home buyer education.

○ Wells Fargo will contribute an additional $3 million for local initiatives related to improving economic vitality, preserving public safety, and increasing financial literacy, with spending directed by the city and county.

○ Wells Fargo also communicated that we have made a $425 million home purchase lending goal for the city and county over the next five years.

From January of 2009 through September of 2012, we have forgiven more than $5.5 billion of mortgage principal for our customers facing financial hardship. We have placed more than 800,000 home owners into active trial and completed modifications.

We are committed to putting people in homes and helping them stay there.

173 **Wells Fargo reported net income:** Company regulatory filings.

175 **drop-down menu offered a unique option:** Exhibit A of Memphis–Shelby County's complaint against Wells Fargo; available at http://media.commercialappeal.com/media/static/Final_Complaint.pdf.

175 **ResCap lost $7.3 billion:** Company presentation for February 4, 2010, p. 16, upper right. Available on the Ally website at www.ally.com/about/investor/events-presentations. I'm indebted to Dakin Campbell for his help in ferreting this out.

175 **Marano was paid $5.6 million:** Dakin Campbell, "Despite Losses, GMAC Execs Get Big Paydays," Bloomberg News, March 2, 2010, www.bloomberg.com/apps/news?pid=newsarchive&sid=aWSrGayNptVs.

175 **Marano received a 14 percent raise:** Data compiled by Bloomberg News from regulatory filings.

175 **ResCap filed for bankruptcy:** Steven Church, Phil Milford, and Dakin Campbell, "Ally's ResCap Files Bankruptcy, Plans Sale to

Fortress," Bloomberg News, May 14, 2012, www.bloomberg.com /news/2012–05–14/ally-s-residential-capital-files-for-bankruptcy -protection-1-.html.

177 **The Uptown development consists:** Interview with Alexandra Mobley.

177 **Rebecca Black was receiving tax and maintenance bills:** Interviews with Rebecca Black.

178 **The blight manager:** Interview with Tim Meulenberg, Kalamazoo's code administration manager and supervisor of the city's antiblight team.

178 **city's planning director told me:** Interview with Russell Claus, Oklahoma City's planning director.

179 **A housing advocate in Durham, North Carolina:** Interview with Peter Skillern, executive director, Reinvestment Partners in Durham.

179 **A foreclosure expert in North Lake Tahoe, California:** Interview with Sean O'Toole, chief executive officer of ForeclosureRadar .com.

179 **A realtor I spoke to there:** Interview with Dawn Lane of the HOPE Home Foundation.

179 **On the night of March 30, 2012:** Carroll, "Police Identify Man."

179 **Police didn't call the killing gang related:** Interviews with Sergeant Alyssa Macon-Moore of the Memphis Police.

181 **has owned at least two houses:** County of Morris Tax Board, New Jersey.

181 **built in 1916 of rough-hewn gray stones:** It's quite beautiful. See a photo of the Madison train station at "About Madison," Borough of Madison, New Jersey, www.rosenet.org/content/about _madison.

181 **Marano bought a home:** County of Morris Tax Board, New Jersey.

181 **sold it to Oldpike Associates LLC:** From Madison, New Jersey, parcel data tables.

182 **on ten acres in Park City, Utah:** Summit County, Utah, public records. Thanks to Shelley Osterloh for eyeballing the place.

182 **bought another home . . . sold his stake:** County of Morris Tax Board, New Jersey.

INDEX

Dave Cross

BOB IVRY is a reporter for Bloomberg News whose awards include the 2009 George Polk Award, a 2008 Gerald Loeb Award, a 2012 special citation from the Goldsmith Investigative Reporting Award jury at Harvard's Kennedy School, the Society of Professional Journalists 2012 Public Service in Online Journalism Award, the 2012 Investigative Reporters and Editors Freedom of Information Prize, the 2010 Hillman Prize, three New York Press Club Awards, two National Headliner Awards, and three awards from the Society of American Business Editors and Writers. He's written for *Esquire, Maxim, Popular Science*, and *Washington Post Book World*; and his short fiction has appeared in *Esquire* and *Ploughshares*. Before joining Bloomberg News, Ivry worked for the *Record*, the *San Francisco Examiner*, and the *San Francisco Bay Guardian*. In 2012, BusinessInsider.com named @bobivry one of "The 101 Finance People You Have to Follow on Twitter."